"Some people strengthen the society just by being the kind of people they are."

—John W. Gardner

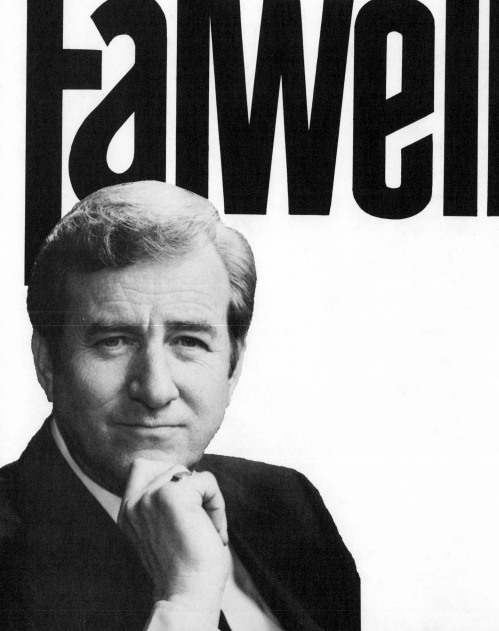

Before the Millennium

A Critical Biography

Dinesh D'Souza

REGNERY GATEWAY • CHICAGO

Published by Regnery Gateway, Inc.
360 W. Superior St., Chicago, IL 60610

Library of Congress Cataloging in Publication Data
D'Souza, Dinesh, 1961-
    Falwell, before the millenium.

    1. Falwell, Jerry. 2. Baptists—United States—Clergy
Biography. I. Title.
BX6495.F3D76 1984 286'.13 [B]   83-43306
ISBN 0-89526-607-5

CONTENTS

Introduction

The roles were reversed when Jerry Falwell spoke at the Harvard Divinity School in May 1983. Falwell was supposed to be the rabid fundamentalist, and his audience genteel and sophisticated. Yet whenever Falwell mentioned God, the family, or the American flag, students hissed and jeered. He defended pluralism and free expression; several Harvard undergraduates responded with chants of "Hitler, Falwell, go to hell." Midway through his talk two protesters from a Harvard "Committee Against Racism" yelled "Racist, Fascist pig" at Falwell and were dragged, kicking, from the hall by security guards.

Harvard theologian Harvey Cox, who invited Falwell to Cambridge, had led off with a nervous disclaimer of his own: "Please understand that my presence here tonight should in no way be understood as an endorsement of what Jerry Falwell recommends." When Falwell took the microphone, he countered, "Thank you for your kind introduction, Professor Cox. Students, please understand that my speaking here tonight should in no way be construed as an endorsement of the Harvard Divinity School." Nervous applause. Some students booed.

Falwell's speech was intended to clarify misconceptions about his political and religious views and also, in Moral Majority official Cal Thomas's words, "to show that our positions are defensible and that

7

Falwell is not an ayatollah."

First Falwell outlined the five main points of fundamentalist doctrine: belief in the inerrancy of the Bible, the deity of Christ and his birth of a virgin, the substitutionary atonement of Christ's death for all sin, the literal resurrection of Christ, and his return to earth in the Second Advent. Various evangelical and fundamentalist groups add corollaries to these five tenets; but all accept them as the bedrock of the faith, and Falwell, as pastor of Thomas Road Baptist Church in Lynchburg, Virginia, is obliged to defend this orthodoxy against competing heresies. Then Falwell described his political views, which he said were separate from his religious beliefs—four principles: affirmed in the charter of Moral Majority; pro-life, which means opposition to abortion and euthanasia; pro-family, "One man for one woman in one lifetime"; pro-moral, which means opposition to pornography and the illegal drug traffic; and pro-American, which means favoring a strong national defense and, oddly, support for Israel and Jewish people everywhere.

Falwell admitted to his audience that his theological roots were narrow and specific, but his moral-political orthodoxy, he said, represented nothing less than the American orthodoxy, the shared values that have sustained this nation since its genesis and enabled it to function as a unitary nation instead of serving as a battleground for tribes of different, irreconcilable values.

Falwell delivered that same speech at Dartmouth College, Yale University, and Princeton University, where he also met a mixture of caterwauling, cynicism, and reserved approval. Students at Yale could not help smiling when Falwell, after meeting with President Bartlett Giamatti (who had publicly excoriated Falwell several months earlier), cheerfully announced that he and Bart had decided *against* merging Yale and Liberty Baptist College, the school Falwell had founded in Virginia in 1971. At Dartmouth, Falwell was challenged by a girl who conceded his First amendment right to speak, a right she said she would extend even to Fascists and Communists, but she objected to Falwell's "strident tone and manner." Falwell replied, "Being from the South, I did not have as privileged an upbringing as you did." Silence. Then a spatter of laughs, some hissing. When at Harvard a student defended Falwell by calling his hecklers "hooligans," Falwell lightheartedly dismissed his student ally, implying that he would be nowhere without his critics.

Watching Falwell's campus performances, I felt he was doing much to erase stereotypes—not only of himself as Hitler, another Jim Jones

of Guyana, or an American Ayatollah Khomeini, but also of fundamentalists in general as backwoods people living among possums and
magnolias, suffused with hate, barely literate. I found it surprising that
Ivy League audiences permitted themselves to be seduced by this
preacher. Admittedly there were some attempts to prevent him from
speaking at Harvard and Dartmouth. At Harvard, divinity student
Stewart Guernsey claimed that letting Falwell speak was "playing into
his hands." At Dartmouth, associate chaplain Richard Hyde called
him "a false prophet," describing his views as "idolatry, pure and simple." But most students and faculty *wanted* Falwell to come, to see him
embarrass himself.

I have in fact seen many an outsider of conservative disposition
saunter boldly to an Ivy League podium, only to be torn to bits by
piranhas in the audience. But Falwell not only deflects the sneers and
wrath of his critics, who are legion, but he turns their attacks to his
own advantage. At Princeton Falwell was nearly prevented from
speaking because of a bomb threat, but he declared that he would
speak, bomb or no bomb, and timorous people could leave. The students regarded this as heroic. In the end, I do not think he won any
converts to fundamentalism, or recruited many members for Moral
Majority, but he did create some shocked admirers, and he aroused the
curiosity of most of the others.

It was this experience of Falwell that provoked me to launch the in-
vestigation leading to this book. I was (and am) not interested in fundamentalism as a personal belief; in fact I was hostile to it. I was raised
Catholic, and hardly receptive to the anti-Catholic fundamentalist
tradition epitomized by the Reverend Frank Norris's famous 1924 sermon deploring "Rum and Romanism." I had other problems with
Falwell. Raised on three continents, I found him parochial. Nonwhite,
I wondered whether his was a Christianity for whites only. Educated in
the Ivy League, I disliked his apparent anti-intellectualism. And I
found him excessively moralistic. But Falwell intrigued me because of
the peculiar, irrational response evoked from his critics.

Confronted with Falwell, urbane men grow hair on their face. Such
notables as Bartlett Giamatti, president of Yale, and Mario Cuomo,
governor of New York, have issued shrill condemnations of Falwell.
And yet both men profess to share several of Falwell's beliefs, and nei-
ther need fear much Falwell support among his constituency. Among
Falwell's detractors are, not surprisingly, Jane Fonda, Ed Asner,
George McGovern, Mike Royko, Ted Kennedy, Carl Rowan, Tip
O'Neill, Anthony Lewis, Jimmy Carter, Mark Hatfield, John Barth,

Paul Newman, Phil Donahue, and Bill Moyers. But his critics also include TV producer Norman Lear, who has accused Falwell of anti-Semitism; the Catholic journal *America*, which charges him with "moral fascism"; and Barry Goldwater, a conservative icon, who said, "Every good American ought to kick Falwell in the ass." Falwell's critics have accused him of rapacity, ignorance, simplistic statements, subverting the Constitution, invading the bedroom, trying to force religion down people's throats, and beating his wife and children. Could these things be true? I wanted a closer look at Falwell.

This book is what I like to call a "current biography." Typically biographies are written late in their subject's life, or after his death. Falwell is a recent celebrity; he has been a national figure for only about five years. Yet in those five years Falwell has altered the political map of America. Pollster Lou Harris credits him with Reagan's entire margin of victory in the 1980 election. Without Moral Majority, Harris believes, Jimmy Carter would have won by one percentage point.

There may be some hyperbole in this, but in general Falwell's critics do not deny his influence. A few of them pooh-pooh his television clout, but most actually exaggerate his power, some accusing him of mind control and forcing his narrow views on the public. As early as October 1978 *Esquire* magazine named Falwell "the next Billy Graham." But since then Falwell has taken another route. While his theological status has remained the same or diminished slightly, his political position has become more important—so important that Harry Cook, religion editor for the *Detroit Free Press*, reluctantly conceded that "Falwell had a larger impact on the 1980 political races than any religious leader in this country's 200-year history."

The media has backed off from Falwell since 1982, so it is little known that his church and Moral Majority have expanded in influence since the last election and are poised to affect the next one even more significantly. Falwell's church budget climbed from $58 million in 1980 to nearly $90 million in 1984. His television network added about 100 new stations in this interval, a viewership increase of 5 million. Moral Majority, which Falwell chairs, expanded its membership from 2 million in 1980 to 6½ million in 1984. After a brief hiatus from politics—Falwell was virtually uninvolved in the 1982 congressional races—Falwell has leaped back into the arena, berating advocates of the nuclear freeze, warning of AIDS and herpes in apocalyptic terms, grading President Reagan's performance every two weeks or so.

Naturally this book focuses on Falwell's glittering years from 1979 to

1984. He regards these as the most important of his life. "What I am doing now is my reason for being," he told a reporter for the *Washington Post* recently. My effort here is to understand the Falwell we see today. Who is this small-town Baptist preacher who has become a political leader thundering at the country and the Congress? What of his fundamentalism, a once respectable faith long cast aside as chaff, but now in a renaissance with startling political and religious implications.

Jerry Falwell and his people cooperated with me in this enterprise; so did his critics. So I have been able to see aspects of Falwell's life that he, suspicious of the media, has heretofore kept from the public eye. I have felt the force of arguments for and against his positions. Few people are reticent on the subject of Falwell, and the challenge of this biography has been to edit bales of material into a book of manageable size.

Conversations reported here are, in most cases, the product of personal interviews; in some instances, I have used quotations from the media. I have read several thousand pages of news stories and TV transcripts about Falwell, as well as the dozen or so books about him.

I have many persons to thank for assisting me in this project. In the main, these are simple folk, allergic to publicity, mostly concerned with the weather and church-going and butterbeans. They could not always see what all the fuss was about, but at the end of my research I could.

Jerry Falwell matters. That is perhaps the bottom line. It is not the most interesting fact about Falwell. I am more intrigued by the contradictions that drive him. Sometimes his entire life seems a giant contradiction—between his faith, which is detached and otherworldly, and his politics, which are ferociously devoted to the here-and-now. Falwell is sometimes temperamental. At times he is militant and divisive. Sometimes he responds angrily to what people have said about him; sometimes he starts it and they respond. At other times Falwell is warm and ironic, making charitable comments about men like William Sloane Coffin, whom he may have called Lucifer just the week before. On occasion Falwell seems reverent of tradition, scourging change-oriented "progressives" who seek to turn society topsy-turvy. But often he is reckless, bounding out of the fundamentalist camp to engage in a politics long eschewed by his peers and spurning stick-in-the-mud preachers who can't change their ways. Falwell is both a prophet of doom and a herald of the Glorious Second Coming. He calls America a divinely ordained nation even while warning, "If

God allows America to continue, He owes an apology to Sodom and Gomorrah."

But for all these paradoxes, Falwell is important to history. Some of his critics say that ten years from now we will have forgotten about him; he says the same about them, but makes it five years. We know only the present—that Falwell has escorted into the political arena some 10 million fundamentalists who now form what he calls "the largest minority bloc in America." This group seems selfishly to demand that the rest of us succumb to its specific agenda. Yet unlike other minority groups, it does not ask for benefits for itself, but for the moral reform of everybody else, of the nation's institutions and people. In this sense it comprises an altruistic majority-oriented minority. Falwell's shepherding of evangelical fundamentalists into politics and the responsibilities of citizenship is his contribution to democracy, and it is not a small one.

Besides that, Falwell presides over what I call "moral fundamentalism" in America; the Judeo-Christian tradition. This is wider and deeper than any religious orthodoxy. Although this tradition has become unfashionable in certain circles—at Manhattan cocktail parties, for instance—it still represents the most powerful current of unity in America, and those who seek to swim against it may find themselves broken by the flow. Jerry Falwell stands today as the strongest and perhaps most articulate defender of this tradition. There is nobody quite like him, nobody who does the things he does.

If Jerry Falwell did not exist, would it be necessary (or possible) to invent him? How valid are the positions he stakes out in his sweeping, controversial rhetoric? Is he whipping up national hysteria by tossing religious potion into the political cauldron? Or is politics diluting his fundamentalist faith? What is Falwell's family like? And what about fundamentalists—the people we think of as wearing Sears Roebuck suits and crew cuts? Is Falwell like these people? If not, what is he doing among them? The rest of this book will be devoted to answering these questions—and to raising some new ones. Through narrative, anecdote, and detail I hope to show this man against the background of the philosophical foundations of American society. Is Jerry Falwell sustaining this society's pillars, or is he tearing them down, Samson-style?

1

A Day in the Life...

Jerry Falwell woke up at 6:00 A.M., turned off the alarm, and climbed into the shower. He emerged well scrubbed and smelling faintly of cologne. His wife, Macel, then got up and woke the children. A little later the family had breakfast together and talked about family matters.

After breakfast there was a flurry of activity. The kids were dispatched to school, and Falwell pecked his wife before getting in his black Buick to ride to the offices of Thomas Road Baptist Church, his $90-million-a-year ministry.

When Jeanette Hogan, Falwell's personal secretary, heard her boss in the outer office she immediately poured him his coffee. Falwell, an inveterate practical joker, sneaked up behind her and yelled in her ear. She jumped, adjusted her spectacles, and gave him her you-do-this-every-day-so-how-come-you-still-think-it's-funny look.

Falwell was not fazed. "Any work for me to do today, Jean?" he asked cheerily. She ran down a long list of appointments: prayer meeting at 8:30; a business session at 9:00; a conference with Cal Thomas, vice-president of Moral Majority, at 10:15; a talk to seniors at Lynchburg Christian Academy, Falwell's school at 11:30; lunch from 12:30 to 12:50; then DeWitt Braud, the Baton Rouge, Louisiana, businessman who manages finances for Falwell's television ministry, would call to discuss those. Falwell would have from 2:00 to 3:00 P.M. to look over the galleys of *Fundamentalist Journal*, a glossy magazine his church puts out. At 4:00, he was scheduled to fly to Jacksonville, Florida, to preach at the fiftieth anniversary of the ministry of Pastor Wendell Zimmerman of the Baptist Bible Temple there. (I was supposed to travel with and interview him on the plane.) Falwell absorbed the details, took his cup of coffee, and went into his office, where the phone was already ringing.

It was a reporter from a New York TV station. A Moral Majority member was quoted as having said that he hoped a cure was never found for AIDS, the fatal disease affecting mostly homosexuals. Falwell sighed. "I don't know the circumstances. I cannot comment on that," he said. "But I myself hope a cure is found." He paused, then added, "Of course the real cure for AIDS and herpes and all those diseases is sexual restraint. I'm talking about traditional morality, the notion that—"

The reporter cut him off. "Thank you, Dr. Falwell, thank you very much."

Falwell put down the phone, shaking his head, smiling a little. Then it was time for the prayer meeting. Each person present prayed in turn, asking for personal blessings, invigoration for the ministry, success in missionary efforts, etc.

The prayer meeting broke up, and the others left, scattering toward their offices in the building. Falwell quickly perused the papers for his next meeting. The business at hand was discussion of the pace of construction for Liberty Baptist College. Charts were laid across people's knees and tables; an architect explained the details. Falwell listened, asking a question here and there. The assembled businessmen seemed impressed by his familiarity with the subject. At the conclusion of the presentation, Falwell said, "Gentlemen, your suggestions are excellent; I accept them. Let's keep on with the construction." As the others started to leave, Falwell added, "Let's keep the work going. Remember, Liberty must have fifty thousand students here by the year 2000. We have got to have facilities for them." The businessmen laughed, but Falwell was serious.

Cal Thomas came in to ask Falwell about Senator Ted Kennedy of Massachusetts. Senator Kennedy had accidentally been put on the Moral Majority mailing list—maybe as a joke—and received appeals for funds: "Please send your contribution today. Your money is urgently needed to help us fight people like Tip O'Neill and Ted Kennedy. . . ." Kennedy, who has an eye for irony, had called the *New York Times*, saying they might find it amusing. When Thomas was contacted by the *Times*, he said he had no plans to remove Kennedy's name from the list unless the senator requested that. Then Thomas sent a.photocopy of the *Times'* little feature to Kennedy with a note saying he'd enjoyed the incident; it was nice that in America reasonable men could disagree. And would Kennedy like to come to Lynchburg and speak at Liberty Baptist College?

"Kennedy says yes—I got a call from his man in Washington," Thomas told Falwell. "Man, this could be a terrific coup for us."

Falwell was not so sure. "Obviously, Cal, it would be publicity, but what will our people think?"

"Bill him as the Antichrist!," Cal joked."

Falwell grinned. "Let's do it—it will give the liberals a hernia. They won't be able to stereotype us like before."

"It could help Kennedy, too," Thomas replied. "He's coming across as anti-God, anti-moral, and he may be trying to prove he isn't anti-family or something."

"Good for him. But let's also bring some good conservative to speak the next week. That way we can bill it as a debate of sorts."

Thomas ran down a list of potentials: Jesse Helms, Richard Nixon-
. . .not Jim Watt—he was here last month. . .Bill Armstrong, Jack Kemp, William F. Buckley, Jr. Falwell selected Kemp and Nixon as his first two choices.

"I think I'll ask Nixon first," Thomas said. "It will be appropriate, you know. Both men are scarred. Nixon has Watergate; Kennedy has Chappaquiddick."

Falwell screwed up his face in mock horror. "Don't even compare the two."

"No, no," Thomas protested. "It will be good for Nixon. I mean, he won't get a single heckler here. Our people will *love* him."

"I'll leave it up to you, Cal," Falwell said.

From 10:30 Falwell answered important phone calls: to a pastor friend in Missouri who wanted to order one thousand "Jesus first" pins; to a sick church member; to a six-figure contributor who was disenchanted with Falwell's support of Israel. He also dictated letters that Jeanette Hogan would spend the rest of the day transcribing. DeWitt Braud called early—he had a meeting all afternoon. He was afraid that Falwell could not afford to expand his radio ministry at the rate he was and race construction of the college at the same time. "We have to strike a sensible middle ground, Jerry," Braud cautioned.

Falwell frowned. "Yes, yes. It's all up to you, DeWitt, you know the ropes. But I think we should keep up with both. The Lord has blessed this ministry; I think He will provide."

"I know that, Jerry, but we must wait for Him to provide *before* we spend."

At Liberty Baptist College, Falwell told students he was expecting an outstanding year from them, that knowledge could not be gained without moral character, and that he was building them a new gymnasium. Applause. Then Falwell and an associate, Don Norman, stopped for lunch at a local diner. Falwell had a salad, Norman a Lynchburger.

During the afternoon Falwell took and made more calls and poured over the copy for the *Fundamentalist Journal.* He thumbed through all the features but paid most attention to his own article on Christian schools, which he knew was the only article critics in the national media would read. In it Falwell denounced secular humanism. "Humanism teaches that man is his own god," Falwell wrote. "Humanism teaches that moral values are relative, and that ethics are situational. The Ten Commandments are viewed as outmoded hindrances to human progress. In addition, naturalism views man as nothing more than a biological and chemical machine." And so on. He also called for a "coalition of Christian educators" to lobby for tuition tax credits, prayer in public schools, and less government intrusion.

At 3:30 Hogan called to him. "The pilots are ready, Dr. Falwell. Duane is here to take you to the airport." Falwell packed his briefcase with work to do on the plane. Hogan reminded him that I would be traveling with him to interview him en route to Jacksonville.

"Oh, that's right," Falwell said, unloading papers. "This can wait until tomorrow."

Our plane touched gently down on the Jacksonville, Florida airstrip. I said "our plane"; it is actually Falwell's ministry plane, a dainty eleven-seater, Israeli-built, purchased for $3.5 million. It had been a ninety-minute flight from Lynchburg; Falwell spent much of the time munching peanuts. He seemed completely rested in the plane, which he called a second home to him, since he travelled so much. Duane Ward, Falwell's puckish, competent aide, who travels everywhere with him and rounds up the press, accompanied us.

We were met by Pastor Zimmerman himself. Falwell told me it was in Zimmerman's church in Kansas City that he had preached his own very first sermon twenty-nine years before. "Zimmerman's a terrific fellow," Falwell said.

Zimmerman turned out to be an elderly, soft-spoken man with a long nose and a peering manner. Falwell hugged him closely. Zimmerman stammered how grateful he was that Falwell had taken the time to come, given how busy Falwell was, and so on, but Falwell dismissed that, preferring to twit Zimmerman on his erratic driving.

Zimmerman outlined the massive orchestration that had gone into the evening's event.

At Bible Baptist Temple we were greeted by several church elders in three-piece polyester suits. They ran up to us with umbrellas to shelter us from a thunderstorm that had just broken.

There were only a handful of protesters, holding signs like "The Moral Majority is neither." They didn't say much, just peered at Falwell and muttered with resentment.

Then we ducked into the sanctuary out of the rain. I hovered in the corridor; Falwell went to the bathroom to wash up. The church was teeming. As Falwell had predicted, a cheeky television cameraman was wheeling his equipment up the center aisle, to the consternation and resentment of the congregation. Some church members came out to see Falwell. One asked him to sign a Bible. An old lady with a hunchback insisted on clutching him but could only hold onto his middle. Pastor Zimmerman's son, a local policeman, punched Falwell on the shoulder and called him "Jerry boy." Falwell smiled. He seemed entirely at home with this crowd. He smiled and shook hands in his curious double-fisted way, called people "brother" and "sister," accepted worthless little mementos, and listened attentively to compliments and comments proffered by the parishioners.

The service had already begun. The choir was singing gospel tunes with more zeal than melody, and every now and then the congregants would bellow out an "Amen" or "Say it, brother." His Bible under his right arm, Falwell marched up the aisle with Zimmerman. All eyes turned, but the people kept singing. The TV man flashed his lights in Falwell's face. Falwell smiled into the camera and kept walking. I sat in a middle row between a square-faced youth with a flower in his lapel and a breathy black woman whose voice sustained the faction singing out of tune.

Falwell preached for an hour. The audience hung onto his words. First he berated the "freezeniks," then said that pornography publishers should be stopped. But mostly he spoke about the local churches—"Bible-believing, God-fearing, soul-winning churches"— and how he believed it was these churches that would turn America around. "The moral condition of a nation is a reflection of the scriptural condition of its churches," Falwell thundered. "Living by God's principles brings a nation to greatness; violating those principles brings a nation to shame." Falwell particularly praised the 110,000 fundamentalist churches in America, with some 20 million members. He said, "I'm glad for the free enterprise system; I'm glad for the state and local government; but as far as I'm concerned, what is happening here at Bible Baptist Temple and at the thousands of fundamentalist churches across America is what is really important."

The church filled with approving murmurs. "Amen, brother." "Say it again." The black woman turned to me. "Ain't he somethin'?" I shrugged my shoulders, a little embarrassed. The woman wiped a tear from her eye and turned her face back to the altar.

After Falwell finished, he and I were whisked off to Zimmerman's house, where assorted church members and officials joined us. We sat around a mahogany table and ate fried chicken and duck, made our own salads, and poured Tab and coffee. People came up to Falwell and told him what a fantastic job he was doing, how they couldn't believe he took the abuse he did, and that they were behind him 100 percent, and they just wanted him to know it.

He told the group that he'd been on a television show in San Francisco recently with three hostile persons—a homosexual rights advocate, a doctor intent on dispelling misconceptions, and a patient with AIDS. By the end of the show, Falwell said, the AIDS patient was taking his side, even asking Falwell to give him the telephone number of his counseling service. The guy wanted to be reborn. Those present said, "Amen," and Falwell added wryly, "When it's the end of the road, man, it's no time for rhetoric."

Then Falwell got a phone call from Lynchburg. Falwell's pilot's son had been injured in an accident—nothing serious, some bruises and a fractured jaw, but the man should know. Falwell seemed shaken. He called the hospital the boy had been taken to. He called his wife to ask her to get information from the pilot's wife, and then to call him back, which she did. He asked us all pray for the man's son, then took a last bite of his chicken, and said we had to leave at once.

The pilot took the news rather well. In fact, he spent a full ten minutes telling us about youthful exploits of his own that had included danger of serious injury. The kid was evidently a real chip off the old block. Soon we were in the air and on our way back to Lynchburg.

2

That Old-Time Religion

U.S. News and World Report named Jerry Falwell one of the twenty most powerful people in America for 1982. Falwell is dearly and sometimes crazily loved—by the 10 million people who watch his television show; by his 20,000 church members in Lynchburg; by the readers of Good Housekeeping, who voted him second most admired American (after President Reagan) in 1983; and by the readers of Conservative Digest, who have for the last three years named Falwell their "most admired conservative not in Congress." Other Falwell aficionados include President Reagan and Vice-President George Bush, who have praised Falwell's emphasis on the Judeo-Christian tradition; former Israeli Prime Minister Menachem Begin, who awarded Falwell the Jabotinsky Award for distinguished service to Israel; members of Religious Heritage of America, who in 1979 named Falwell clergyman of the year; and the board of Food for the Hungry International, who gave Falwell their humanitarian award that same year. A more recent admirer was Newsweek columnist Meg Greenfield, who has named Falwell, Jesse Jackson, and Ronald Reagan the three best politicians in America. Comparing the three to the more usual "steady, flat, safe, uneventful" politicians, Greenfield called them "stock car racers. They engage the attention, they terrify, they entertain, and they move like hell."

Falwell also boasts a bipartisan and heavily populated group of detractors. He doesn't worry much about most of them. "When you call sin by its right name, you can be assured of all kinds of reprisals," he says. "I don't care about popularity. Christ was crucified—that's how he ended his career."

Among Falwell's foes are former President Carter, who accused Falwell in 1980 of putting forth "a narrow definition of what a Christian is, and also what an acceptable politician is." This definition excluded Carter, so naturally he "didn't want to see that happen." Carter's second, Walter Mondale, wrote a fundraising letter for the Committee on the Future of America, arguing that Falwell "operates outside the normal parameters of our political system." This was because, according to Mondale, Falwell "identifies his positions and candidates as moral and American. And he implies that those who differ are immoral and un-American."

Scientist Isaac Asimov went further. He warned that there was "no way" America could retain its lead in technology "if we follow the dictates of the Moral Majority." Asimov was joined by Ira Glasser, president of the American Civil Liberties Union, who felt there was a "strong anti-Bill of Rights movement building in America" and that Falwell was at the head of it.

The Media has collaborated with Falwell's critics in attacking him and his values. But despite attack—or perhaps because of the exposure—Falwell's influence continues to increase; and his organizations have doubled and tripled in size.

Since 1979 Falwell has been featured in the following magazines—in many more than once: *Esquire, Harpers, Atlantic Monthly, The New Yorker, Playboy, Chic, Hustler, Screw, Penthouse, Time, Newsweek, Life, U.S. News and World Report, The Economist, Le Monde, Le Express, Le Point, Stern, Conservative Digest,* and the *Village Voice.*

Falwell has appeared in front page stories in most national and international papers, including the *New York Times,* the *Washington Post,* the *Los Angeles Times,* the *London Observer,* and the *Jerusalem Post.*

He was a guest on "The Phil Donahue Show" eleven times, on "The Tom Synder Show," "The Today Show," "Tomorrow," "Good Morning America," "Meet the Press," "Nightline," and "CBS Morning News."

Several books have been written about Falwell and the evangelical right, virtually all of their authors displaying remarkable capacities for rage. They carry such titles as *God's Bullies, Holy Terror,* and *Thunder on the Right.*

Fortunately, on his television show, "The Old Time Gospel Hour," Falwell is able to counter some of the barrages fired at him. The program is broadcast weekly to four hundred stations across the country, and also to stations in Canada, Bermuda, Haiti, Australia, the British Virgin Islands, and the Philippines. In addition Falwell syndicates his Sunday church service from four to five hundred radio stations, and Moral Majority's politically charged *Moral Majority Report* boasts a circulation of one million.

The avalanche of criticism set off by Falwell's enemies and sustained by the media is intended to bury him politically and to shatter and disunite his constituency. His detractors often treat him with condescension, prefacing their attacks with "Of course Jerry Falwell is overrated" or "I dislike to give Jerry Falwell more publicity with this, but I feel an obligation. . . ." The urgency and bitterness of their polemic nevertheless betrays the realism of their fears. These are not necessarily fears that Falwell is going to take over the country and run it from Lynchburg—make everybody pray by day and lynch blacks by night. But there is at least the fear that Falwell, as a formidable force in American politics, can administer severe whacks to the backsides of liberal legislators and summon a powerful coalition to oppose heretofore privileged programs and opinions. Falwell's power is well illustrated in the defeat of the Equal Rights Amendment. As Falwell puts it, "The ERA was a piece of anti-family legislation. It was supported by all three networks, by every daily newspaper in America except three, by liberal politicians, by three presidents of the United States, by most of the members of Congress, by most of the governors, by most of the radio stations and the media, by almost everybody on the left, by most of the labor unions. Yet we stopped it." Except for Phyllis Schlafly, Falwell has probably done more than any individual to defeat the controversial amendment. And he has demonstrated substantial political clout on other issues: the nuclear freeze, homosexuality, abortion, school prayer. Those who admire, as well as fear, the forces of moralism would do well to beware of Jerry Falwell.

Media attacks on Falwell have been orgiastic, in part because of media feeling that he is what he is because he has manipulated them so effectively. In the *Washington Monthly*, journalist Tina Rosenberg attributed Falwell's national reputation mostly to a sleight-of-hand pulled on the networks and the print media. Media attacks on Falwell at times exude a sense of frustration because reporters see that trying to pull Falwell down often just unites and incenses his supporters, provoking them to write checks to Lynchburg, Virginia. Many conservatives who don't particularly identify with Falwell will send money to him because they detest the way he is roughed-about in the press.

Nevertheless, attacks on Falwell persist, most of them alleging that Falwell wants to establish a theocracy or "impose his morality" on an unwilling America. The media has had some success in efforts to cut Falwell off from mainline Christians, his natural allies, by implying that he is some sort of demon who wants to overthrow the Constitution. Reporters I have talked to admit that they routinely go after him but justify this by pointing out that Falwell, like Hitler, is a dangerous man who should be stopped. Who would want to give objective press to Hitler? They also claim their campaign to be a necessary antidote to the self-promotion Falwell does through his own radio and television show. And yet this campaign has backfired in unforeseen ways. In 1980 Falwell told Roger Mudd, "The media has done more to turn this country toward God than any one aspect of the propagation of the gospel in this century." Nothing infuriates reporters more than the thought that they and their medium raised up Jerry Falwell. They reserve the unqualified right to undo him if they can.

Falwell showed his political muscle in 1980, when Moral Majority joined other groups to defeat the incumbent president and left-leaning senators like Birch Bayh, Frank Church, George McGovern, and John Culver. President Reagan courted the evangelical vote, which he was told was enormous—between 20 and 50 million people. Reagan appointed Robert Billings, the executive director of Moral Majority, as religious liaison for his campaign. Falwell promised to deliver evangelical and fundamentalist votes to Reagan if the Republican platform reflected moral conservatism, which it did—reversing its position on the Equal Rights Amendment, strongly opposing abortion. And Falwell made good. In 1980, evangelicals voted for Reagan over Carter by 56 percent to 34 percent. Reagan signaled his awareness of Falwell's power by consulting with him about appointing George Bush as his running mate. He also phoned Falwell to explain his appointment of Sandra Day O'Connor, whose pro-life views were suspect, to the Supreme Court.

Although Falwell's group was not active in the 1982 election, Falwell's 1980 successes continue to project him as the national spokesman for morality. He, not William Sloan Coffin or the Berrigan brothers, is now consulted on the moral implications of euthanasia or homosexuality. And Falwell's recent activism on behalf of Reagan's defense policies and against the nuclear freeze suggests that he and

Moral Majority intend to be actively involved in the 1984 election campaign.

What is the source of Falwell's influence? Obviously some of it derives from his personal charisma and leadership. But Falwell is also a fortunate man standing at a crossroads of history; so let us consider the social currents that made room for him.

Jerry Falwell grew up in a fundamentalist milieu. Before he was born, fundamentalism was an intrinsic part of American culture, the dominant faith even. By the time of his youth and early adulthood, it had become a secessionist and truant faith mainly for zealots. Now, in Falwell's prime, fundamentalism is a moral tentacle re-entering mainstream culture, wrapping around its soft and wanton flesh, threatening to squeeze it back into shape.

Fundamentalism is much misunderstood in America today. Most people think of it as a way of doing things rather than as a system of beliefs. No matter what you think, if you rave and rant, seek to control and oppress your audience, and burn books in the process, you are a fundamentalist. Taking this approach, some have linked "fundamentalism" in Iran, Saudi Arabia, and America.

Naturally such comparisons are odious to fundamentalists in this country. Fundamentalists no more appreciate being likened to the Ayatollah Khomeini because he was a critic of modernism, than liberals relish being compared to Stalin because he was a critic of private property.

Fundamentalism in America is a concrete and coherent philosophy. It developed out of peculiar American circumstances and shares little in common with many of our own religious traditions, much less with Iranian or Saudi Arabian models. It is important to understand Protestant fundamentalism to see why, in the 1980s, some 20 million Americans have risen out of political apathy to institute what they consider a moral reformation of this country.

The term "fundamentalism" comes from *The Fundamentals: A Testimony to the Truth*, a set of twelve paperbound volumes published by the Bible Institute of Los Angeles between 1909 and 1919. Edited by Amzi Dixon, the purpose of these volumes was the defense of traditional, orthodox views of the Bible. Several distinguished theologians contributed essays which were not always in agreement. However, they did concur that orthodoxy was imperiled by creeping liberalism, which they equated with secularism. Thanks to two Los Angeles financiers, *The Fundamentals* was distributed to some 3 million people. Every pastor, evangelist, missionary, theology professor, theology student, and Sunday School superintendent whose address could be obtained received a copy. The tone of *The Fundamentals* was erudite, not hortatory, but its message was urgent: Theological liberalism must be repealed.

Of course there were fundamentalists before Dixon got around to publishing his volumes, but they were not a united group and squabbled endlessly about fine points of doctrine. Precursors include Dispensationalism, Revivalism, pietism, the Holiness movements, Puritanism, Reformed Confessionalism, and the orthodox Presbyterian theology of the so-called Princeton group. Basically, what is important to remember is that contemporary fundamentalism developed in reaction to theological liberalism.

Theological liberals like to think of themselves as just nice guys applying modern insights to old-fashioned theology. But fundamentalists do not accept this innocuous image. They see the liberal agenda as a deliberate attempt to erode the authority of Scripture. The key issue between fundamentalists and modernists from the start has been the accuracy of Scripture.

Fundamentalists feel that the Bible is without error. Liberals admit that, ahem, it is the word of god, but, you know, transcribed by simpletons, so there is understandable confusion. Liberals "update" Scripture by ignoring certain things they don't like and adding relevant data collected by science. They are sure that the Author would be pleased with the corrections. The fundamentalists violently object. After all, if the Bible is not infallible, it is like any other book, say the "inspired" writings of Shakespeare. If people can pick and choose what is and is not true in the Bible, the authority of Scripture will be undermined seriously.

The liberal program has not been restricted to attacking the credibility of Scripture, but that was the essential first step. Scripture was the lone sentry at the gates of modernism, which liberals wanted open. Liberals have always denied that they want to substitute secularism for Scripture, but that is what they appear to have done. First they said that while the Bible was infallible, certain beliefs were not incompatible with science. Then they said that certain passages should be discounted in favor of scientific explanation. For example, creation was best explained by the scientific theory of evolution. Next they discounted miracles described in the Bible as metaphorical and hyperbolic, mere expressions of belief by illiterate people. Then it was no longer necessary to believe that Christ literally rose from the dead, in the sense that he left an empty tomb. The Resurrection could be understood as a spiritual metamorphosis. Next they said that while Christ was the son of God, beliefs intended to corroborate this, such as the virgin birth, were superfluous. It was the essential credo that mattered. Then we read that while the Bible seems to say that Christ is the only way to salvation, what that means is problematic. And the term *saved* itself was ambiguous. Some people don't feel the need to be saved. Shall we ostracize them from the Church? Certainly not, so now Christ was better understood as a great moral teacher from whom we could all learn much. Then they said that Christ's moral teachings were in no way superior to the proclamations of Hindu and Buddhist teachers. Each guru was great in his or her own way. Finally the liberals announced that the concept *God* was itself obscure, used in different ways by different people. All one needed to acknowledge was that it refers to some creative process.

Fundamentalists saw this coming for a long time. Many of them sounded paranoid. They had reason to be, although invoking paranoia is not the best way to win an argument. Fundamentalists were scorned for equating Darwinism with Satanism. Liberals, urbane in their unbelief, could easily portray their critics as deep-South rustics living amongst armadillos and practicing religious literalism. And some were, although this does not mean they were in the wrong. Unfortunately, few fundamentalists were stylish enough to compete against the liberals on liberal terms. Whether or not fundamentalists may have been right all along, they became unfashionable. They were thought of as ignorant. Liberalism came to be thought of as sophisticated and superior.

Early fundamentalist preachers came in different sizes and colors. The Reverend Dwight Moody, who preached just after the Civil War, was moderate and bashful. Moody hated controversy. His message— "Ruin by sin, redemption by Christ, and regeneration by the Holy Ghost"—was relatively bland. Contrast him with pastors like Frank Norris or Billy Sunday, both early twentieth century pastors. Sunday brought the techniques of vaudeville to revivalism. His characteristic response to questions on theology or history was "That's too deep for me," or "I'll have to pass that up." Sunday was, like many of today's fundamentalist preachers, also patriotic. He fanned the flags of anti-German sentiment during World War I. "If you turn hell upside down you will find 'Made in Germany' stamped on the bottom," he once said.

Norris, a leading Baptist during the 1920s, was also a bit of a show-

man. During the evolution controversy, Norris brought apes and mon-
keys into the pulpit and introduced listeners to their "kinfolk,"
according to Darwin's thesis. He campaigned hard against Catholic
presidential candidate Al Smith in 1928 and is credited with a big role
in Herbert Hoover's victory. Norris' sermons struck panic in liberal
hearts. He spoke on such topics as "The Ten Biggest Devils in Fort
Worth, Names Given" and "Rum and Romanism."

Norris was a lively change from liberal theologians, who were bland
and verbose. The most eminent of these was Harry Emerson Fosdick,
who in 1922 preached a famous sermon entitled "Shall the Fundamentalists Win?" Fosdick concluded that they wouldn't and shouldn't
and was subsequently forced to resign from the First Presbyterian
Church in New York.

The antics of such as Norris and Sunday may give the impression
that fundamentalists, as a rule, were hostile to reason. Certainly some
were. "We study only the Bible" was, in fact, the motto of a church
where Falwell himself taught Sunday School in the early 1950s. Yet
fundamentalists who detested learning did so because they were envious of intelligent men; many of them never had the opportunity to be
well educated. The scorn they invited from the liberal Left only exas-
perated their prejudices, because they did not know how to reply.

Fundamentalists also found that liberals, who spoke passionately
about the poor and uneducated, were very illiberal in their treatment
of fundamentalists. They began to suspect what today is less secret:
that liberalism is regarded as liberal only by its friends. To others it displays great intolerance. This point was made as early as 1923 by J.
Gresham Machen, whose book *Christianity and Liberalism* is perhaps
the finest defense of fundamentalism ever written. Machen and his
colleagues at the Princeton Theological Seminary spearheaded the intellectual wing of fundamentalism while involved in bitter polemics
with their liberal counterparts, they were as knowledgeable and tren-
chant as any of them.

Contrary to popular belief, fundamentalism was not opposed to reason and science from the outset. There is a strong empirical common-
sense strain in fundamentalism. Fundamentalists embraced the
inductive techniques of Francis Bacon because they were sure these
would validate Scripture, not refute it. Scholar Ernest Sandeen comments that fundamentalists "never wavered from the fundamental
tenet that if the Bible was to be proven to be God's word the demonstration must be made on the basis of reason, through the use of

authenticity—not inner convictions." With Aquinas, fundamentalists held that reason and revelation were never in conflict.

But fundamentalists were opposed to the "authority" of speculative science. That is why they found Darwinism so incomprehensible and threatening. Darwin had done more than anyone else in history to make atheists out of Christians. In this sense, who cared if Darwin's theories were right or wrong? As Mordecai Ham said, "To hell with science if it's going to damn souls."

Darwin's theory was more than a threat to the biblical account of creation, as most preachers understood it. Darwin's speculative framework threatened the entire epistemological approach of fundamentalists. George Marsden believes that this epistemological challenge was more serious than the attack on creation for most fundamentalists, because it threatens their entire basis for knowledge. That is why for many fundamentalists the evolution controversy was not just a question of two conflicting accounts. It was science versus Scripture, fact versus theory, darkness versus light, barbarism versus Western civilization.

In 1925 John Scopes, a biology teacher in Dayton, Tennessee, was charged with violating a state anti-evolution law. The American Civil Liberties Union and liberals across the country rallied to his defense. Hundreds of reporters showed up at Dayton, including the inimitable H.L. Mencken, a newspaper comedian who aspired to be acclaimed an intellectual. Mencken spurned the fundamentalists in order to gain credibility with the city elite. Most of the media saw the Scopes trial in terms of backwoods preachers against city sophisticates, ignorance against knowledge, Southern myth against scientific laws. I list these contrasts to show that the media, no less than the fundamentalists, saw the trial in Manichean terms: absolute good versus absolute evil.

As far as the jurors were concerned, Scopes did not stand a chance. All twelve jurors were local farmers of strong religious bent. They found Scopes guilty in short order, and he was fined $100. But right from the start, fundamentalism did not have a prayer in the media. Reporters disliked fundamentalists. They were furious with them, if for no other reason than that many fundamentalists did not bother to read major city newspapers like the *New York Times*, if indeed they had heard of them. It was no surprise when the *Baltimore Sun* put up the $500 bail money for Scopes.

Of course media condescension was not the only reason fundamentalists lost at Dayton. How could they win, when their religious beliefs were subjected to an exclusively legal and scientific examination? Fundamentalists thought of religion as a synthesis of reason and revelation. Certainly some biblical claims were enigmatic, but these were the province of revelation. Who needed to prove in scientific terms that Eve was made from Adam's rib? And yet fundamentalists believed it. Even their finest spokesman, William Jennings Bryan, could not justify these mysteries at Dayton. In fact Scopes' attorney, Clarence Darrow, forced Bryan to admit that his belief in the biblical account of creation was essentially dogmatic. Previously Bryan had held that Christianity was scientific, that if science said otherwise, it was speaking unscientifically. But when it was all over, Darrow had made a monkey out of Bryan.

Scopes ended in a tremendous psychological defeat for fundamentalism. Bryan died shortly after the trial, a broken man. But fundamentalists refused to give up on their beliefs. They held, with Bryan, that "It is better to trust the Rock of Ages than to know the age of the rocks." Most other Americans reacted by drawing a Kantian line between science, based on reason, and religion, based on faith.

The creation controversy was only one of several breaking points with modernism. Fundamentalists also objected to biblical criticism that subjected the Bible to vagrant theories of psychologists and literary critics. These men claimed to use their disciplines to wring higher truths out of the Bible, but fundamentalists viewed them as charlatans.

There was also a battle in the religious press about social gospel ministry. This was prompted by Walter Rauschenbusch's A Theology for the Social Gospel, written in 1917, which implied that charitable works were the conduit to salvation. This for fundamentalists had rings of the Catholic heresy of works. Did not Luther and Calvin maintain that we are justified by faith and not by deeds? Certainly fundamentalists believed that faith in God spawned altruism, and before 1917 fundamentalists were actively engaged in social work. But when they saw a social gospel substituted for Christian belief, they abandoned social activism in order to more strongly emphasize the need for a personal acceptance of Christ and a personal morality.

Before long, fundamentalists were linking social gospel with Marxism. They saw more and more liberal churchmen employ Marxist analogies. Marxists maintained that God was essentially a class concept. For fundamentalists this was no better than Darwinism which seemed to say that an indifferent Nature was as close as one could come to God. But fundamentalists did not have battles with social gospel advocates or Marxists that were as bitter as the battle at Dayton.

After Scopes, fundamentalism developed strong separatist tendencies. Many saw the trial as a confirmation of their suspicion that the world itself was evil and that the Second Coming of Christ was imminent. So fundamentalists withdrew from involvement with secular institutions of American life to prepare for the end. They were helped along by liberal spurs. Fundamentalist educators were kicked out of the universities. The media proclaimed fundamentalism intellectually discredited. Politicians no longer took fundamentalists seriously, even in their own constituencies. They were outcasts, shoved out of society, not because of low birth or skin color, but because of alleged stupidity. Maybe it is not so surprising that after 1925 many fundamentalists withdrew their children from secular schools and founded their own institutions and academies. Many of them did not vote any longer. They refused to marry outside their denomination. They had washed their hands of this world.

Historian David Harrel writes: "It was widely assumed that the Dayton debacle had killed fundamentalism. It was never so. The fundamentalists were still there—up in the coves and hallows, milking the cows, driving the trucks and tractors, in the cinder block churches that lined the railroad tracks. Mencken mused while riding the train back to Baltimore from Dayton that one could throw a brick out of the window almost anywhere en route and hit a fundamentalist on the head. But they seemed remote and bizarre, and they talked funny, generally with a Southern drawl, so they were ignored." The 1930s were a time for rapid, independent growth for fundamentalist institutions. The fundamentalists, like the Catholics and Jews and Mormons before them, established their own schools, summer Bible camps, colleges and seminaries, and their own radio stations, magazines, and picture companies. During this time they were concerned not with controversy, but with nurturing the flock. Their characteristic expressions changed from bitter doctrinal disputes to tambourines and entertainment.

As a firm institutional base was consolidated, fundamentalists once again turned their attention outward. Unlike the Catholics and Mormons, who sought multiplication mainly through reproduction, the fundamentalists tried to live up to the biblical command to evangelize. During 1936 the Moody Bible Institute held five hundred Bible conferences throughout the country. Numerous associations were founded: the American Baptist Association, the World Baptists Fellowship, the Independent Fundamental Churches of America.

Some preachers adopted radio ministries as a way of evangelizing the world. While radio might seem a compromise of the withdrawal from a corrupt material world, in fact it proved a way for preachers to reach out to unbelievers without actually confronting them. Fundamentalists were fearful of venturing out into the world after Scopes. There were nasty liberals out there waiting to ambush. Radio provided a way to avoid this trap, to speak to the masses without a few slick upstarts spoiling the show.

The Second World War was a blow to the solar plexus of liberal theology. It exploded the liberal dream of creating a heaven on earth. World War II reminded liberals that there is a hell and life is tragic. Religious orthodoxy benefited from this return to realism—witness the popularity of theologians like Reinhold Niebuhr and Paul Tillich.

In 1941 the American Council of Christian Churches was founded by Carl McIntire. It grew quickly. In 1942 the National Association of Evangelicals was born. It grew, too. These two organizations reflected a brewing dispute between fundamentalists and evangelicals. There was no disagreement over doctrine; evangelicals objected to the methodology and style of the fundamentalists. Theirs was a watered-down fundamentalism. Its strength was its broader appeal, its ecumenism. Its weakness was its coupling of a stern absolute doctrine with sweet proclamations, what Samuel Butler called "brimstone and treacle."

Both fundamentalists and evangelical churches experienced brisk growth through the 1940s and 1950s. In 1949 a Baptist preacher named Billy Graham catapulted to fame when he converted 1500 people at a three-week tent crusade in Los Angeles. Graham was friendly to both evangelicals and fundamentalists, although he drew fire from zealots in both camps for, alternately, strident rhetoric and excessive ecumenism. By 1980 Graham was the best known evangelist in the world, and had witnessed Christ to more than 900 million people.

In the 1950s two preachers, Billy James Hargis and Carl McIntire, made an attempt to draw fundamentalists out of their political apathy. Hargis founded the Christian Crusade in 1949 in Tulsa, Oklahoma. He was vigorously anti-Communist and proved it by floating more than a million gas balloons carrying Bibles over into the Soviet Union. Hargis and McIntire were conspiracy theorists on the order of Joseph McCarthy. Like the Wisconsin senator, they were basically correct about Communism, but tended to exaggerate. In the 1950s McCarthy's followers attacked fluoridation as an attempt to advance socialism under the guise of public health. Similarly Hargis and McIntire saw a Lenin in disguise on the altar of every liberal church. But not many fundamentalists followed Hargis and McIntire. Their priorities were focused on nurturing their own congregations and converting others to Christ. All else was subservient, if not a sheer waste of time.

Most people see the 1960s and 1970s as a great time for secularism and liberalism. In a sense, they were. Liberal policies were put into effect with minimal resistance. All loci of power—the universities, the cultural elite, government—were dominated by liberals. The mainline churches bolstered the secular spirit of the times, hoping thereby to wring some religious concessions from the secularists. But the 1960s also saw liberalism fail. And as its failure become more evident, more and more people who were unsure about liberal fancies from the outset began to defect to the conservative camp. Most conspicuous among these defectors were the neoconservatives, erstwhile liberals who are now the most formidable opponents of a government-dominated society.

The orthodox fundamentalist churches enjoyed mammoth expansion in the late 1960s and early 1970s. The First Baptist Church of Hammond, Indiana, had 700 members in 1959; twenty-three years later its average attendance was 15,000. In 1942 the Highland Baptist Church in Chattanooga, Tennessee, had 470 members. Now it has 33,000. Now, these are exceptional figures, not typical; but the rapid growth of fundamentalist churches overall is undeniable. A curious thing was happening. Liberal churches, who were spending so much time making their religion "relevant" to modern needs, were losing members rapidly. Conservative churches, which persisted in holding "antiquated" doctrines in the face of inevitable change, were doubling and quadrupling in size. This has been a source of great chagrin to liberal churchmen. Their secular allies expected more from them.

By 1980 as many as 100 million Americans espoused traditional religious or moral views. They were ripe for political picking. Liberals, still intoxicated from victories among the intellectual and government elites, were largely ignorant of this massive shift, at least initially. They did not know that the ground had slipped from under them. They thought they were invulnerable. But it was not so.

It is not that all evangelicals and fundamentalists who are politically conscious today were defectors from the liberal camp. Indeed many of them resisted liberalism from the outset. But they resisted it only theologically, not politically. And most of their resistance took the form of keeping liberal theology from invading their churches. They did not bother to tackle liberalism in hostile territory. They didn't challenge the National Council of Churches and the World Council of Churches when these two bodies issued vigorous defenses of Marxist governments, social gospel theology, or the New International Economic Order. There were a few fundamentalist activists in the 1960s, but they were never able to convince their fellows to abandon prospering enclaves and enter the messy real world. It was comfortable concentrating on Sunday church-going and organ music. Who wanted to combat pornography, sex education, and defense policies when these did not threaten the fundamentalist subculture?

Then along came Jerry Falwell. His power over the fundamentalists has been enormous, not only because of his mesmerizing speeches, genial manner, and his tireless working, but also because he truly is one of them. Until the mid-1960s Falwell, like most fundamentalists, was against entering politics. It was biblically verboten; it took time away from evangelization. So then when he stood up and asked fundamentalists to get out and vote, telling them it was their duty as Americans and Christians, that "it is a sin not to vote," people took notice. they had felt hurt from political blows against their cherished beliefs. They were not initially interested in politics, but then politics became interested in them. It took prayer out of their schools and placed pornography and drugs in reach of their children. It condoned vice in schools in the name of liberality, and vaunted skepticism. It denounced religion as antiquated and oppressive. The fundamentalists were paralyzed until Falwell told them not only that it was okay for them to hit back, but that it was positively a biblical command to do so.

The entry of several million evangelicals and fundamentalists into politics came as a surprise both to liberals and to the fundamentalist leaders who had been counseling separation from politics since the middle 1920s. Each group attacked Falwell as a false messiah, but without success. The time was ripe for fundamentalists to get back into the social fracas, and Falwell was the man to draw them into it. Falwell's enemies have discovered how difficult it is to beat the combination of a troubled people and a charismatic leader.

Falwell has not only been able to tap into fundamentalist alienation and frustration; he has also proved able, despite his narrow religious orthodoxy, to attract followers among the majority of American Christians and Jews worried about the moral slide of their society. This is because he has been willing to forge both religious and political alliances, the letter based solely upon a moral consensus. Moral Majority, the organization Falwell started in 1979, is a political alliance of Roman Catholics (who comprise 30 percent of the membership), evangelicals, conservative Jews, Mormons, and nonreligious people concerned with morality. These people share little, if any, religious doctrine, but they do agree that America should be strengthened militarily, that abortion should be stopped, that drugs and promiscuity are scarring our society, that the family is the defining unit of our society.

Besides politicizing fundamentalists and unifying moralists of different faiths under the Moral Majority banner; Falwell has accomplished more. Daniel Yankelovitch observed in *Psychology Today* (November 1981) that Falwell appeals to many more people than send $25 to his church or Moral Majority. People unaffiliated with Falwell, who may be embarrassed at identifying with him, nevertheless sympathize with many of his positions. Opinion polls show that Americans rank the decline in morality as the single greatest problem facing the country today—worse than the arms race, the rising crime rate, the racism and sexism said to dominate our society, or unemployment.

The people concerned about the nation's moral slide, then, are Falwell's larger constituency. Falwell doesn't care whether they like him personally—he isn't running for election—but he does affect the way they think and act. He puts their fears into a political context; then he encourages them to express this political feeling. Most often this is done through voting for conservative politicians either Republican or Democratic.

I watched Falwell in action during the week of October 4-11, 1983, and had a chance to see how he exploited his political base. On October 10 I traveled with Falwell and Moral Majority officials to Raleigh, North Carolina, and then to Toledo, Ohio. At Raleigh we were met by the Reverend Lamarr Mooneyham, a youthful pastor who is also director of Moral Majority for the state of North Carolina. Mooneyham took us to the Galeria restaurant in Raleigh, where Falwell and he discussed the crucial senatorial race between Jesse Helms and Governor Hunt.

"Can you give me two hundred thousand people, Lamarr?" Falwell asked.

Mooneyham hedged. He explained difficulties with registering voters. He said he was still setting up an organizational base. And he didn't think it would need two hundred thousand to get Helms re-elected. "The man who can deliver one hundred thousand votes can deliver the state," Mooneyham said.

Shortly before our conversation, Jesse Jackson had appeared in North Carolina to help register black voters and defeat Helms. Jackson had raced through the state, raising a lot of dust and generating media coverage, but his people weren't doing much, according to Mooneyham. "We're having some problems, but we're doing much better." Moral Majority's slogan for the North Carolina race was "Do you want Jesse Jackson of Illinois or Jesse Helms of North Carolina?"

Mooneyham called Jackson a "racist" and Helms a "God-fearing man." Falwell said Helms was probably the only man he would entrust his kids to. "We've got to win this one," he told Mooneyham. "This may be even more important than the presidential race."

We left Raleigh at 11:30 A.M. and flew to Ohio, where Falwell preached to some eight hundred pastors from Ohio, Michigan, and Indiana. The talk, sponsored by the Toledo Baptist Church, was being held under the aegis of the Bible Baptist Fellowship, a fundamentalist organization. Falwell's talk to these pastors was important because it would have a multiplying effect. These pastors each had churches with anywhere from sixty to five hundred members. If what Falwell said had an effect on them, they would spread it across their congregations. So in effect Falwell was reaching as many as one hundred thousand people that day.

His mood was aggressive and optimistic. "I am often charged with trying to establish a Christian America," he said. "I don't want a theocracy, but yes, I would like more people in this country to live Christian lives." Outlining the nation's Judeo-Christian heritage, Falwell said, "While many of our founding fathers were deists, they nevertheless respected the ideas of God, decency, and morality." He denounced the wanton murder of unborn infants, promising, "We're going to stop the carnage. Whether they like it or not, we are going to stop the murder of one and a half million babies a year. It's going to happen. It's not a matter of how, it's a matter of when."

Sounding the hopeful note he has echoed since 1982, Falwell thundered, "I'm glad things are changing in this country. That's why they're marching in the streets. In a couple of weeks the atheists, the American Atheist Society, will be marching on our sidewalks, and, let's see, in another week we have the gays who are coming to march. We had the feminists a few weeks ago. And then the Communists and the Nazis will come, no doubt. They're coming from everywhere. That's wonderful. You know why they're marching? You know why the pornographers and abortionists are angry? Because they're losing." The pastors began to applaud. "Do you think for one moment that the liberals don't know the tide has turned? Do you wonder why there are forty-eight groups formed last month to combat just Jerry Falwell and fundamentalist Christians?"

Ed Holland, the pastor of Toledo Baptist Church, told me that Falwell was having a powerful effect in getting his people to "stand up for the issues." After Falwell's speech, Holland congratulated Falwell but indicated problems with mobilizing a political force in Toledo. "Toledo is largely Catholic," Holland complained; then he began to denounce the Catholic bishops.

Falwell tempered what was becoming an anti-Catholic tirade. "I bet I could get a big crowd of Catholics and Jews out here. Hey, those people have a common cause with us on the moral issues."

Fundamentalists have entered the political ball game; that is the reality. Falwell has shown what a promising, and punishing, reality it can be. Liberals try to ignore this. They make much of the inconsistency of other-worldly preachers talking about current affairs. Despite the 1980 defeat of Church, McGovern, and Brademas, they have concluded that fundamentalism is an evanescent phenomenon. Falwell may have created a hullaballoo in 1980, but he is pretty much deflated now. The Liberal establishment need not fear the Southern crazies now. They have also decided that Falwell has no supporters outside the fundamentalist movement.

Of course this was all said in 1980, when Falwell, Richard Viguerie, and others predicted what was to come. But liberals do not want to remember 1980, which they are convinced was a freak shift, not a major political realignment. In fact the moral indignation of Christian America has *not* subsided. So to the extent that the Left ignores Falwell, which is really to ignore moral America, it stands in serious jeopardy. In a 1977 article in *New Times*, Andrew Kopkind wrote, "To disregard [fundamentalism's] authentic roots in home-town America is to misread the new national mood, and to become its most vulnerable victim." It could happen again.

3

Growing Up Wild

On August 11, 1933 (eight years after the Scopes trial) Helen Falwell of Lynchburg, Virginia, went into labor prematurely. Opening her eyes wearily after the delivery, she asked her husband Carey, "Is it a boy or girl?" To which he replied, "Two boys, dear. Two boys." Helen lay back and went to sleep with a smile on her face.

Carey Falwell was forty and Helen was thirty-eight. They hadn't expected another child, let alone two. But after the death of a daughter, Rosha, two years earlier of appendicitis, the replacements were appreciated.

There were four children in the Falwell family now: Virginia, age sixteen; Lewis, age six; and the twins, with no score yet. The family had scores of relatives living in and about the town, all descendants of Charles Falwell, landowner, dairyfarmer, and atheist. They came around to get a look at the twins. There had never been twins in the Falwell clan before.

The curly-haired twin, Jerry; took after his father. You could see it in the set jaw and aggressive hand movement. The other baby, Gene, was passive and content. He took after Helen's family, the Beasleys, no doubt about it.

Their father, Carey Falwell, was a well-known local businessman whose trucks hauled fuel for most of the local automobiles and mills. The Falwell family had been part of the original community of Lynch-burg, founded in 1757 when John Lynch, son of an Irish tobacco farmer, established a ferry at a ford along the James River. The ford be-came a popular trading place in Virginia, and soon people from differ-ent parts of Virginia, the North and Europe settled in the area. The settlement was named Lynchburg after its ferryman-founder. During the American Revolution Lynch and his brother Charles took to seiz-ing Tories and hanging them by their thumbs until they yelled "Lib-erty forever." This practice became rather common in the area, giving rise to the term *lynching*.

Alexis de Tocqueville passed through Lynchburg early in the nine-teenth century, gathering material for his classic *Democracy in Amer-ica*. It impressed Tocqueville, in Lynchburg as elsewhere, that America distinguished herself not by her aristocracy or religious establishment, but by her voluntary associations, mainly independent churches of ex-traordinary strength and vitality. Despite Baptist predominance, the town was, from the start, lenient about its denominational orthodoxy. Quakers set up shop here from the beginning, and the first Catholic church was built in 1843, decades before one was built in the nation's capital. Before the American Revolution Thomas Jefferson and Pa-trick Henry often used the Lynchburg ferry, and Jefferson praised the town highly for its "enterprise and correct course." During the Civil War Lynchburg was, of course, a Confederate stronghold.

The City of Lynchburg is self-conscious about its heritage. Grand monuments honor its founder and its importance during the Civil War. Lynchburg looks what it is, a manufacturing town. It was dusty and smoke-filled already fifty years ago, when Carey's father, Charles Falwell, owned a good deal of it. Lynchburg was then, as it is now, a conglomeration of rednecks and aristocrats, Southern crazies and Southern belles, white trash and old money.

The Falwell family has always been concentrated in and around Lynchburg. Jerry Falwell's grandfather was a landowner, and his father before him a slaveholder, but the wealth handed down to Carey was as much a wealth of memories as of provisions. However, Carey, a lean, hard entrepreneur, took what little capital his father had provided him and turned it into real money, *noveau* money, so that even in the worst of the Depression he still owned several cars and regularly ate venison. He was, according to his relatives, a scrupulous trader and parent . . . and a mean bootlegger. His wife, Helen, by contrast, was the epit-ome of the stern Christian woman—Victorian manner, painfully pious, strict with her children, yet patient and submissive toward her husband, whose boisterousness she could never control.

Carey Falwell and Helen Beasley grew up some forty miles apart in the Lynchburg area. Carey was raised outside the church; his father felt that religion was an obstacle to ambition. One of sixteen children, Helen was raised in Appomattox County. Her father, King David Beasley, sent her to Sunday School regularly. Both Carey and Helen walked several miles to school as children, but apparently neither found it worth the trek, for they both dropped out after the seventh grade. Then they went to work. They were married in 1913. Virginia was born shortly after and christened in a Christian ceremony. Helen insisted on it. Carey, an agnostic indifferent to religion, didn't care.

At first, they lived on the family property with Carey's three brothers, one sister and their families and worked the land. But this was the dawn of the automobile age, and Carey soon became fascinated with four-wheel frames that moved and kicked back smoke. He borrowed money from his father and started Power Oil Co., a company that delivered gasoline for local consumption. The fuel came in to Richmond on barges where Carey's men loaded it on a train to Lynchburg station to be stored in large tanks in the Falwell back yard until trucking companies made orders. Carey, who had a virtual monopoly, made quick profits this way, so he soon expanded into the trucking business himself. He also pioneered the first bus lines in Virginia in the late 1920s.

By the early 1930s Carey controlled most of the transportation industry in Lynchburg. It was time to enjoy life, so he constructed the Old Fort Hotel on a historic site in Lynchburg where the South had put up a fortress to keep out Union soldiers during the Civil War. Here he began his first bouts with liquor, while his wife stayed home meticulously conserving their newfound resources, darning the children's socks.

In late 1931, two years before Jerry and Gene were born, Carey and Helen lost their second daughter, Rosha. She came down with appendicitis; the family doctor diagnosed it as pneumonia. Carey refused to take the girl to the hospital. Like many, he distrusted hospitals. Subsequently Rosha's appendix burst, and she died of blood poisoning. That same year, Carey shot his younger brother, Garland, in a duel. Garland allegedly challenged Carey to a shoot-out in the family-owned restaurant. It was a fatal challenge.

Jerry Falwell and his sister, Virginia, feel that it was these two incidents that drove Carey to drink. He had begun swigging in the bootlegging days, rebelling against the Prohibition that his wife's family and fellow fundamentalists had lobbied for. His drinking was chronic by the late 1930s, when Jerry and Gene were in their early years of school. Jerry remembers that Carey Falwell always talked about his dead brother and daughter after bouts of drinking.

Gene Raymond was named after the movie actor who bears that name. The name Jerry was picked simply for the sound, and Jerry's middle name, Laymon, was selected to rhyme with Gene's middle name, Raymond.

Gene and Jerry are not identical twins. Everyone says Jerry takes after his father—he is hard-driving and aggressive, a business whiz, done-up and sophisticated yet bafflingly naive, a workaholic. Gene, they say, gets his easygoing ways from the Beasley family. He is sensitive, mechanically minded, likes to work with his hands, and walks away from fights. He hates the city, the squabble, and the rat race, preferring to fish and grow vegetables. "Jerry has always been a firecracker," says his uncle Calvin Falwell. "But now Gene, he wouldn't raise his voice if the roof fell on his head." Gene was bigger than Jerry in their early years, however, and dominated their relationship. "We had many fights," Jerry recalls. "Luckily my father would stop them, because I would have gotten creamed." Jerry was the one who provoked most of the fights.

The twins were registered at Mountain View Elementary school in Lynchburg. Their father was prosperous, and they were driven there by a black servant, Dave Brown. Falwell remembers Brown as a soft-spoken, wise man who was blind in one eye, wore suspenders, and carried the twins on his shoulders. "I learned my right jab from him," Jerry says, speaking affectionately of Brown, who is now retired and living in Stamford, Connecticut. There were about thirty kids in Jerry and Gene's class, and the twins soon beat up the males to establish rank. At school, Jerry discovered that he had an aptitude for math and science; Gene hated class and frequently did not attend. Jerry liked to play pranks, some of them a little cruel, but Gene very often took the blame. It was not just because of brotherly love. Gene hoped they would kick him out of school.

In the second grade, Jerry once locked a new teacher in a closet. "She was a math teacher, fresh out of college, and it was her first day," Falwell recalls. "We didn't intend anything mean; we just wanted to have fun." Jerry and another student lured the woman into the closet, then skipped out and locked the door. She remained there until the end of class; crying out, but not loud enough for anyone to hear. When she was finally rescued, she was too frightened to be able to identify the culprits, whom she described only as "young and bad boys." The school principal, however, was less diffident and began an inquiry to locate the rogues, promising stern punishment. When the pressure had built to a point where Jerry was about to confess, his brother, Gene, to Jerry's astonishment, stood up and said, "I did it, sir. I am responsible for this." "He was like that," Jerry said. "Always looking to get whacked and expelled."

After school the twins played two-man baseball in the cow pasture or wrestling in the barn with Pep, their terrier. Often on Thursday around 3:00 P.M. the twins would go down to a nearby ravine and lie on their stomachs to thrill to the sensation of a train thundering over their heads, filling the ravine with noise and shaking the earth under them. In more serene moments they went walking on Candlers Mountain, now part of Falwell church land. There they nibbled on strange plants and looked for insects and animals.

At times Gene and Jerry also accompanied Virginia on dates with her fiance, Lawrence Jennings, who insists he did not find their company iritating. (Jennings was to be Virginia's second husband. Her first marriage, at a very young age, had already soured.) "They were devilish, wide-awake kids," Jennings remembers. "They looked on me as a real buddy." Virginia says, "They followed us everywhere. They wanted to know what we saw in each other. I suppose, in a way, we were happy to have them along." The young couple took the twins to movies—wild Westerns were their favorite—or on picnics. Jennings, possibly to impress his girl, taught them skills like how to tie various knots and how to cure meat. He also taught Jerry to shoot an airgun at an early age, and then regretted it because Jerry used the airgun "to blow up all the windows on the Falwell property and in Lynchburg," in Jennings' words.

Jerry Falwell had a happy childhood, but he didn't see much of his father, even before the latter's hard-drinking years. Carey Falwell, Jerry remembers, woke up at four in the morning, read the paper, had breakfast at five, which his wife diligently prepared for him, and was in the office by six. He returned home late to gulp down his dinner and then sit outside the house. In a rare and inexplicable moment, Carey put one hand on Jerry's head and the other on Gene's and said, "This one will be my preacher, and this one my doctor." The first part of the prediction eventually came true although why an agnostic would wish that is unclear. Virginia Falwell remembers the incident distinctly.

As a father, Carey was usually affectionate, although he could be draconian. Serious pranks of the kids were referred to him by Helen.

She herself set minor offenses right with her switch. Carey's hand was infinitely heavier, though, and the twins avoided his wrath. "My father was two hundred ten pounds and hefty," Jerry Falwell says. "By the time he finished with you, rebellion was out of the question." Carey was a short-haired and clean-shaven man who, according to Calvin Falwell, his nephew, hated beards and mustaches because "they gave you a kind of careless, hippie look." So the twins grew up clean shaven too. They shared an awe about their father and respected his power, although it was exercised relatively infrequently.

Carey mostly drank in the late evening, although it sometimes carried over into the early morning. He drank vodka, rum, whiskey, beer, or a potpourri of these out of a large earthen mug. Friends who saw Carey say he could often hardly move, but his mind was always sharp. He could make business decisions in the most comatose-seeming state. Nor did drinking make him noisy or fitful. He just sat there, wobbling his feet, nursing his bottle, sipping himself unconscious. Naturally, the drinking was a source of embarrassment to Helen and the children, but they treated Carey with unfailing respect, even when he would not recognize it. Helen was a teetotaler all her life. Jerry and Gene, however, admit that their father's habit led them to sample liquor, and the two quaffed a lot at Pickreal's Cafe in Lynchburg, even at a young age.

Helen Falwell understood her sons' vagrancies; she was not naive. But neither did she see human failings as an excuse for having lenient rules, or none at all. Mrs. Falwell had been raised in a strict home. As a child, her parents took her to Hollywood Baptist Church—Hollywood was the name of the county—and even after she married the religiously indiferent Carey, Helen attended regular service at the Franklin Street Baptist Church, where pastor Robert Randolph delivered kindly sermons. Randolph was well respected in Campbell County, where the Falwells owned property, because he preached a practical faith that most people could live by. Helen seldom missed a service.

She made Jerry and Gene attend Sunday School at Franklin Street Church. The boys protested wildly, asserting their right to make up their own minds, proclaiming their maturity and independence from religion, but to no avail. Dave Brown drove them to church each Sunday morning at 10 A.M. But no sooner did his car sputter away than the twins would skip into the brush. Often they went to their Uncle Matthew Ferguson's house and read the comics, but this practice stopped when Ferguson began reporting their presence to Mrs. Falwell. After that they went walking around the neighborhood, returning to church in time to be picked up by an unsuspecting Brown each week.

"I found Sunday School boring, the few times that I went," Jerry says. "But that could be because of my father. Since he didn't go to church, Gene and I didn't see why we had to go." Falwell says he also regarded religion as "something women did." The twins "attended" Sunday School until age thirteen. They were baptized at age twelve, but Jerry says he had no "personal relationship with Christ"—it was "purely ritual." "We went in dry sinners and came out wet sinners." Shortly after this, he and Gene dropped out of church. "My father said we could make up our own minds," Jerry explains. "Mom couldn't force us to go to church anymore."

Helen adopted a new proselytization strategy for the twins. On Sundays she would wake up early to fix Carey breakfast, she would turn on the Charles E. Fuller radio broadcast from Long Beach, California. Fuller's "Old Fashioned Revival Hour" was broadcast coast to coast and also reached out to the southernmost tip of South America and to islands of the Pacific. Although Fuller was not a hoarse preacher, screaming and having fits on the air, Jerry and Gene both found his voice extremely irritating. It spoke to them calmly from the radio across the room. The twins, half asleep in their beds, were too lazy to get up and turn it off. "My mother was smart about Dr. Fuller," Jerry says. "She knew that our laziness would win over our exasperation, and we would keep listening to him."

For a time it was not clear that these tactics of Helen's would work. There was something of the hell raiser in her boys, especially Jerry. Both Jerry and Gene were driving cars by age ten. They had to stretch their necks to see the road and their feet to reach the brake, but they drove fast on back roads nevertheless, scaring workers and sending children scuttling. Jerry was fond of automobiles for their slickness and speed. Gene liked to take them apart piece by piece and then put them back together again. "He was a real genius with his hands," Jerry says, but he often fought Gene to prevent him from taking apart his car. Their father didn't mind them driving. In fact, he viewed it as a sign of maturity and he got state licenses for them when they were thirteen by lying about their age. Years later Jerry went back to the state motor vehicles department and told them he was three years younger than his driver's license said. They asked him where his father was; Carey could be prosecuted for lying. Jerry told them he was dead but offered to tell them where his grave was. They laughed, changed his recorded date of birth, and left it at that.

The twins soon put their talents to profitable use. They seined for minnows in nearby creeks and sold them as bait to local fishermen. The neighbors did not mind the boys messing about in their creek. Since their father provided the cars to drive around, and the neighbors let them fish for free, "they had no overhead cost, and Gene and I made between us, oh, thirty dollars a week," Jerry says.

By the time the twins were at Brookville High in Lynchburg, they had a successful bait business going and were experienced drivers. Academically, Jerry had surged ahead of Gene (he'd skipped a grade in elementary school) and had near-perfect grades. Gene knew everything there was to know about automobiles and tractors. Their father, Carey, was known about town as a good, honest, rich and frequently drunk man. He always treated his children well, however, and never flew into inebriated rages. He did often curse at his wife, who ignored him when he did so. "Carey was rough when he was drunk," says son-in-law Jennings, "but when he was sober, there wasn't a finer man in Lynchburg."

At Brookville Jerry scored the highest marks in school for math, and he came in second at a statewide spelling bee. He edited the high school paper, *The Brookville Bee*. During most of his junior year he wanted to be a journalist. From pesky items in *The Bee* that made his principal jump, he realized the power of the media. His goal, after high school, was to enter Lynchburg College and later Virginia Polytechnic Institute. His high school counselor said he had the necessary ability. As class valedictorian and a good athlete, he thought briefly of applying to Harvard or Notre Dame, but he was warned that these schools were inhospitable to Virginians, so he let his parochial instincts triumph.

Shortly before graduation from Brookville, Jerry had an accident while driving a partly repaired Austin convertible that Gene had recently wrecked. He lost control and it flipped over several times. Lawrence Brown, who was in the car with Jerry, was flung from it but only suffered bruises. Jerry was taken to the hosptial with a broken nose (he still carries the scar), broken arms, fingernails ripped off, and blood all over his chest. Jerry had to take his final exams orally. He appeared to receive his diploma in a cast and bandages.

"That was embarrassing," Falwell remembers. "But it was not the greatest insult. The greatest insult was that I was prevented from giving my valedictory address because I played a prank." Falwell had worked out a scheme for school athletes to eat without meal tickets at the dining hall. When the scam was exposed, he was penalized for the offense, one of many, by having to watch the boy ranked second in the class deliver the valedictory. A mention in his local paper, *The Daily News and Advance*, was Falwell's only recognition for topping his senior class. Falwell did get to deliver an address at Brookville, but not until thirty years later, in 1980. That was at the invitation of then Principal William Wright, who had learned of Falwell's youthful prank and penalty. Falwell told the Brookville students that his address to them was belated. When he said why, they laughed and cheered.

Despite the Falwell money, life was rather dull in Lynchburg. The high school girls were sweet and just blossoming, but strictures against hanky-panky were numerous. It was considered effrontery even to speak to a girl outside of necessary conversations—"May I borrow your book?" "No, we don't have school tomorrow." Gene found solace in insects and technology. Jerry developed a practical joker's temperament, which he retains today. He also became what he calls a "sports addict" and played as if his life depended on it. "Studies were not a challenge for me, but athletics were." He played intramural basketball and baseball in high school and was captain and fullback for the football team. He was large and all-American and made up with vigor what he lacked in talent. Friends who played with him or against him say he was a boisterous athlete—but not unfair. During his high school and college years, Falwell says he looked forward to a professional baseball career. He was disappointed that he couldn't make it. "I had visions of making a lot of money by playing professional baseball but I was never good enough for that, I discovered."

In the evenings Jerry regularly met his friends across from the Royal Cafe on a brick construction reverently referred to as "the Wall." Here he met Jim Moon, a square-faced, rowdy kid from across town who was to become his closest friend and later an associate in his ministry. Moon says he befriended Falwell because "Jerry owned an aluminum-top 1934 Plymouth," which, Falwell admits, was a major reason for his popularity. The car carried not only sports equipment and other baggage for the denizens of the Wall, but also brought them to and from it and carried them, ten or twelve at a time, on country road spins.

Otis Wright, a member of the Wall group, remembers that Falwell would take "oh, ten to fifteen of us" down to Timber Lake to fish and swim. There would be a boy on each back and front fender and two on top of the car. That would not deter Jerry from driving fast, however, and he once actually sent a lad hurtling into a bush.

Listening to members of the Wall gang today, one cannot help but be amazed and a little skeptical of their accounts of past doings. They are like the tales of a well-meaning father who each year lengthens the distance he says he walked to school in order to impress his offspring with the hardship of old times. Clearly Jerry was leader of the gang— "instigator," Moon calls him. Some of their exploits are on record. On Halloween in late 1949 the group set some fifty railroad ties on Campbell Avenue in Lynchburg on fire, diverting traffic down Sackett Street while they enjoyed the warmth and esthetics of the blaze. "The problem was, we didn't know we were sending the traffic down a dead end road," Falwell confesses. Also the asphalt on Campbell Avenue caught fire. "So the police were called soon, and we had to run." One of the gang, "a real tough girl named Rags," stayed behind as an informant. When the police arrived she said she had seen the whole thing; the culprits went that-a-way. Then, having sent the police on a false trail, Rags told the gang, hiding nearby, to come out now, but they had better all get home.

Another common ploy for the Wall gang was to get Ray "Buttercup" Bell, a puny kid, to stand before the Royal Cafe and pick fights. As college boys and men came out of the movie and bars late in the evening, Buttercup would wave his fists in challenge at them, or at passing cars. Every now and then somebody would throw down a beer to take up the challenge or a car would screech to a halt and several guys would get out and seize Buttercup by the collar. "At the moment they got Bud," Falwell says, "about forty of us would come over the Wall, and the fighting would start." It was never vicious—"no knives, guns, that sort of thing,"—but when it was over, lips had been split and sometimes noses were broken. "It taught me the importance of overwhelming superiority in number of forces," Falwell laughs. "Overwhelming superiority is why we almost never got hurt—really hurt, I mean."

Fortunately Falwell was never arrested, but, according to Jim Moon, "he's bailed a few people out.""We didn't do anything bad," Moon insists, "But we didn't do much good either."

At various times Falwell did things like tie a friend to a basketball hoop overnight; take the furniture off a friend's porch and put it on his roof; turn over outhouses with people in them; and provoke the family goat in attacking Lawrence Jennings when he came by to court Virginia. There were pranks like setting off fire and burglar alarms, tying people to trees and posts, and calling friends on the phone and giving ridiculous messages in disguised voices. Falwell insists this was all in good fun, prompted partly by the boredom of youth, but there is a hairiness about some of these pranks that perhaps mirrors Falwell's more outrageous proclamations these days. Close friends say there is a sense in which Falwell's entire political career is a prank, although he is genuinely concerned about the nation's moral slide. His strategies are theatrical, campy, out of the ordinary—for example, penning the "95 Theses for Return to a Moral America" and mimicking Luther at Wittenberg, nailing them to a door of the Capitol building.

Falwell does not seem ashamed of his childhood antics. "I was quite wild," he admits, "and I attracted friends of similar proclivities." He says he drank a lot with the others "because I didn't want to be a loner" but insists he was never a heavy drinker. "The memories of my father were too strong. He died when I was fifteen, and it's not something a kid forgets the next day, you know." Falwell retains a good deal of his teenage rowdiness, even as a national figure under constant watch by the press. Sometimes his aides still have to hold him back from implementing an idea like showing up at Norman Lear's home and challenging him to a debate on his front porch. "I get some crazy ideas," Falwell admits, "but I have a better sense now of my position and responsibilities. I can control myself much better."

Otis Wright, a friend from those days, remembers Falwell as a very intelligent gang leader. Teenagers would come from the other side of town, and the Wall group would defend their property against these invaders of their turf. Compared to New York gang fights, these were gentlemen's wars, to be sure, but boys ended up unconscious all the same. Falwell was "aggressive beyond belief," Wright says, so he often prevailed in battles. "Also he used his head when the rest of us only used it for butting." Falwell's intelligence was a kind of street canniness that had nothing to do with pedagogy. Yet, Wright recalls that Falwell also spoke elegantly and would have been regarded as hifalutin if he hadn't been so tough. "Jerry spoke good English when the rest of us were talking street language." He admits that Falwell often used obscenities but says he always couched them in good grammar.

Falwell says his martial weakness was his doggedness. "When I got into a fight with somebody, it didn't matter who was getting beat, the fight would never stop unless it was absolutely impossible to go on." He adds something that may be relevant for him today, "I have always been too aggressive."

The worst day of Falwell's youth was October 10, 1948. His father, Carey Falwell, died that day, entirely spent with alcohol. He succumbed to cirrhosis of the liver. Falwell maintains that his father did not die an agnostic. He says he knows someone who told Carey about the redemptive power of Christ shortly before his final illness, but this account remains unverifiable and is perhaps colored by Jerry's desires retroactively imposed upon his parent. Who wants to think of one's father searing in the flames of hell?

Helen Falwell took her husband's death stoically. She stood still, refusing to blink or shed a tear as they carried Carey's body out of the family home. Then she said a short prayer and began to clean up the house. There would be folks coming by all that week, and it would never do to have the house unkempt.

Jerry Falwell was chastened by his father's death. It taught him, he says, the risk of alcohol. But it did not cause him to stop drinking. Jerry says he never smoked a cigarette in his life, however, "because dad wouldn't allow it." His mother detested the smell of smoke and prohibited anyone from smoking in the house. Jerry and Gene recall that their elder brother, Lewis, on returning from the Navy, lit up a cigarette at the dining table, upon which Carey Falwell, without looking up from his meal, punched the cigarette out of Lewis' mouth, sending the young man tumbling to the floor. "Nothing's changed, son," Carey said, and kept on eating. Lewis stood up, spitting through bloody lips. But he did not take his father on. He simply crushed the cigarette under his foot and walked out the door. "It was a lesson to us," Jerry says. "Mind you, Lewis was a full grown man when this happened."

Although Carey Falwell was a self-made entrepreneur, he was a lifelong Democrat, as Southerners generally were in those days. In the main, he seems to have been indifferent to government—suspicious of it, but willing to let it runs its affairs, which did not really intrude upon his life. Jerry himself had Democratic sympathies throughout his high school and early college days. He remembers opposing Thomas Dewey at the tender age of eleven and having "heated arguments" with friends at school about the awful Republicans. "I grew up during the Roosevelt dynasty," Falwell says. "I can hardly remember a time in my early years when FDR wasn't president.

Nor was the young Falwell much of a patriot, at least in the histrionic sense. He supported the U.S. effort during the Second World War but wondered whether the war was a political move to divert attention from domestic problems. He wasn't a wild flag-waver, just "paid my respects," he says, and that was that. He did admire General Patton and Winston Churchill for their wartime valor. Now he thinks Patton should have moved his army toward Russia in 1945, but at the time "I didn't think of it." Falwell says he was suspicious of the patriotic fervor aroused by the war because, although he was not religious, he was raised in established fundamentalist tradition of ambivalence toward politics and patriotism. Fundamentalists of the day held that politics was morally corrupt and that patriotism was often a surrogate for devotion toward God. While religious people did not share this theological interpretation, they too regarded nationalism as vulgar. Jerry says his father felt that since the United States was in the war she "might as well finish off everybody else." Young Jerry agreed completely. "My father and I had one mind about the war," he says now.

Falwell freely admits similarities between him and his father. "I took after my father, and Gene after my mother and her side of the family. No one has doubts about that."

Carey Falwell was an intuitive businessman who, in nephew Calvin's words, "started new businesses overnight," although he occasionally overstepped himself. Financial pressures and drinking troubles forced Carey to sell the Merry Garden Nightclub, which he built to liven up night life in Lynchburg, to his brother Warren. Then Carey took up bee-farming and built an apiary. Jerry Falwell has similarly acute business instincts, but sometimes he likewise plays too easy with money. This is partly due to his conviction that "God will provide." Jerry and his father were alike in many ways: hard-driving yet straight, impetuous yet level-headed, and initially irreligious—not out of a militant atheism, but because of a vague sense that religion stultified.

"My father didn't like to be collared," Jerry says simply when asked about his father's agnosticism. "And neither do I. I don't like to be collared." He now remembers his father as a "hard man, a moral man" who "deserved to be head of our household." Without embarrassment he refers to Carey Falwell as "my male idol." He says, "I attribute my own tenacity to my father," adding, "He couldn't admit he was a failure in anything, and he was always certain that there was a solution to every problem and an answer to every question." Jerry Falwell believes that, too, for theological reasons, although he admits, "I feel that it may take years to find the solution. But you have to operate from the premise that there is a solution."

Carey Falwell found answers within himself, much in the manner that modern psychology books recommend, but Jerry Falwell, at least since his conversion, looks to God for answers. Although he is still fiercely independent, a self-made man by any definition, Jerry feels that the self-help philosophy is, in the long run, nihilistic. "Many motivational organizations tell people that all the necessary resources are within themselves, and all they have to do is tap that well," he said in a sermon at Thomas Road. "I don't believe that. I don't accept that for a moment. We need God." However, he does not interpret his relationship with God and his obedience to divine commands as constricting. He feels that Christianity is incredibly liberating spiritually. "Everyone talks about freedom," Falwell told me, "but spiritual freedom is the highest kind of freedom. And it comes only from a personal relationship with Jesus Christ. And no one can take that away from you, either in Lynchburg, Virginia, or in the Gulag."

Falwell credits his moral values to his mother. "I owe all my character to my mother," he says. "I owe everything I know about right and wrong to her." This is typical hyperbole. Surely he derives much of his moral teaching today from the Bible and books on theology. But he feels a fierce loyalty to his parents and cannot praise them enough, even for things they may have done badly.

Jerry graduated from Brookville High School with a 98.6 percent average. In math and the sciences he had a 100 percent score, and his teachers urged him to become a professor. Falwell's friends say he is intellectually and athletically gifted, but Falwell himself insists, "I was never outstandingly smart. I just made up for it with hard work, spending more time than others." He thinks this is the secret of his ministry today. "I do not believe that I am a more talented minister than many who have smaller ministries than I do. But I do believe I work harder than they." But, he adds, "I never think of it as work, you know. I have always liked what I do, whether it is sports or being a minister. I have always been full of ambition." Falwell's critics, who are only too conscious of his ambition, wonder whether that and not the Holy Spirit is what spurs his activities today.

Falwell's companions also describe him as an incurable optimist. Despite his bleak predictions for a nation that he describes as "morally sick," he himself admits, "I never see the glass as half empty. It's always half full." Gene, by contrast, remains a philosopher of endurance. "Life is tough, but we've got to stick it through; we're all we've got" seems to summarize Gene's perspective. Jerry Falwell is amused, sometimes impatient, with his brother's unruffled, somewhat pessimistic view of the world. Gene is baffled by Jerry's presumption that he can change the rhythm of society.

Jerry graduated from Brookville in the spring of 1950. (Gene was dropping out.) Now he was grown up, really grown up. He was—dare he say it?—a Southern gentleman. He had top grades, and he was an accomplished athlete. Girls whispered to each other and smiled at him bashfully, and he had fast cars to take everyone to Roanoke and Charlottesville. Things were looking good for Jerry Falwell as he stepped into early manhood.

4

The Irreverent Convert

In the fall of 1950 young Jerry Falwell entered Lynchburg College. Jerry had charted a career plan—Lynchburg College and then on to Virginia Tech to study engineering. His brother Gene was confused about what he wanted to do, and enlisted in the Navy. Lewis, their older brother, had served several years in the Navy and described it as hardening but full of thrills. Not that Gene was a thrill-seeker like Jerry, but he decided to experiment.

Jerry was a little envious. Sure, he was the one going to college, but it was Lynchburg College, the college on the block, a ten-minute drive away, and he was going to live at home. Jerry wondered about signing up with the Air Force. He wanted very much to fly a plane—it would be so much more exciting than a car—but his drive to become an engineer was strong. And he knew he was cut out to be a college man—not bookish perhaps, but one of those all-round campus figures, playing hard on the athletic field, dating the pretty girls, and studying in a last stretch for exams.

Lynchburg College was founded in 1903 as Virginia Christian College. It was established to teach men to be preachers and women to be preachers' and missionaries' wives. It boasted a Georgian campus, spotted with a few more modern buildings. Its first preacher-presidents were of a fiery stripe, but gradually the school succumbed to the new scholarship. The old religion courses were rooted out and chapel attendance ceased to be mandatory. The college was determined to contend with "new realities" whatever they were. The younger faculty, liberated Southern pedants who had studied out of state, decided that their own culture was too parochial. So Lynchburg became a liberal arts college, devoted to the proposition that all norms must be subjected to intellectual scrutiny. Students and faculty were supposed to cultivate an "open mind." Lynchburg College didn't want to be like the other fundamentalist schools in the area: narrow, orthodox, regulated. It wanted to be avant garde, the beacon college in Virginia. So courses in parapsychology and Chinese studies were introduced. More students from other towns were recruited for "diversity." Religious traditions, while respected, were treated as trivial, mere symbols of a buried past. That was Lynchburg College when Jerry Falwell arrived on campus, but throughout his college career he was never to notice it.

He took courses in mathematics, physics, English, and engineering the first year and went to classes regularly, which was a change from high school. He did not involve himself in numerous extra-curricular activities. He did play briefly on the college basketball team but found the team going nowhere, so slid out. He studied between three and four hours a day, usually at odd times, in the early morning or midafternoon, and in odd places, sitting with a goat or lying on top of his car.

Helen Falwell was ambivalent about Jerry's studies. On the one hand she saw college as a sign of success. But on the other she feared that college would take Jerry away from her and make him materialistic and pseudo sophisticated. She reacted to her fears by imposing strict rules on Jerry—no smoking, no alcohol—and encouraged him to hang out with his old gang. She frequently invoked memories of Jerry's father, who, despite his failings, had been an honest Southern gentlemen.

Helen Falwell need not have feared, for Jerry never let himself be seduced away from his roots. He retained his ambition and his playfulness which inclined toward the same slapstick he did in high school. He often called his mother from college and reported tragedies in a disguised voice. It got to the point, according to his sister, Virginia, that Helen Falwell at times mistook other people for her son playing a prank. On one occasion a relative called to report his daughter suffering from bronchitis. Helen laughed and kept imploring Jerry to call off the joke, because she had figured it out. After that incident, Helen asked Jerry to control his childishness. He laughed and said he had better think up something to fool the piqued relative. He grew closer to his mother during this time, because her usual favorite, Gene, was away at sea, and Lewis and Virginia were by now married and out of the house.

Falwell did stay with the Wall group even after entering college. At first the gang feared that he would moderate, that creeping respectability would set in for the Wall gang, but that never happened. He stayed as raucous and full of pranks as ever. The boys in the gang regarded him with a mixture of awe and envy, partly because now the girls in the gang were regarding him with coy affection. The tomboys were starting to slip out of jeans and into dresses. Even though the gang retained its identity, the chemistry was beginning to change. The old superficial ties could not remain for long.

The girls Falwell dated were local or college girls, usually around his age, and he liked them blonde and giggly. He did not go out with girls from his own gang, although when Rags, the roughneck of them all, asked him to a school dance, he went, just to show his admiration for her. Falwell claims to have dated most of the cheerleading squad at Brookville High School. He took his dates to the drive-in movie theater in Lynchburg or for long drives. Sometimes he just sat and listened to music with his girl; his favorites were Frank Sinatra, Tony Bennett, and Perry Como. He insists he did not date more than twenty girls during his freshman college year, and none for more than a month.

Sometimes Falwell double-dated with Jim Moon. Moon was a real skirt-chaser and often schemed with Jerry about how to get girls; occasionally he schemed about how to get Jerry's girl. The two young men became close. They discovered that they not only shared a penchant for creating scenes, disrupting equilibrium, they also liked the same kinds of sports, books, and women.

Falwell studied for two years at Lynchburg College. At the end of his first year he was awarded the B.F. Goodrich Citation for superior grades in mathematics. He scored the highest average in math at the college that year. He also did well in engineering and found himself in the top eighth of his class. His teachers assured him that he would have no problem getting into Virginia Tech.

Falwell entered his sophomore year expecting it to be much like the first, with an assortment of exams, gang doing, and dates, but things happened that changed the course of his career and his life. He did not expect these things to happen, but he felt swept up by an irresistible tide of events.

The main event was his conversion. This occurred on January 20, 1952, and Falwell now says it was the most important day in his life. Ironically, Falwell was prepared for his conversion by radio preacher Charles E. Fuller, whose "Old Fashioned Revival Hour" Helen Falwell had subjected Jerry and Gene to each Sunday morning.

Fuller was a tall, dark-haired man with deep-set eyes. A graduate of Pomona College, where he was a star football player, Fuller worked in a California gold mine for several years. He had lost his faith in Christianity because he'd come to accept the Darwinian account of evolution. This he subsequently rejected upon his conversion which infused him with a desire to study and teach Scripture. He began with that in Placentia, California.

While attending a Bible conference in Indianapolis in 1927, Fuller was asked to give a short homily on a radio program in place of the regular speaker, who was on vacation. He was reluctant but finally agreed. He felt he stuttered throughout the sermon. When the regular speaker returned and asked him what he had spoken about, Fuller embarrassedly inquired whether there had been many complaints. No, the preacher said, but there were several letters of praise. This inspired Fuller to begin a series of broadcasts from Calvary Church in Placentia over MGER radio in Long Beach. These continued until 1933, when Fuller moved to San Marino to devote himself to full-time radio broadcasting. These details bear an uncanny resemblance to Jerry Falwell's media ministry later on.

Fuller's "Old Fashioned Revival Hour," after which Falwell's "Old Time Gospel Hour" is named and patterned, was a sixty-minute melange of music, prayer, and preaching. The program began with the hymn "Jesus Saves." Then Fuller spoke his opening words. He had a calm, modulated voice that set an intimate atmosphere. The choir was an essential part of his ministry. His wife led the singing. The second half of the program was devoted to a Bible message and reading of letters. The letters were many and spoke of dramatic conversions and deep edification.

Jerry Falwell's TV show today is an hour long, like Fuller's program, but it is a regular church service, not a staged event. Like Fuller, he practices a confident, low-key style of Bible preaching, issuing no threats of damnation or plague, but he is sometimes heated about political issues. Although Fuller's outreach was much smaller than his successor's is, he was the major media minister of his day. By 1940 Fuller's radio show was broadcast on all 152 Mutual stations, and he was reaching an audience of nearly five million listeners. He got nearly four hundred letters after each broadcast, and his annual budget was more than $1 million per year, making him one of the nation's top broadcasters, secular or religious.

Like Falwell, Fuller was very concerned about his ratings. He was agitated when they tumbled, although he tended to downplay them in public. "I'm not interested in figures," Fuller once told a Boston rally. "I'm interested in souls. Some people say I reach twenty million people. I don't know. All I know is that I preach the greatest message in the world. There may be greater orators, but nobody can preach a greater message because I preach from the world's greatest book. It is the old gospel, the simple gospel that pulls."

Compare this to what Falwell says. "I'm trying to reach as many people and tell them about God as He will let me. I cannot make them accept Christ, but I can tell them about Him. I can give them the good news, the only news that's worth hearing these days. . . . The media is God's way of getting his message out. I am only His minister."

Fuller was strongly opposed by other envious preachers and by liberal church groups, even though his message was nonpolitical. The Federal Council of Churches, who placed competing programs on the NBC and CBS networks, accused Fuller of exploiting his medium when their efforts were unsuccessful. Some Federal Council members also allied with advertisers, who felt that radio preachers were driving up the price of air time, and secular groups to remove religious broadcasting from the media on the grounds that it violated the constitutional principle of separation of church and state. Fuller had a nervous moment in 1941 when a group called the Institute of Education by Radio proposed that the networks refuse to sell time for religious programs. This recommendation was accepted by Mutual, but after a bitter struggle between the network and the newly formed National Association of Evangelicals, which supported Fuller, the "Old Fashioned Revival Hour" was back on the air. Falwell is a student of these controversies, for they closely parallel those he is engaged in today. "The attacks haven't changed," he says. "They are made by the same people on the same grounds. These are the people who hate religion or who are jealous of successful ministries."

When Helen Falwell put on Fuller's broadcasts, Jerry and Gene paid as little attention to them as possible. But in retrospect Fuller had a great, if subconscious, effect on him. In fact, a major reason he seldom attended church was that the preachers at Franklin Street Baptist Church, where his mother went, did not compare with Charles Fuller. When Falwell did go to church at college, he looked for a preacher like Dr. Fuller. Finally he found one in Reverend Paul Donnelson, pastor of the Park Avenue Baptist Church in Lynchburg.

On Sunday, January 20, 1952, Jim Moon drove up to Falwell's house and told him that they should go to church that evening. Naw, Jerry said, he wasn't up to it, and besides, he wanted to take the evening off to sit on the Wall and watch girls and drink. (His mother's stricture against alcohol applied only at home, as far as he was concerned.) Moon said he had heard that there were some attractive girls at Park Avenue Baptist Church. Really? Moon said he had told Otis Wright this and Wright had said he would go for a look. "Are you in or out, Jerry?" Moon wanted to know. Falwell shrugged. "I guess it's church for me," he said. Moon said he would be back to pick Jerry up at six.

When the boys arrived at church, the sanctuary was almost full, so the ushers led them to the front row. They were uncomfortable about this, never having taken front row seats before. ("When we came early, it was to catch a back seat," Falwell jokes.) But they noticed that the closer they got, the better the scenery. There were two pretty young women at the altar; Delores Clark and Macel Pate—Delores at the organ and Macel at the piano.

Falwell and Moon independently resolved to go up to the pastor and express interest in joining the church, hoping during the course of this to be introduced to the girls. Reverend Donnelson unintentionally thwarted the game plan with a good sermon.

He spoke about the relationship of truth to simplicity, Falwell remembers. There may be an inverse relationship between esoteric knowledge and religious truth, Donnelson said. But he was not crude and demeaning toward science. He merely defended what Bruno Bettelheim calls "the informed heart," which takes precedence over the analytical mind. Falwell was reminded of the sermons of Charles Fuller. Fuller was an uncompromising fundamentalist, yet his sermons had a certain charm. They were stylistically unorthodox, and here was pastor Donnelson with the same kind of delivery.

Falwell and Moon were so taken with Donnelson's sermon that they made no effort to get introduced to the two girls afterwards. Instead, when Donnelson, after his homily, invited people to "come up the aisles and receive Christ," Falwell and Moon did. They hesitated at first, but a deacon took their shoulders and went to the front with them, opening his Bible to Romans 10:13—"Whosoever calls on the name of the Lord will be saved." After the service, both young men received Christ as their personal savior and joined Park Avenue Baptist Church. Falwell describes his conversion as "unemotional," adding that while it did occur in a single moment, it was also a realization of the truth of Christianity, and his personal need for it during the course of Donnelson's homily. "I was converted to the view that my life had a purpose," he says. "Before that I lived in a wild manner, but I didn't know what for." He stresses that he was not previously anti-clerical, but that his attitudes to the church were ambivalent. On the one hand he respected preachers. On the other, he was often intimidated by their yelling and put off by their legalism—don't do this or this or this—which affronted his mischievous nature. All hostility toward the church dissipated that day, Falwell says, and at the end of the service he resolved to buy a bible. He had never studied one in his life.

Macel Pate, whom Falwell had initially hoped to meet that day, was the daughter of Sam and Lucille Pate. Sam Pate was a builder, Lucille worked at a Lynchburg shoe factory. The family lived on Munford Street in Lynchburg and initially attended Munford Street Baptist Church three times a week. But there was a controversy at the church in Macel's youth over some fine point of doctrine, which was compounded by personality disputes. The result was that Macel's parents and others left the church and joined Park Avenue Baptist Church.

Macel attended the E.C. Glass High School in Lynchburg. She proved an above average student. Her family was strict with her and hardly let her out on dates. In school Macel is remembered as a pretty girl with brown, shoulder-length hair who hardly talked to boys. Macel's parents did not permit her to see movies or go to dances, a rule they modified eventually. In her high school days recreation for Macel consisted of going to choir practice at the church and for an ice cream after. "Our whole life revolved around the church," Macel says. "We were in there whenever the doors were open. We didn't know any other way of life. She was working as a teller at the First National Bank at this time and had been seeing another young man for almost two years. She admits to noticing Jerry Falwell in church that Sunday evening.

But Falwell left Park Avenue Church resolving only to buy copies of a Bible, a Bible dictionary, and *Strong's Exhaustive Concordance*, all of which Donnelson cited that Sunday. Macel hoped to see Falwell come back. At least he had signed up for membership. (Jim Moon and Delores Clark subsequently developed their own relationship and are happily married today.)

Falwell spent most of the next week reading his newly acquired books and urging friends to come to church the next Sunday. This, he found, was not easy. Otis Wright and Jim Moon tried it, too, and they found it even harder. "We would ask a friend about coming to Park Avenue Church, and he would laugh, so we would become very defensive," Moon says. Falwell was more confident about persuading friends to get religion, but he, too, met with ridicule and contempt. Wright says the moment Falwell converted to Christianity he lost his position as leader of his gang.

Falwell did induce six or seven guys to attend the next Sunday, however. He promised it was a one-time deal, it was fun—if not would he, Jerry Falwell, be in this—the service was shorter than you might expect. The next Sunday the group, six young men besides Falwell and Wright piled in Falwell's car and drove to church, arms and legs sticking out of the car's windows. Religion does not instantly make one less nonchalant. Buddy McCauley and Otis Wright were "saved" that day.

Falwell says that since his conversion, "I can honestly say that all I have ever wanted is to glorify Jesus Christ through moment-by-moment acknowledgement of His lordship in my life." As if to confirm this, he gave up drinking and movies at once, although it was too much to renounce practical jokes. He began to devour the printed sermons of the great fundamentalist preachers: Frank Norris, William Jennings Bryan, Clarence Macartney. Suddenly he cared more about his church than his gang. The guys and gals in the gang felt a sadness, because they knew Falwell's attempt to recruit them really constituted a parting. New guys began to vie for leadership position in the gang.

Falwell's conversion also drew him away from a potential career he was pursuing in baseball. He had been an outstanding athlete in high school and college, but he reached his pinnacle as the star hitter and outfielder for the Lynchburg City League, at the time a very good team. In early 1952 Falwell was invited by the St. Louis Cardinals to try out for a professional baseball contract, and he did. "I wasn't good enough," he says, "so I didn't make it, and that was the end of that." However, he also says that if he had been offered a deal, he would certainly have accepted, and if he had not become a Christian, he would probably have pursued a baseball career anyway.

At Park Avenue Church Falwell began to work actively with the youth group at church. He also began going out with Macel on short double dates with Jim Moon and Delores Clark. The four of them went for spins on the mountainside, engaging in trivial conversation about how beautiful it was, how spacious the mountain ranges were, how quaintly the car chugged. They talked about everything but themselves.

Macel remembers Falwell as a gruff sort who was "not really ill-mannered. . .but he had a lot of rough edges." Macel doesn't feel he was really destructive, although "he did get drunk and play pranks and all." What Macel remembers most about their early courtship was Falwell's atrocious taste in clothes, which persists today to some extent.

Macel's mother was initially nervous about her dating Falwell. The Pates did not know the Falwell family—they lived way across town. Sam Pate carefully monitored his daughter's coming and going. He required Macel to return home at absurdly early times, so dates continued at her house. Then around eleven Mr. Pate would call bedtime, so Falwell would have to leave. This strictness was in part provoked by Mrs. Pate's concern that Falwell's conversion was perhaps not genuine. She knew something of his reputation with the Wall gang. But when he dropped out of Lynchburg College to begin studying for the ministry, she was happily convinced of his religious transformation.

In the fall of 1952, Jerry Falwell enrolled in Baptist Bible College in Springfield, Missouri, as a junior. This was at the suggestion of Pastor Donnelson, whose father, Fred Donnelson, was a professor at BBC. Falwell's decision surprised virtually everyone. He was convinced that God wanted him to drop out of Lynchburg College. God might even want him to enter the ministry, but he didn't know that yet. He just had to do what God was asking. Macel, familiar with this kind of theological reasoning, did not question his decision.

Before taking off for Springfield, Falwell confessed his conversion to his mother, whom he had not previously told. To his wonder she merely smiled to herself, as if she had expected it all along. He bade good-bye to Donnelson, to whom he said he owned everything, but Donnelson waved him off—it was God, not he, who worked miracles. Donnelson also told him, "Falwell, I think you will bring many to God. You're the kind of man He chooses for that." Falwell didn't know what to say. He said he would try to get good grades at Baptist Bible College.

Jim Moon, already enrolled at Baptist Bible, showed Falwell around the campus. It was a real change from Lynchburg College. Falwell found a "drastic difference" between the religious outlook of faculty and students at Lynchburg College and those at Baptist Bible College. He admits this could partly reflect his own change of heart. "I went to Lynchburg College to get a liberal education," he says. "I went to Baptist Bible College with the specific purpose of preparing for Christian ministry." Baptist Bible was characterized by the austerity of a religious institution. Falwell wondered whether he would find this stifling, but Moon said, it wasn't so bad once you got used to it. There were rules, but as long as you observed them, you could do pretty much anything else. Most of the rules concerned smoking and drinking, which Falwell had given up anyway. He settled into his room. After he had unpacked, Julius Blazs, his roommate and also from Lynchburg, came in and said a big hello. Falwell nervously shook his hand. Blazs was coincidentally a previous suitor of Macel's.

At Baptist Bible College Falwell and Moon took mandatory courses in Bible history, church history, theology, music, speech, and English. He studied under pastors well known among fundamentalists: G.B. Vick, Noel Smith, W.E. Dowell, and F.S. Donnelson. There were three hundred or so students in their class, mostly fundamentalist children from the Midwest and South. Falwell found the atmosphere a little stuffy, but his curiosity for understanding the Bible, which he describes as obsessive, sustained him. He also played basketball for Baptist Bible, making forward and captain of the varsity team.

Although he abided by most of the rules of the college, Falwell could not forego his own brand of jesting. The officials at Baptist Bible were not really accustomed to a young man driving a motorcycle through the boys' dormitory at midnight. Nor did they expect him to run a garden hose to a friend's dormitory room. In the latter case they made him clean up the flood, but the floor was barely dry when he came back and emptied a five-gallon can of water on the floor. "Falwell was just a run-of-the-mill guy here," remembers W.E. Dowell, president of BBC, then faculty chairman. But, he adds, after a moment, "He was kind of a mischievous fellow at school."

Falwell learned some of his antics at BBC itself. There he read about the old fundamentalist pastors and their pulpit chicanery—about the Reverend Frank Norris introducing apes on his pulpit as "Mr. Darwin" and "Mr. Lamarck"; about the Reverend John Roach Straton referring to Harry Emerson Fosdick, the prominent liberal theologian, as "a Baptist bootlegger...a Presbyterian outlaw...the Jesse James of the theological world." In fact, Falwell, twenty-five years ago, was something of a latter-day Norris or Straton. But he has since been tempered by more sophisticated people, both conservative and liberal. He has also come to realize that knowledge does not necessarily connote liberalism.

Falwell also discovered the intellectual heritage of the fundamentalists. As the scholar Sandeen wrote about the post-Scopes era: "It is clear that the fundamentalists, although alarmed and dismayed by the teachings of the modernists, were not ill informed or ignorant...their movement at this time possessed great vigor, particularly in evangelism and world mission. The stump preachers had their appeal, but they were in the minority, Falwell discovered. They taught him that one can be pious and playful at the same time.

The Reverend Truman Dollar, now pastor of Kansas City Baptist Temple, then a classmate of Falwell's, says Falwell was simultaneously devout and irreverent, citing his lighting of firecrackers in the corridors as an example. Dollar says Falwell was "a constant problem to the administration." The deans forgave him, however, because of his excellent academic record and affectionate nature. After an outrageous gambit, he would appear at President Dowell's office looking so stricken and contrite that Dowell would laugh and ask him to get out before he was expelled. Dollar and Moon insist that Falwell was also capable of truly selfless behavior. Not only would he help other students at the cost of his own studies, but he would spend time listening to them when they were discouraged and feeling the need of sympathy or encouragement.

During his first year at BBC, Falwell went to High Street Baptist Church in Springfield and asked if he could teach Sunday School class. The superintendent, Max Hawkins, used to seeing overzealous Bible students turn up at his door, asked Falwell what made him think he could teach what he didn't know. Falwell replied that he wasn't studied in the gospel, but he knew Christ, if that's what the superintendent was talking about.

Hawkins reluctantly gave him one eleven-year-old boy to teach. After several weeks, the class had grown to two boys. Falwell was discouraged. He went to Hawkins to resign the class. Hawkins told Falwell he wasn't all surprised with his failure; he rather had expected him to flop from the beginning.

Falwell was stunned. He went to the dean of BBC and asked for the key to an empty dormitory room. There he prayed for hours each weekday, expressing frustration with his own garbled Bible presentation, pleading with God to fill him with energy and inspiration. Then he went out into the ball fields to play baseball with the local young boys, who found in him a curious affection and intensity. They drew close to him, fascinated by his stories about the man eaten by a whale, the woman who ate the apple, and other tales they thought he had made up.

In nine months time, Falwell had fifty-six kids in his own Sunday School class. He went back to Hawkins at High Street Church, who told him he'd figured all along that the challenge of rejection would inspire him to do great things. Falwell was doubtful about this, but appreciative when he was given legitimate church space in which to conduct Sunday School from then on.

Jim Moon says that he and Falwell sought every occasion to drive from Springfield to Lynchburg to see their girls. It was a thousand-mile drive and the roads were uneven, but Falwell was a driver who knew no speed limit, and there was a will and a way.

In 1954, two years after he entered BBC, Falwell decided to take a year off and return to Lynchburg. He had heard that attendance had dropped in the youth group at Park Avenue Baptist Church. He also missed Macel. Moon continued at BBC and finished a year before Falwell. Jerry didn't like to see his buddy finish before him but he felt the need to return home too strong to resist. But he did not waver in his commitment to his faith. He went energetically to work in the youth program at the Park Avenue Church. At the end of that year, its attendance was up to 250. There was something obsessive about the way he worked. He seemed to need measurable indices of his success: ten more students this week, four people accepting Christ after a service, etc. For Jerry Falwell at Park Avenue Church, it was as important to count new heads as it had been for his father to count income at the end of a workday.

In the fall of 1955 Falwell returned to BBC to finish his education for the ministry. He took a weekend position teaching students at the Kansas City Baptist Temple, whose pastor was Wendell Zimmerman, already a well-known itinerant pastor. Falwell had to drive four hundred miles round trip to Kansas City each week, but he didn't mind, because Zimmerman awed him with his all-knowing theological convictions and witty preaching style. Because Falwell fared so well at Zimmerman's church, Zimmerman asked him to become youth pastor.

Three weeks before Falwell's graduation, Zimmerman asked him to preach at the morning service at Baptist Temple. Falwell had never preached to a full church before. Besides, as he says, "This was Baptist Temple, not any church. Some of the great preachers of all time had preached in Baptist Temple. I did not know if I dared preach there." But Zimmerman insisted. He would be away that weekend, and if Falwell didn't preach, he would use someone else. Falwell rushed back to his room to pray for several hours. "I realized that it was not accidental that Pastor Zimmerman asked me to preach in that church. I thought it may be God's way of telling me something."

Until then Falwell was uncertain about what to do after graduation. Most of the BBC seniors had already found positions in various ministries, but Falwell, the college's top student, was without a job. He had thought about becoming a preacher, of course, but felt no clear calling in that direction. He was afraid that it was going to be business as usual after graduation—that is, that he was going to have to work in a lumberyard or bus route or farm when he returned to Lynchburg. He prayed that God would reveal some sign if he wanted him to take up the ministry. Otherwise he would understand that God wanted a layman's virtue from him, and he would return to the Falwell enterprises in Lynchburg after graduation.

That Sunday the church was full. Young Falwell, standing at the pulpit, felt the people look him over strangely. He opened his Bible to Hebrews chapter 9 and 10, and began to preach. "It was a beginner's sermon and it didn't start off well, because just when I started talking two people stood up and left, but God honored His word." At the end of the sermon, nineteen people came to the front at Falwell's invitation to receive Christ. Falwell knew that some of these were already born-again believers simply marching up for rededication. But one woman whom he prayed over especially moved him. She told him she was a charter member of the church and had attended for all those years, but until that moment she had never accepted Christ as her personal savior. Falwell thought to himself "If the great preachers—B.R. Lakin and Wendell Zimmerman—couldn't do this, if God chose me to convert this woman. . . ." His prayer had been answered." Falwell would do what he set out to do when he came to BBC, become a soul-winner for Christ.

Since leaving BBC, Falwell's feeling for the college has grown ever more intense. His annual contribution to BBC have grown; they were at the $50,000 level in 1982. Although rules at Falwell's own Liberty Baptist College are more liberal than those he suffered at BBC, Falwell never condemns BBC. Instead he expounds on the efficacy of rules in building character.

When Falwell told Reverend Zimmerman of his decision to become a pastor, Zimmerman was joyous and wished him the best. "To start you off, I'm going to offer you a position here, at this church," he said. Falwell's face fell. He said he appreciated the offer very much, his experience at Kansas City Baptist Temple was terrific, but he felt he had to start anew. He thought of himself as a pioneer, kind of like Zimmerman himself. Zimmerman said he understood perfectly. The two men shook hands, and Falwell drove back to Lynchburg. He planned to stop there briefly, then drive on to Macon, Georgia, where his friend Bill Lynes, now married, lived with his wife, Iona, and managed a shoe store. When Falwell called Lynes up and told him of his decision to win souls for Christ, Lynes had become very excited and invited Falwell to start a church in Macon. He had promised to get some money together, and Falwell was on his way to set up a new church. But elaborate plans have a way of being thwarted by the vagaries of fate, or, as Falwell would say, the ways of God are inscrutable.

5

Pastor of the
Donald Duck Church

Falwell spent more time in Lynchburg than he'd planned to. One reason was to be with Macel. He wanted her to marry him. They talked about it; and Macel said yes, of course she would marry him.

Falwell started attending Park Avenue Baptist Church again. He soon discovered that things were not quite the same. Pastor Donnelson was gone. A group of church members had become somewhat alienated from Park Avenue Church. They attended but complained about the new pastor.

Falwell felt uncomfortable in this altered setting. His friend Otis Wright advised him to forget it and to go with him to Macon, Georgia. "All good things finally end," Wright said. "Park Avenue Church will never be the same."

Falwell was then approached by thirty-five adults from Park Avenue Church. They were going to split from Park Avenue Church and wanted him to found a new church for them. Falwell was horrified. He couldn't do it. God would not want that. The dissidents countered that Pastor Wood did not have a monopoly on God. Falwell told them he would have to think about it. They asked him to pray about it, emphasizing at the same time that they wanted a place to worship and were definitely not going back to Park Avenue.

Falwell talked to Frank Wood to see if he could resolve differences, but he found Wood unconcerned about the dissident members. If they didn't like the way he preached, they didn't have to listen, Wood said. Falwell called them God-fearing people, sincere in their faith, and said Wood should pay attention to them. Wood was unsympathetic.

Falwell left the meeting with Wood dejected. He was more determined than ever to leave for Macon. All this cast a pall over memories of his conversion and everything else surrounding Park Avenue Church.

After deliberating and praying, Falwell told the church dissidents he would spend an extra two weeks in Lynchburg and help them found a new church—nothing fancy, just a place to meet and pray. And he would deliver the first few sermons, but after that it was up to them to find a new minister. He was going on to Macon. The dissidents said they understood.

The first thing to do was to find a meeting place. Dan Dunaway, one of the thirty-five members, called an insurance agent, who set off around Lynchburg with them to look at vacant properties. It was raining, and at one point the insurance man's car stalled. As the agent puttered with the engine, Dunaway noticed a funny little building by the side of the road. Without saying anything, he got out to look at it. It was about 35 feet by 50 feet, and it was empty. An old sign outside said "Donald Duck Bottling Company."

Dunaway beckoned to Falwell and the insurance man to take a look, which they did. The agent said it seemed a sturdy little structure. The rent probably would be affordable, and he would inquire further. Falwell said he was anxious that the new location be across town from Park Avenue Church—"I don't want to damage attendance at Park Avenue Church." And this site fitted that concern. The three men went back to the car, which started immediately. Falwell and Dunaway still interpret this set of circumstances as providential, God's way of directing them to the right place.

The rent turned out to be $300 per month, which the thirty-five members said they could afford between them. They also offered Falwell a salary, but he said he couldn't accept. It was not that he didn't need the money. Rather, he was afraid the position might become permanent if he accepted it. The next week the new church members, Macel, and Falwell showed up at the old bottling company building with mops, pails, sandwiches, lemonade, and a radio. The floor was still sticky from the bottler's soft drink syrups. There was also syrup on the walls and ceilings.

On June 28, 1956, the first service was held in Donald Duck Church. The church wasn't named yet, but that's what most people called it—its members from affection, the Park Avenue Church skeptics in derision. Falwell preached at the service, and all thirty-five adults and their children attended. He predicted that this small church would soon explode out of its walls. They were going to be "on fire" for Christ. The congregation said Amen.

The next week Falwell went out and bought a map of Lynchburg, tacked it on the wall and drew concentric circles, with the church location in the middle. He gave biblical names to the area within each circle: Jerusalem, Judea, and Samaria. Then he began his rounds, first knocking on each door within the first circle, then the second, and so on until, in his words, "I had knocked on nearly every door in Lynchburg." He introduced himself and talked not only about his church, but also about the family, their kids, their garage repairs, etc. He did not take up their time, but left after a comfortably brief visit, inviting those he spoke with to stop by his church on Thomas Road. When he stepped back out into the driveway, he wrote down all the information he had gathered.

Falwell almost immediately began a radio and TV ministry. He was inspired to this by the example of Charles E. Fuller. Fuller was off the air now, and nobody had replaced him. It was not that Falwell expected to fill Fuller's shoes, but he saw radio as a powerful way to reach people, to convert them in their homes and cars and also to steer some in the direction of Thomas Road. "I had no doubts about whether to start a radio ministry," he says. "I wanted to reach as many people as I could."

He convinced the deacons of his church to put up the $7 it cost each day for thirty minutes on local radio. Soon he added television (black and white) at a cost of $90 per half hour. He appeared live on Sunday from 5:30 to 6:00 P.M. on WSET Channel 13 and delivered the sermon he would preach one hour later at the 7 o'clock service at Thomas Road.

Falwell's radio ministry had a positive effect on his members. They now regarded him as a big-time preacher. Within a month, the church had grown from thirty-five members to nearly a hundred. Already the room was far too small to hold the Sunday congregation. Falwell promised that construction would begin soon on additions to the one-room church.

Sam Pate, Macel's father and a builder by profession, agreed to help Falwell add on to his church. For this he was paid $2 per hour. Everybody else worked alongside him for free. About a hundred seats, some broken, were salvaged from an old theater and arranged in horseshoe formation. Using $4500 worth of materials, they added on several rooms—two more for worship services and one or two classrooms for Sunday school.

It was at this time that Falwell agreed to stay on and accept a salary. He was pastor, janitor, handyman, plumber, public relations man, and accountant for the church. His salary was $65 per week, with no expense account. He provided his own car, and he had to pay for gas. The phone bill was his. Pretty soon Falwell found his tasks too pressing on his time. So he began to delegate. Macel was, from the start, pianist at the new church. Now she was pianist and accountant. Otis Wright was put in charge of the youth program. "I knew nothing about youth," Wright told me, "but I said I'd do the best I could." Other church members also volunteered to assist with aspects of church-work.

When Falwell's church started there were already about a hundred churches in Lynchburg. The people who came to his church came for two reasons. First they were taken by the energy of the young pastor, whose devotion to the ministry they could not help but notice. The second reason was that the church, now called Thomas Road Church, was small and embattled. It's members worked together in competition with the larger, softer, richer churches in town.

The church members crowded in around 10:00 on Sunday morning. First he sorted out his books, then he led the singing of the opening hymn. Macel played the piano. Otis Wright sat in the first row and sang loudly, forcing those around him to raise their voices and keep up. Falwell had no firm time-table. The congregation sang as long as they liked, and then he delivered the homily.

Falwell typically preached the saving gospel of Christ and the importance of growing spiritually: how to develop stable family relationships, how to pray, how to handle failure and disappointment, how to deal with human vices like alcoholism and marital infidelity. Although he had his shrill moments, he was, in general, a homey preacher, much like Charles E. Fuller. He was an intelligent preacher, in the manner of Dwight Moody, not anti-intellectual in the tradition of many fundamentalist pastors.

After the service the church members milled about the yard, chatting with each other, and with Falwell, who would quickly put away the podium ("I was afraid it would be stolen"), take off his jacket, and come outside to joke with his parishioners. Because he has established a good rapport with his congregation, he has never been involved in a squabble of the kind that precipitated the split at Park Avenue Church. (These squabbles occur frequently in fundamentalist churches because of their doctrinal hair-splitting and fetish about proper conduct.) At the end of the first year the church committee voted to raise Falwell's salary by $20 per week, but he declined. He didn't object to taking money, but the church could not afford it then. But the committee said it could—membership was up to 864 just twelve months after founding. Falwell gave in.

Finally Macel and Jerry set the date for their wedding day. The entire church was excited about the coming event. Much of the congregation was elderly, and they treated their engaged-to-be-married preacher with almost parental concern. Several church members stopped to talk with Helen Falwell about the wedding ceremony. She told them that it was the bride's family that took care of these things.

One day Helen took her son aside and asked him, "This girl you're after, it's for life, isn't it?" It struck Falwell as a stupid question, and he said so. But his mother reminded him that all people getting married regarded such questions as foolish, whereas few people who were divorced or separated did.

Falwell turned a quizzical eye toward her. "What are you saying, mother, that Macel isn't good for me?"

His mother laughed. "Don't be silly, Jerry, she's too good for you—that's what I'm saying." Falwell just looked at her. "Don't you be a preacher to her."

"Who's being a preacher to her?" he asked.

His mother replied, "Just don't let it happen, Jerry. You're a preacher to the people in the pews. You're going to be a husband to Macel. There's a difference." He shrugged. "You'll never find another one as good as Macel, that's all I'm saying," she finished. Jerry knew that she was alluding to the divorces of his sister, Virginia, and his brother Lewis, which had pained her greatly. Her own husband had sometimes been difficult, often perhaps, but she'd never shown any sign of thinking of leaving him.

The day of the wedding, April 12, 1958, finally arrived. Falwell woke up early that morning and prayed for two hours. He asked that his marriage be blessed and sustained through time.

The ceremony was held in the Thomas Road Baptist Church. Pastor John Suttenfield, who led a church Helen Falwell often attended before she joined her son's congregation, agreed to unite the young couple. The church was packed that Friday evening. Everybody wanted to see the strange sight—the pastor, usually large and looming at the pulpit, now walking bashfully down the aisle with a girl on his arm.

The reception was held in the church itself; around two hundred people came. Calvin Falwell, Jerry's first cousin, remembers it as a jocund occasion. Not only church members were invited. The large Falwell family drew in various acquaintances, who ranged from upright church members with cross pins on their lapels to others who were relative strangers in church. No alcohol was served.

Macel wore her white lace wedding gown throughout the evening.

Also at the wedding were several of Falwell and Macel's youthful friends and relatives who had at one time or other been the butt of Jerry's practical jokes. They decided that the young preacher's wedding day was a perfect time for retribution. So phone calls were made back and forth. There was the guy Falwell had once locked in a car with a stink bomb. There were victims of "anonymous" phone calls and midnight firecrackers tossed through open windows. These conspirators settled on a plan to be executed after the ceremonies. Jerry Falwell would learn that they were not to be messed with.

The festivities continued late into the night. Jim Moon and his wife, Delores, made jokes about the first time Moon and Falwell met Macel and Delores. Pastors B.R. Lakin and Wendell Zimmerman predicted a healthy family and ministry for the young Falwell. Alumni of the Wall group, some of them turned respectable and speaking in correct idiom, some restive in their unaccustomed suits and dresses, mingled with the others.

As conversation finally began to die down and people started to leave, a group of conspirators cast knowing looks at their watches and each other. They knew that one of them was outside taking apart wires in Falwell's car. This was the car Falwell was to use to drive to his mother's house, where he would pick up his packed suitcase prior to leaving on his honeymoon. The conspirators included two Lynchburg policemen, under less rigorous rules in those days, who were to capture Falwell as he vainly tried to start the car, and take him into custody for several hours. A separate kidnapping was planned for the new bride. She was to be taken unsuspectingly to a friend's house, where she would be held overnight.

It was a pretty serious plot. One of those involved now says, "It was only fair that Jerry's punishment fit the crime he had done to us."

However, shortly before the reception ended at 10:00 P.M., the two policemen who were to take Falwell were called to the station. Ironically, a liquor raid was taking place at a restaurant in town. The police-men left, to the consternation and frustration of the others. But they decided to continue with the plans. Falwell could not be taken now; he was too burly and they were short-handed. But he would not be able to move his car, and carrying out the rest of the plot would be just as effective.

So that is what they did, spiriting the bride away and leaving the bridegroom to his own devices.

When Falwell turned the ignition on his car, nothing happened. He tried again. Just a spluttering sound. He wiped his forehead, sat back, and rubbed his arms. Maybe he was too excited to keep his hand steady. He tried once more. Nothing. He got out of the car and opened the hood. He puttered around, then sighing, went down on his back and wriggled under the car, still in his black tuxedo. He saw what was wrong. The car had been sabotaged and would not be starting in a hurry. And then it struck him. Suddenly he realized the joke being played on him.

Falwell ran into the church and dialed his sister, Virginia, who must be home by now, on the church phone. Her husband answered. "Who is it?"

"Jerry Falwell."

"Jerry?"

"Lawrence, is my sister, Virginia, home?"

"Yup."

"Can I talk to her?"

"All right, if you want. Virginia!" Faint voice. "Jerry wants to talk to you . . . Jerry Falwell."

Virginia came to the line, puzzled. Falwell told her of the mean-spirited prank being played on him. "It's all the tricks I've played on them, Virginia," Falwell said, slightly remorseful.

Virginia, a justice of the peace, said she would do what she could. Falwell should go with his mother, get his bags together, and wait at the house. She would try to get things straightened out, "but I don't know how long it's going to take. Watch TV and wait, Jerry, that's all I can say."

So Falwell sat through the late news . . . then a sitcom, . . . then a late evening current events analysis. His mother consoled him that things would be rectified soon. She said she might as well call up Un-cle Carl, who was a mechanic. Maybe he could fix Jerry's car. Falwell said it was hopeless. But Helen made the call anyway, and Carl Falwell said he would be right over.

Falwell put in a couple more calls to Virginia, who said she had police cars tracking down the vehicle. She had given descriptions of all those under suspicion and all the cars she remembered. She couldn't resist telling her brother that for once he was feeling how much a practical joke could sting. He knew what she meant but replied, "Virginia, what are you talking about?"

"I'm talking about justice," she said. "That's my business, to figure out justice."

"Well, it's not being served in this case," he snapped. She laughed. He went back to watching television.

The kidnappers were found at 3:00 A.M. They were spotted by a policeman who had pulled off the road for a smoke. He put in a call to his mates, and they screamingly converged on the kidnappers' car. The practical jokers were arrested. They protested. The police couldn't arrest them for taking a friend for a spin! The police replied that they could and were. At this the plotters became rather sour and asked the officers if Falwell had put them up to this. The cops said no, they were just answering a kidnapping report. It was off to jail for the perpetrators, but before long they were let go, and no charges were filed.

It was four in the morning before the young people were able to commence their honeymoon trip to Miami.

6

Trouble with the Feds

It was a wonderful honeymoon for the young couple from Lynchburg.
Now, Falwell had to be getting back to his church. As it is, the members had to recruit a visiting pastor for one Sunday.

Falwell recalls a strangeness about being in Florida. In a sense, it was
a journey abroad for him. Florida was different. Florida was neon lights
and azure sky, tall hotels and bellboys, shysters and people in multicol-
ored shirts, boozing and wenching in the resorts and on the beach.
The young couple stayed away from the area's more worldly attrac-
tions, secure in their new faith and their new bond of marriage.

Soon it was back to Lynchburg and the ministry. There were nearly
one thousand members of Thomas Road now, and the two main employees could not afford to take a long vacation. It was back to preaching and prayer meetings, to potluck suppers and Sunday school.
"Those early years were probably the busiest time in my life," Falwell
remembers. "You think I'm busy now, but there was no end of things
to do then."

The years before his eldest son was born were important years for
building Falwell's ministry. He devoted time to little else. His church
was growing, taking in more people and more money each year. There
was competition from other fundamentalist churches, which were also

aggressive about proselytization. But few of the other preachers were as "hungry" for souls as Falwell.

In order to bring as many people to Christ as he possibly could, Falwell developed the concept of "saturation evangelism." (This term has now become part of the theory of evangelistic ministry.) Basically, this means no-holds-barred "soul-winning." Falwell refused to pick just one strategy for converting people; he embraced them all. He used every available means to get to people. This included his radio ministry, his television ministry, door-to-door canvassing and handing out of Bibles, rallies and prayer sessions in public places, publishing pamphlets and books about Christ to distribute and sell, talking about God in casual conversations, and sending out direct-mail letters inviting people to attend Thomas Road. This zeal to convert led Falwell to plow most of his own time and much of that of his church members into a desperate effort to preach the saving gospel of Christ to a lost world. After all, that is the biblical mandate. It may only have been a Virginia ministry then—already it was swelling out of Lynchburg—but he certainly planned to export it across the country, if not abroad.

Aggressive though his people may have been, Falwell admits he would not have been able to stimulate the church growth he did without radio and television. At first he was relatively relaxed about getting into broadcasting. He felt it was important, because you could reach more people than you could see, but he did it without much planning, almost reflexively imitating Charles Fuller. In 1962 "The Old Time Gospel Hour" expanded to Roanoke, Virginia; the next year it was being broadcast over most of the state. In 1968 Falwell changed the format of his show, abandoning his variety-style program for a taping of his regular Sunday church service.

Television preaching was not a fundamentalist innovation. Already in the 1950s Catholic Bishop Fulton Sheen had established a national ministry with his weekly show. He converted famous people like Clare Booth Luce. He brought an urbane religious consciousness to television that charmed even liberal sensibilities. People cheered when he won an Emmy for his television performances; the bishop cheerily gave all credit to his script writers—Matthew, Mark, Luke and John.

The fundamentalists were accomplishing something different than Sheen, however. They were not using television to give religion a sophisticated allure, to endear it to armchair esthetes and trend-followers. Many of the fundamentalist TV evangelists were without wit and refinement. They were thunder-preachers, howling out the unadulterated word of God. And people warmed to this message. For all its stridency, it was secure; it guaranteed salvation. All the talk about the complexity of moral situations, the interrelation between religion and psychiatry, and the value of self-help religiosity had its audience, but to many simple folk it only made things worse. The role of religion was to enlighten, they felt, not to confuse. Also they regarded television as a passive medium from which to imbibe entertainment and knowledge. They did not want questions, they wanted answers. And the fundamentalists provided answers in the most important realm, the moral realm. It was simple: Accept Christ and you are saved. Acknowledge your sinful condition. Wash away your sins in His blood. It was a fantastic product to sell over television; eternal salvation now, the only price being acceptance of Christ.

Falwell acknowledges the role television played in transforming his ministry. "Without the media we could not have made an entrance into the lives of people so quickly. When we knocked on doors and introduced ourselves, the people already knew us. We were welcome. The media became a tool for building the church." Being a media figure also gave Falwell a sense of success and importance. His church was invigorated too. People liked to hear that their pastor was just finishing his radio program and heading down to Thomas Road. They liked to turn on the car radio and hear the familiar voice say the familiar things. They liked to flip their TV channels and locate Brother Jerry. "Between the local radio broadcast every day and the weekly telecast, Thomas Road came alive," Falwell says. "Our sense of mission was increased. The conquest of the city was in sight."

Thomas Road Church grew during those early years at a rate of six or seven times higher than other fundamentalist churches. Given the fact that some of these churches pursued many of the same soul-winning strategies as Falwell, except for radio and TV, those media must be credited with much of the difference in results. Growth at Thomas Road was nothing short of amazing for a new church in a town that was not growing bigger, that already had more than a hundred churches in it.

Meanwhile, outside the Bible belt, liberal religion had resolved on an entirely different method for recruiting souls. Its pastors largely accepted the secular criticism of religion: too narrow, dogmatic, simplistic, etc. They were adapting their product—salvation—to the new consumer. This involved numerous biblical sleights-of-hand in the name of progressivism. For example the notion that God is love, that God loves sinners, was worded around to "The world is complex. God is love. There are no easy answers. We sin. But that's okay. God is

love." There was a sense that the more one sinned, the more one discovered just how much a God of love Christ was.

The liberal churches also rid themselves of narrowing
requirements—anything that would offend or alienate people. There
were no mandatory, doctrinal tenets, as long as religious striving, the
search for truth, persisted. Liberal theology was relativistic—it held
that truths were not absolute, but conditional on the situation, the individual, the society. The only imperative was "freedom," academic
freedom in the case of theologians. The liberal presumption that there
were no certain truths to be found invalidated the entire procedure of
free discussion as a goal to arrive at truth.

All this provoked a sharp reaction from fundamentalists, but they
were not the only ones protesting. In the 1950s Reinhold Niebuhr and
Paul Tillich, two renowned theologians, chastised liberal ministers for
their diminished sense of the sacred, their one-sided emphasis on
God's love without mentioning his justice, the persistent confusion of
the image of God in man for God himself. "The cross is a revelation of
the love of God only to those who have first stood under it as a judg-
ment," Niebuhr wrote.

This was the fundamentalist position. Anyone who acknowledged
his sinful condition and accepted Christ as savior would bring on divine grace. No matter how heinous the sins one committed, no matter
how heinous the sins one continued to commit, salvation was there for
the asking. It was not for fundamentalists to fall into the Catholic
"heresy" of works. They did not reckon virtuous deeds as counting toward the salvation scoreboard. Rather, they viewed good deeds as ema-
nating directly out of commitment to Christ but of themselves
somewhat irrelevant to the person's eternal fate. No group so much as
the fundamentalists is conscious of the fallen human condition. That
is perhaps why they emphasize so much salvation by faith alone.

What galled fundamentalists was that liberal ministers talked about
God's love without stressing the need for it. They treated sin as a trivial annoyance, in some cases something forced by the wealthy classes
upon the poor. Liberal ministers preached about "corporate" sins: the
capitalist system, global inequities, pollution of the environment. This
was a politicization of the concept of sin that fundamentalists simply
could not bear. If only those ministers conceded the fall from grace, if
only they preached the saving blood of Christ. But instead they
preached a halfhearted gospel about halfhearted sins (most of which
social conditions were responsible for anyway). No wonder they had
problems enlarging their following. As Ed Dobson, dean of Falwell's

college, puts it, "Why should people who are not in need of salvation put their faith in a Bible that is not infallible, in a God who is not omnipotent, in a Christ who did not literally die or rise and isn't coming back?" The great weakness of liberal theology was that it amounted to a social agenda in which religion was not necessary at all. The liberals feared dogma because it divides, but they did not realize that it also defines. Without dogma they lost their identity.

Fundamentalist dogma is based on a simple biblical progression that Falwell has articulated in various forms and adaptations over twenty-five years. A. "For all have sinned and fallen short of the glory of God" (Romans 3:23). B. "The wages of sin are death" (Romans 6:23). C. "I [Christ] am the resurrection and the life. He that believes in me, though he were dead, yet shall he live" (John 11:25-26). D. "Except that a man be born again, he cannot see the kingdom of God" (John 3:3). E. "For by grace are we saved through faith, and not of ourselves. It is the gift of God. Not of works, lest any man should boast" (Ephesians 2:8-9).

This is the entire fundamentalist orthodoxy. Falwell believes it with his whole heart. He has undergone many shifts of opinion over the years, but never once since his conversion has he renounced or compromised a single one of these tenets. The doctrines of fundamentalist Christianity have become the raison d'etre for his life. He claims that to this day he has not spoken in public on a single occasion when he has not preached the saving gospel of Christ—including secular talk shows and press conferences where the audience was hardly interested. "Who knows but that there may be someone listening to me who may never turn on that TV set again, may never hear my voice or any fundamentalist pastor, who may be dead tomorrow without having heard the saving gospel of Christ. I never want to be responsible for letting that happen." Falwell is willing to endure the risk of contradicting principles of separation of church and state, principles he says he espouses, to follow through on his irrepressible desire to preach the basic gospel.

"Fundamentalism is not a feeling, it is doctrine," Jerry Falwell has said. Indeed it is difficult to locate Christians more picky about doctrinal nuances than fundamentalists. For many fundamentalist preachers doctrine is everything. But Falwell is of a different temperament, which has led some to speculate that he is not a true-born fundamentalist. For Falwell doctrine means a great deal, but not everything. It may not even be the most important thing. The most important thing is the born-again *experience.* "Just as there is no other way to get into the human family except by birth, there is no other way to get into God's family expect by the new birth," Falwell writes in *Finding Inner Peace and Strength.*. The born-again aspect of Falwell's Christianity stresses experience over doctrine: Get to know Christ personally. Set up a relationship with Him. Through his dual emphasis on doctrine and experience, Falwell seems to have found a middle ground between those who stress only rigid principles on the one hand, and those (for example charismatics) who reject stuffy doctrines altogether and proclaim their personal chumminess with God Himself.

The Falwell formula worked wonders at Thomas Road, which entered the 1960s as a vibrant Virginia church aspiring to become one of the great churches of America. That was the goal. The church membership was far removed from other things and knew little of the happenings of the day. In 1960 they turned a sour face toward candidate John F. Kennedy, more because he was Catholic than anything else. Some fundamentalist pastors fulminated on the evils of Catholicism, warning that Kennedy in the White House could mean a direct line between Washington and the Vatican. But Falwell, although he opposed Kennedy, says he did so for political and not religious reasons, and in any case, he never preached about politics. In retrospect he feels "Kennedy did a good job. He was strong against the Soviets. Some of his actions would give liberals today a hernia. He produced the downfall of Khrushchev. But I disagree with his economic policies." Falwell does disagree now, because he now has views on the economy. At the time it was unclear that he was aware of the concept of capitalism, except as it worked in his everyday life.

Falwell's view of Eisenhower's two-term presidency is similarly uninformed and impressionistic. "I was glad about Ike," he says. "He was the first Republican I liked." Falwell says he was impressed by Eisenhower's war hero status, but "After eight years in office, I found him too complacent. A little too much golf." Kennedy's election, even though, it produced ripples of resentment among some fundamentalists, went mostly unnoticed at Thomas Road Church. "We felt then that the country could take care of itself. Many times we disagreed, but we didn't care enough to speak up," Falwell says. "Our goals had to do with the local church."

The local church building was starting to split at the seams. The people came from all over. Most, of course, were Lynchburg residents. But some came from as far as Roanoke and Charlottesville, piling out of their cars and filing into the pews to hear the dynamic young pastor whose voice they had heard on the radio and whom they had heard so much about. Falwell's great asset in drawing people has always been his sermons, which are full-throated and inspiring. He is low-keyed enough to make people comfortable and not offend them; he is strong-jawed enough to warm their hearts to the unyielding doctrine of God. He is simple enough to stir passion in the hearts of working folks, who love having their simplicity exalted to virtue; but he is quick-minded enough to be considered intelligent, someone with real insights into the Bible.

Falwell is also witty, which is perhaps his biggest selling point. Not in the coarse sitcom sense, but in a genuine, down-to-earth sense, making people laugh about the little things they feel and do, even about their own religious pretensions. Some fundamentalists, for example, are very concerned with personal appearance. Modesty in dress, proper formal wear, and hair length have always been sticky points with fundamentalists. Falwell, who is more easy going about appearance, has told fundamentalists to "worry a little less about the length of your son's hair, whether it's two inches or three, and worry a little more about the grey hair, the lack of hair, or someone else's hair that's on your head." He routinely makes jokes about age. "That was a wonderful song that Don Norman just sang. I just wish that I can sing like that when I get Don's age."

By the fall of 1957 the Donald Duck building had been enlarged from fifty feet by thirty feet to eighty-eight by thirty. The church also bought a small parcel of land as an investment. Within months another 50-by-30 Sunday school unit was built at the back of the church for children. So then the building was 138-by-30 and "looked like a long warehouse," in Falwell's words. But more people came, and so the sanctuary had to be extended. Falwell decided to build down Thomas Hill Road. It took several months to enlarge the existing sanctuary, and the new one was only ready by March 1958.

In June 1959 Falwell bought a 165-acre farm in Appomattox County near Lynchburg and set up the Elim Home for Alcoholics. He had wanted to do this for some time. He had been haunted since 1948 by the memory of his father's final alcoholic maunderings. The Elim Home is not intended for random drunks, however. It is for people who have made up their mind that they want to reform. Conversion to Christ is not only a prerequisite for admittance to Elim; it is the cure. Falwell is convinced that a genuine spiritual turnaround will rid a Christian of alcoholic addiction. It seems to work at Elim. Some eighteen to twenty people at a time are housed there and live a Spartan life that includes prayer and exercise. It does not include much entertainment and certainly no alcohol. Thomas Road Church bears all of the expense for Elim even today; the patients pay nothing for room and board.

The Falwells had their first child on June 17, 1962. Falwell describes himself as a "not nervous but excited" father that day. It was a boy, and after some discussion, they decided to name him after his father. The other two children were born soon after: Jeannie on November 7, 1964, and Jonathan on September 7, 1966.

Falwell's children have been second in his life only to God. To this day he protects his private life with them and treats them with unabashed favoritism. "What does it profit a man if he gains the whole world but suffers the loss of his children?" he asks. The children in the Falwell home have always enjoyed a fair measure of liberty, but there has never been any doubt about who is in charge. "There was never a vote on the issue. What dad wouldn't allow wasn't done," says Jerry Jr.

Falwell was not involved in politics during these years as he now is. He voted for Goldwater for president in 1964, but halfheartedly. Goldwater was not someone he regarded as a genuine conservative, being wishy-washy on moral issues and seemingly concerned only with the Soviet Union and Vietnam. The real political issues of those early 1960s, the issue which touched people's lives, was racial segregation. The effects of *Brown vs. Board of Education* were being strongly felt in the South. Adjustment was difficult for people who had been raised all their lives to believe in segregation.

"I grew up from infancy believing that segregation was right and Christian," Falwell admits. He preached against the *Brown* decision in 1958, saying, "If Chief Justice Warren and his associates had known God's word, I am quite confident that the 1954 decision would never have been made." He was particularly opposed to interrracial marriage.

In 1965 Falwell preached a sermon called "Ministers and Marches," in which he inveighed against liberal clergymen getting involved in the politics of racial equality. Falwell's position was that the Bible forbids Christians to get involved in politics. "We have a message of redeeming grace through a crucified and risen Lord," Falwell said. "Nowhere are we told to reform the externals. We are not told to wage wars against bootleggers, liquor stores, gamblers, murderers, prostitutes, racketeers, *prejudiced persons or institutions*, or any other existing evil as such. The gospel does not clean up the outside but rather regenerates the inside." Furthermore, he said, "believing the Bible as I do, I would find it impossible to stop preaching the pure saving gospel of Je-

sus Christ, and begin doing anything else—include fighting communism or participating in civil rights reforms. Preachers are not called to
be politicians but soul-winners."

Falwell now jokes about trying to buy back that sermon, which was
published in pamphlet form in the mid sixties. Its objective was clearly
to dissuade preachers from agitating for civil rights reforms, which
Falwell opposed. "Being a segregationist I naturally wanted to uphold
the status quo," he admits. But this position is articulated in a larger
context—that of religion being apart from politics, of separation of
church and state. Here he was in the long fundamentalist tradition of
interpreting church-state separation so broadly as to leave little common ground between religion and politics—"Preachers are not called
to be politicans but soul-winners."

Obviously Falwell's position has changed. He no longer opposes racial integration—in fact he says he strongly supports it—and he believes that preachers should be actively involved in political
discussion. "It took me several years to get segregation flushed out of
my soul," Falwell told me. "Through my Bible reading and spiritual
development, I began to confront this issue in my own life. I realized
that I was completely wrong, what I had been taught was completely
wrong. For me it was a scriptural and personal realization that segregation was evil. I realized it was not taught in the Bible. In fact, the opposite is recommended. Then I had to teach the church."

It was a painful process, and it took at least until 1968, the year
Falwell enrolled the first blacks as members of Thomas Road church.
Not many blacks had tried to join before that. Thomas Road, like
many churches in Virginia, had the reputation of being a "white
church," and so it was. Falwell says, "When I began to repudiate segregation, it cost me. Many of my friends thought I was becoming liberal." Don Norman, Falwell's associate pastor, says if Falwell had
admitted black members to Thomas Road before he did, "the church
would have experienced turmoil."

There were a few ugly racial scenes in Thomas Road in the 1960s.
On several occasions black radicals "who had no interest in religion,"
according to Otis Wright, one of Thomas Road's original members,
would saunter down the aisle and sit in between two white women.
"They just wanted to be provocative," Wright says. "They had no interest in praying or anything." And Thomas Road had no interest in
letting them stay. Almost on cue, burly church members would get up
and escort the troublemakers out. They were not there to be violent,
only to have a cause for complaint; now they could go on local TV

channels and complain about being chucked out of Thomas Road Church.

Falwell worked to change his people's views on segregation first by bringing in black preachers of unquestionable fire and orthodoxy from large black churches to preach. This raised eyebrows, but the preachers were so thunderous and dogmatic that the people quickly warmed up to them and wanted them back. Pretty soon Thomas Road had a small group of black members. Interracial dating or marriage is still a sore point with most members, however, "I think it goes against Scriptures, you know," Otis Wright says.

Falwell believes discrimination and prejudice will always be present to some degree and he still has to fight racism in church and school. "Now we are a generation away from segregation, and when people talk about racism as if it were a thing of the Dark Ages, they don't realize that it is very recent. It is still very present." Falwell has gone from sworn segregationist to avid reformer. He speaks of race almost in the vocabulary of civil rights leaders, and he supports affirmative action up to the point that it becomes deleterious for the minority groups themselves.

Falwell also changed his position on clergy participation in politics, but not until 1973. In the 1960s he felt a visceral distaste for what was going on across the country—the Vietnam protest movement in particular—but he did not oppose the radicals. In retrospect he feels that Lyndon Johnson was "a strong leader and an excellent politician" but "totally wrong about Vietnam." He regards the war as a "necessary struggle," saying, "It was a mistake for us not to win." It was certainly not a mistake to get in. "Had we fought hard from the start in Korea, there would not be a Vietnam." He adds, "And had we done it in Vietnam, there would not be a Nicaragua." Falwell believes the Vietnam war could have been won conventionally; he does not think chemical weapons or nuclear explosives should have been used to expedite victory. "The Vietnam war was lost in Washington." He blames Congress for being "not willing to make the commitment to democracy and freedom." Of the tragedy at Kent State, the killing of student protestors by police, Falwell says, "It was very sad, of course, that students were killed. But there is no getting around the fact that the students brought the tragedy upon themselves. When you burn campuses, defy authority, break the law, whether you are young or old, you risk getting hurt."

Falwell describes the student rebellion of the 1960s and 1970s as "a predictable rebellion against a materialistic society that recognized no values." His theory is that after living through the Depression and fighting World War II, realizing the horror of deprivation, American grandparents and parents resolved that their children would never go through what they had to. So they bestowed on the next generation all the material benefits of the post-war economic boom, but without simultaneously teaching them the values that had sustained their fathers and grandfathers through hardship. As a result, Falwell says, "we got a generation of kids with money but no morals, with material things but no happiness." The discontent of the students was thus a natural expression of their spiritually impoverished condition. He feels it was exploited for political ends by radicals but concedes it was headed in that direction anyway. "Materialism failed as it has always failed," he says. "The young people turned against their religion, their parents, and their country."

As the youth drifted away, the liberal churches drifted with them. Because the presumption of liberal theology is that the church must adapt to the world—go with the flow, so to speak—liberal clergymen were unable to distinguish between correcting the prevalent vices of society or encouraging them. Part of the problem was that the liberal church tended to be excessively subservient to its members. Thus expressions of student vulgarity were treated as sacrosanct by liberal clergymen—not just as problems to be understood and rectified, but as displays of legitimate,if not heroic, dissent from which the Church itself could learn. The attempt by the liberal church to ride the shirttails of the hippie culture took on a tone of the farcical. In the 1960s couples were being married in balloons or in carriages; readings in church included passages from Timothy Leary and Kahlil Gibran; at one wedding in New York the bride wore a G-string; at a Northeastern seminary the students prepared for the Eucharist by smoking marijuana; a Baptist clergyman came on national TV to play the guitar with his toes ("God has given me this gift, and it brings me closer to people," he said); a Catholic priest in Colorado had a sex change operation. These stories suggest the lack of order that characterized many of the liberal churches in the 1960s.

The fundamentalist reply to the protest movement was to grow more rapidly than the protesters. Construction at Thomas Road had been going on almost nonstop since 1957. In 1964 a thousand-seat auditorium was built. In 1965 the Spurgeon and Brainerd buildings were added.

In 1967 Falwell invited A. Pierre Guillermin, formerly president of Southern Methodist College in Orangeburg, South Carolina, to set up a school for his church. They agreed, in Falwell's words, "to set up a total education for young people, from kindergarten through university, so that the kids would get academics and also catch the vision for Christ." So Lynchburg Christian Academy was set up in the fall of 1967, enrolling about one hundred children, mostly of Thomas Road church members, in grades one through five. Grades were progressively tacked onto LCA. In 1968 the sixth grade was added, in 1969 grades seven and eight. By 1971 LCA was an elementary school, grade school, and high school rolled into one.

Fortunately, in the late 1960s Falwell got the financial backing to initiate new projects like LCA. In 1967 "The Old Time Gospel Hour" was being aired in only about a dozen cities around Virginia. But those who listened to Falwell sent in generous contributions, and members of Thomas Road made great sacrifices to launch their pastor's vision. Falwell took this money and immediately invested it, not in generating more money, but in recruiting new members and television viewers. That proved even in financial terms to be a smart approach.

In 1969 Elmer Towns, the Christian educator, came to Lynchburg while writing a book on the ten largest Sunday schools in America. Thomas Road, with 2,640 members, was the ninth largest church in the United States, with the eight largest Sunday school. The leap in membership kicked off a rise in the funds. In 1970 Thomas Road already had a budget of $1 million, mostly from local contributions. Falwell had identified some wealthy gentlemen among his members. He needed money to execute two large plans he had been developing: to start a college and to launch a national television ministry. "The money was not for me," Falwell says. "It was for Christ." He was making $22,500 with small benefits, in 1970.

In 1971 Falwell brought back Dr. Towns to help him found Lynchburg Baptist College on land the church had purchased and named Liberty Mountain. (Pierre Guillermin, meanwhile, left Falwell for four years to help the Reverend Jack Dinsbeer found Christian schools in Florida.) Towns recruited a small born-again faculty and announced the opening of the new Baptist school in local papers. The initial facilities were scanty. When the college opened in September 1971, there was no real campus—no dormitories, no ivy-covered walls. But the faculty quickly grew devoted. The rules were strict, if not draconian, and pretty soon the fundamentalist students who came from Virginia and nearby states began to refer to the school as "Boot camp, Lynchburg."

Jerry Falwell referered to the college from the start as the "University of God." He has fantastic plans for his college, whose name was changed to Liberty Baptist College in 1976. "The fundamentalist kid will look on Liberty Baptist the same way a Roman Catholic youngster looks on Notre Dame," Falwell predicts. At the rate LBC has grown since 1971, from a "boot camp" with a few hundred students to a 4,400-acre campus with five thousand students and several graduate programs, Falwell will accomplish his goal before his deadline of 2000 A.D.

Towns and Falwell started Thomas Road Bible Institute (now Liberty Bible Institute) in the fall of 1972. A home Bible study program was also instituted. It presently enrolls fifteen thousand families. In October 1973 Lynchburg Baptist Theological Seminary (now Liberty Baptist Seminary) was opened to prepare students, mostly LBC graduates, for the ministry. Numerous other facilities were added around these core institutions and more staff was added to man these various activities. In 1967 Jim Soward came to Lynchburg to head Sunday school administration. In 1971 Don Norman joined the "Old Time Gospel Hour" crew.

Sports programs were introduced on a large scale, partly because Falwell was an aficionado, but also to attract the energies of fundamentalist kids to athletics. Falwell has developed an entire theology of sports, which he metaphorically extends to the rest of his ministry. He preaches sermons advising his people to be "champions for Christ"; he did a series on his television show called "Ten Champions of the Bible"; he asks his sports team to "win titles in Jesus' name." Falwell feels that "Christians are called to be winners" and likes to quote Vince Lombardi—"If winning isn't important, why do they keep score?" In view of this attitude toward Christianity, it is not surprising that Falwell resents pictures depicting Christ as a skinny, long-haired man with flowing robes. "Christ wasn't effeminate; Christ was a he-man."

Continuing construction at Thomas Road, Falwell constructed a four thousand seat auditorium for cultural performances and religious programs. The program in communications at the college was linked to Falwell's television ministry, so that students could help orchestrate, and sometimes appear on, "The Old Time Gospel Hour," by now airing on nine hundred TV and radio stations. "We wanted to develop an educational system that began at the cradle," Falwell says. "We wanted to meet all the spiritual and intellectual needs of kids." Says Eldridge Dunn, who runs the children's ministry at the school, "We want to compete with the world." Apparently Falwell was com-

peting effectively: In 1972, on the sixteenth anniversary of his ministry, he was able to produce nineteen thousand people—adults and
students—at Lynchburg Municipal Stadium for a Sunday school
celebration—he called the "the biggest Sunday school since Pente-
cost." *Newsweek* in a July 1972 story billed Thomas Road Church as
"the fastest growing church in the United States".

I asked Falwell why he was not provoked into politics by the candi-
dacy for president of George McGovern in 1972. Falwell says simply,
"I saw him as a politician with absolutely no chance of winning." The
utter futility of McGovern's campaign made Falwell doubly disappointed that Nixon, whom he supported, acted unethically to secure
the election. Falwell calls Watergate "a national tragedy. Watergate
set back the conservative trend for several years and gave us Jimmy
Carter." He views Watergate as a typical example of the media double
standard. "They weren't very much upset about Billy Sol Estes and
Bobby Baker." Falwell complains. Yet "no one can be blamed more
than Mr. Nixon for Watergate." These views, which Falwell offers
now, are the product of retrospective analysis; at the time he reacted
to national and world incidents from instinct, confining himself to a
brief comment or derogatory remark when he heard the news on the
radio. But he never spoke about these things in public. They were regarded outside the domain of life in Lynchburg.

Many dramatic things happened in 1973, which changed the fate of
Thomas Road Baptist Church. Of these, the most serious was a fracas
with the federal government that almost closed the doors of Falwell's
booming ministry. In January Falwell got a call from a representative of
the Securities Exchange Commission and was informed that the SEC
had filed suit against Thomas Road Church, charging the ministry
with "fraud and deceit" in its financial operations. Specific allegations
were that Thomas Road had filed inaccurate and improper bond pro-
specti, that records of the church were not submitted correctly and
that the church had more debtors than creditors. Falwell, who takes
money seriously but who has never been a meticulous manager of it,
was distressed. Was almost two decades of labor and devotion to go
down the drain?

Until 1973 Thomas Road Church maintained a typical small church
financial bookkeeping office. Falwell remained the principal employee, in charge of everything from ordering coffee to supervising
construction on the college. Volunteers handled functions ranging
from janitorial work to accounting. No wonder that the books were in
terrible shape. But Falwell turned the SEC charges somewhat to his

advantage, charging that "the devil" was after Thomas Road Church. His volunteer bookkeepers did not intend to defraud anyone, and the government officials had acted rudely and presumptuously. But it was true that the church had raised $5 million from big contributors without even issuing a prospectus. Bonds were being sold without proper records being kept. Nobody could tell exactly how much had been raised by the church that year or where the money came from and where it was going. Falwell and his church officials were scheduled to appear in federal court in August before Judge James Turk, who had the reputation of being a hardnosed purveyor of justice.

Falwell and his wife describe the controversy with the SEC as most traumatic for themselves and the ministry. Falwell, who had never appeared in court before, found the experience most humiliating; he sought refuge in prayer.

"He was depressed a lot," according to his personal secretary, Jeanette Hogan. "Everything mushroomed so fast." Although Falwell now concedes his negligence, at the time he regarded the SEC action as a plot to close down a successful ministry. He did not realize, he now says, that sincerity does not substitute for proper management.

Any successful ministry makes enemies, and Thomas Road Church had its detractors in Lynchburg and across the state. Some of these were fundamentalist churches envious that they had been surpassed by Thomas Road in membership. Some were liberal churches whose pastors despised the "dogmatism" and "narrowness" (and the popularity of these evils) at Thomas Road. There were those who counted the financial success of Thomas Road against its pastor. Judge Turk listened to the accounts of error and the explanations proferred by Falwell and his attorneys. He concluded that while "there is no evidence of intentional wrongdoing" and "nothing that has been said from the witness stand that in any way taints the good name of Thomas Road Church," nevertheless Thomas Road would have to turn over its financial operations to a board of five prominent Lynchburg businessmen. They would institute modern-day practices of accounting and fiscal efficiency. At the time Falwell and his associates bitterly resented the intrusion. Now Falwell feels the SEC scandal was an educational experience for Thomas Road because "it forced us to move from a one-horse church to a corporate position." The volunteer treasurer gave way to an "accounting department."

The five businessmen who took over financial management for the church quickly transformed it from a catch-as-catch-can ministry to a sophisticated one. First they looked for evidence of fiscal malpractice at Thomas Road. They found none, only waste and sloppiness. They fired unnecessary employees and some excessively well-meaning but incompetent volunteers. Experts were hired in areas like accounting and public relations. An advertising agency, Epsilon Data Management, was recruited to coordinate fundraising. The businessmen also adopted a cost-efficient way to purchase television time for Falwell, previously bought on an ad hoc basis at much higher cost. Also, stations whose local broadcast did not prompt an inflow of revenue in excess of cost were taken off the Falwell list. These measures worked. From 1973 to 1977, revenues at Thomas Road rose from $7 million to $22 million. The businessmen, receding from the scene already as early as 1975, turned back the church's financial affairs to Falwell, who now relies on competent administrators to prevent another SEC situation.

7

The Preacher
Turns to Politics

Falwell's salary, $22,000 in 1970, was $42,500 in 1980. His benefits also rose substantially over that ten-year period. Whereas in 1970 he had to be content to drive a Buick, a decade later he was being flown around the country in a Jet Commander owned by the ministry. So the time from the SEC crisis until the 1980 election was one of prosperity for the Falwell family. The kids were eleven, nine, and seven years old in 1973. All were enrolled in Falwell's school, Lynchburg Christian Academy. They strolled about the campus, frolicking with the other fundamentalist children.

Falwell's children have not benefitted from enrolling in their father's school. The straight-A grades of Jerry Jr. or Jeannie are legitimate. Falwell wants no special treatment for his three children—neither does he allow unusual and special demands to be made of them. He wants only fair and equitable treatment so that they will not be embittered or spoiled. Whatever the advantages and disadvantages of attending Falwell's school and then his college, the Falwell children clearly had no choice. It would never do for Falwell to set up a new school and proclaim his faith in its academic standards and then send his children elsewhere.

The Falwell children lived in a closed world, to be sure. They were exposed only to their born-again teachers and parents. Jerry Jr. admits that, until he attended summer school at Yale in the summer of 1983, his only influences were his LCA teachers, his parents, and some right-wing activist friends of his father. Falwell and Macel were careful never to quarrel with each other before the kids. Falwell says his chil-were given sex eduction at an early age, but "with moral values, not in a vacuum." Sex is also taught at LCA, but strictly as a biological science—none of this "values clarification" humbug.

One only has to talk to Falwell for a few minutes to detect that the issue of sex is a primary one. Why it should be so is not clear. The Bible condemns fornication and adultery, but only as one sin among many. Yet Falwell seems to hold that sexual wrongdoing is a far greater sin than, say, feeling anger or jealousy. Falwell admits to going to much greater measures to ensure that his children and his students were morally pure than to ensure that they did not criticize or connive or talk behind each other's backs. This is because he views sexual order as the heart of social order. He does feel that it is possible to separate the pleasurable and reproductive aspects of sexuality, and he favors contraception. "The bed in marriage is holy. Husband and wife belong to each other. Pleasure as well as procreation are part of their sexual relationship." One gets the impression that Falwell's peculiar protectiveness on the issue of sex is less a theological view than a social one. Faithful sex within marriage strengthens the institution of the family.

Overall, Falwell opposes hedonism, because he holds, with Aristotle, that happiness is an activity of the soul in accordance with virtue. He interprets happiness in a long-term sense, in the sense of eternal happiness. Attempts to obtain this-worldly happiness can prejudice one's chances in the next world.

In 1973, shortly after the SEC crisis, Falwell and his family moved from their home on Grove Road to another on Chesterfield Road in Lynchburg. The new home was somewhat larger than the other. It had a swimming pool and cost $80,000. His congregation appeared pleased that their "first family" was being cared for. Despite his material success, Falwell insists that neither he nor his family have become materialistic.

In 1970 the Federal Communications Commission decided that paid religious broadcasts would no longer be considered partisan announcements subject to regulation and the rule of reply time. Rather, they would be treated as public service announcements. Network affiliates immediately began to sell off their Sunday morning hours. Soon even some prime time slots were sold to preachers who could afford it. Because Sunday morning was considered a "ghetto period" of television, rates were extremely low, and Falwell was easily able to take in several times what he spent. Even as late as 1979 he spent only $9 million to broadcast for one hour nationwide.

Since 1970 there has been continued opposition by liberal groups, especially church groups, to the FCC decision. Liberal and atheist groups have requested free equal time for time sold to fundamentalists. Falwell views this as absurd. "We believe that time should be made available to whoever can pay for it." He admits that "conservatives tend to be able to raise more money and buy more time," and that "liberals cannot do this," but feels that "that's their problem." He believes that his religious and social agenda is very much in the public interest. He does not see why free reply time should be doled out to clamoring opponents when he is paying precious dollars for this television hour. Falwell is now especially grateful to Mark Fowler, director of the FCC and a Reagan appointee, who has successfully fended off efforts to regulate paid religious time.

During the 1970s liberal churches experienced a steady decline, while fundamentalist churches grew rapidly. From 1970 through 1977 the United Methodists lost 886,000 members, the United Presbyterians 526,000, and the Episcopal Church 467,000. By contrast Baptist Bible Fellowship, with just 200 preachers in 1950, had over 3000 churches in 1977. The National Religious Broadcasters Organization, mainly comprised of evangelical-fundamentalist preachers, grew from 49 members in 1944 to more than 1800 in 1980. Record enrollments were reported in 1980 at fundamentalist seminaries: Dallas Theological Seminary (1500), Grace Theological Seminary (500), Southwestern Baptist Theological Seminary (3700), Trinity Evangelical Divinity School (1800), Baptist Bible College (2500), Bob Jones University (6000), Calvin College (4100), Cedarville College (1500), Liberty Baptist College (4400) and Tennessee Temple University (5000).

Fundamentalist churches reported huge memberships. In 1980 the First Baptist Church of Hammond, Indiana, had 15,000 members. Highland Park Baptist Church of Chattanooga, Tennessee, had 11,000. Thomas Road Church was third with just over 10,000 members. Next came First Baptist Church of Dallas; Akron Baptist Temple of Akron, Ohio; Canton Baptist Temple of Canton, Ohio; Calvary Temple Church of Springfield, Illinois; and Landmark Baptist Temple of Cincinnati, Ohio. These, the eight largest churches in the country in 1980, were all fundamentalist. And the next twenty-five largest churches were also fundamentalist or evangelical. No wonder that pollster George Gallup observed, "It would be difficult to identify a decade that incorporated more crises and change for the churches than the 1970s. Yet the 1980s may far surpass the tumultuous furor we have just completed. Staggering membership losses suffered by mainline denominations have not yet turned around in a positive growth direction. The Presbyterian, Episcopalian, and United Church of Christ communions cannot long exist as viable church organizations nationally if the declines of the 1970s persist in the 1980s. On the other hand, the conservative churches appear to be in an up-period, with the Southern Baptists and a variety of fundamentalist groups setting attendance and membership records almost hourly."

The fundamentalist churches were full and the fundamentalist TV programs were growing in viewers. The liberal pews were empty. No wonder that liberal clergymen turned their resentment on their successful counterparts. It was a common complaint during the 1970s that TV ministries were bad because they sought to take people away from the local church, which was the venue of true communion with God. The Reverend William Fore of the National Council of Churches wrote a vituperative article in *TV Guide* titled "There Is No Such Thing as a TV pastor." Pressed to explain the popularity of TV preachers, Fore theorized that they purveyed ideas that the people wanted to hear, not necessarily the message of a God who requires justice, humility, and love.

Falwell denies that he is taking people away from the local church. "We encourage the local church," he says. "We are careful to schedule our TV slots at times when Sunday morning services in local churches are not going on." Not all TV preachers do this, but in general, it does not seem that the electric church detracts much from local church attendance.

In the letters provoked by his *TV Guide* article, Fore discovered another possible cause for diminished local church attendance. There were more than 300 angry letters, so many that Fore was compelled to write a shocked reappraisal in *Christianity Today.* "The local church simply is not meeting the needs of many, many people." he admitted. And the television ministries were. The people who wrote to Fore said they found their local preachers self-righteous, this-worldly, concerned more with social justice than salvation, and sticking their hands in people's pockets at the same time they denounced greed, capitalism, self-aggrandizement, etc. The letter writers found a simplicity about the TV preachers. They might be wealthy, but they were frank about it. At least they built prayer towers and cathedrals. They didn't drink gin and tonics like the liberal clergymen. They didn't wear tweed coats. They didn't pretend they knew Kierkegaard.

Four television preachers who were to have a pronounced effect on the 1980 election came to prominence in the 1970s. They were: Falwell, Pat Robertson of the Christian Broadcasting Network and the 700 Club, James Robison of the Religious Roundtable, and James Bakker of the PTL Club. These preachers displaced the older TV ministers who had reigned on the air since the 1950s: Billy Graham, Oral Roberts, Rex Humbard, and Robert Schuller. These early ministers were more genial and saccharine. Schuller was an updated Norman Vincent Peale. Roberts was all flowers and arm-raising—just look to the ceiling and a loving God will answer your prayers. Humbard's ministry was similarly reassuring, with a Nashville country style and none of the threats and wildfire that characterized the younger preachers' shows. Curiously, it is the older preachers who have acquired a reputation for affluence among their viewers, even though the media treats the new preacher as money-grubbing outsiders. In fact Bakker, Robison and Falwell live in miserly fashion compared to Roberts and Humbard and Graham. Humbard, for example, recently purchased a home and condominiums valued at $650,000. When asked about the ethics of allocating church money for personal use, he observed. "My people don't give a hoot what I spent that money for."

The story of all the television preachers is, almost without exception, a kind of religious Horatio Alger story. Humbard led off his television programs, now broadcast on 650 stations in 18 countries, with a modest $65 paid up for a radio program. Pat Robertson filed a charter for CBN in January 1960 and opened a bank account with a $3 deposit. Now CBN owns four TV stations and five radio stations and has a staff of eight-hundred. Oral Roberts' first television program on January 10, 1954, was broadcast on 16 stations; in early 1980 "Oral Roberts and You" issued from 165 stations and took in $50 million a year. James Bakker, a former employee of the 700 Club, cleverly mastered the technological skills and started his own PTL Club, now a multimillion-dollar ministry. And, of course, Falwell began with thirty-five adults at Thomas Road Baptist Church.

Falwell, Bakker, Robison, and Robertson began to pile up a huge viewership in the early 1970s, unnoticed by the national media, who regarded the alarm of the mainline churches over fundamentalist television ministries as undue paranoia. Louis Harris calls the power of re-religious television the "most neglected story of our time," and so it is.

In 1973, however, it was a nascent power, a power that only found expression in calls to conversion and awaited opportunity for some more concrete form of self-expression.

In 1973, by a seven to two decision, the Supreme Court of the United States ruled that states could not make laws regulating a woman's "right" to an abortion during the first trimester of pregnancy. The decision stunned many across the country, but none more than the fundamentalists. Jerry Falwell remembers that he was at home and heard the news on the radio. It took a moment for it to sink in, he says. Then he felt sick. All he could feel was numbness and shock. His sense of America was of a basically good nation, perhaps unsaved and insensitive to the fundamentalist gospel, but nevertheless a basically moral and upright nation. After the *Roe vs. Wade* decision on abortion, Falwell knew he would have to rethink his relationship to his government.

Falwell did not immediately act upon his consternation and horror. It is doubtful that he could have then, although he thinks he could. The liberal establishment, backed by the liberal churches, built a powerful cordon around *Roe vs. Wade*. The objective from the start was to acquire for the abortion decision the same sullen acquiescence that come with *Brown vs. Board of Education*, the desegregation decision of 1954. The liberal church praised *Roe vs. Wade*, as a show of moderation on the part of the Court and hailed it as a unifying decision. This would cut down on the number of back-alley abortions and would extend the privilege of pregnancy termination to the poor. The liberals also maintained that opposition to the abortion ruling was mainly from Catholic sources and could be dismissed because it was based on theological, not rational considerations. Antiabortion people were described as authoritarian types who wished to "impose their morality" on the rest of society. No one seemed to remember that a court of seven people had just imposed its view of morality on an entire nation, had just reneged on a tradition of several hundred years, had just reversed several precedents. All that was okay in the interest of progressivism. Those who wished to reverse *Roe vs. Wade* were denounced as reactionaries who wanted to "turn back the clock." In Falwell's analysis, "When liberals say that it is impossible to turn back the clock, they mean that nobody should try and undo their errors." But in fact, the clock had stopped for unborn babies in America, and he could not stand silent. A baby's pain may not cause much suffering to the ideologically anesthetized, but Falwell could not block out the agony he saw inflicted.

Falwell immediately began to condemn abortion in his church. This was a surprising move, in a sense. Since Falwell's father's day, fundamentalists had stuck pretty much to gospel preaching. Even Falwell defined a church as a "body of born-again believers who have banded together for the purpose of world evangelization." Other purposes were hardly acknowledged. But here he was, blasting the Supreme Court for its abortion decision. His people did not mind, because they were outraged, too.

Falwell was never staunch on the civil rights issue, but he found a powerful analogy for the abortion decision: the nineteenth-century *Dred Scott* Supreme Court decision denying civil rights to blacks. "Did you know that abortion was illegal in this country for one hundred ninety-three years?" Falwell fulminated in a mock address to the Supreme Court. "For one hundred ninety-three years it was against the law. It was a crime to kill an unborn baby. Suddenly by a seven-to-two vote you decide that little unborn babies are not human beings and therefore have no human rights. Strange that in 1857, by the same seven-to-two vote, you held that black people were not human beings, that they had no human or civil rights, that they could be bought and sold as cattle. You were wrong then and you are wrong this time. History will prove you wrong."

This is a strident stuff. In fact, I have never heard a Catholic priest preach against abortion as forthrightly as Falwell. Falwell himself expresses strong gratitude to the Catholic Church. "For years they stood alone and fought the abortion issue. We, the Protestant ministers, were negligent. It is their moment of glory and our moment of shame. But we have good news for them. We are not going to be silent any longer. We have joined the fight."

Falwell expresses particular outrage that most liberal churches have come out in favor of abortion. He cannot comprehend the logic of those who say they are "personally against abortion" but don't want to impose their views on others. Using his favorite analogy, Falwell wrote in *Fundamentalist Journal*, "That is like saying you are against slavery but do not mind if other people keep slaves." Similarly, Falwell blasts the clergymen who "are pro-choice when it comes to killing fetuses, but don't favor choice when it comes to a child praying in a classroom."

There are a number of reasons for Falwell's entering the political arena, but none as influential as the Supreme Court ruling on abortion. Sure, he was piqued at efforts to control his paid religious programming. He was miffed about the derogatory opinion of religion held by most intellectuals. He found the federal government meddlesome in church and private school affairs. He grieved at the expulsion of prayer from schools. But the 1973 decision, he says, "was all I could take. That was the straw that broke the camels' back. Then I was convinced that government was going bad. And I realized that it was, in part, because we had absented ourselves from the process."

In 1973–74 Falwell realized that organizations claiming to represent moral and religious interests were, in fact, behaving in what he regarded as a terribly immoral manner. The World Council of Churches and the National Council of Churches, for example, had succeeded so well in their effort to be "relevant" that they were virtually indistinguishable from the societal ills they were supposed to combat. Falwell feels that the Church should change the world, not be changed by the world. And the WCC and NCC were reacting to the political scene in an opposite way from what he considered moral. As early as 1958 the NCC advocated the admission of Red China into the United Nations. In 1972 the NCC urged support for "liberation" forces in Angola and South Africa. In 1973 Claire Randall, the NCC's general secretary, expressed support for the Supreme Court decisions on school prayer and abortion. Both the WCC and NCC vigorously opposed the Vietnam War. In 1975 the NCC's governing board resolved that homosexuals were entitled to full membership in the Church. Another NCC conference declared that "There is a basic conflict between capitalism and biblical justice, mercy, stewardship, service, community, and self-giving love." In 1981 the WCC's Central Committee denounced the U.S. role in El Salvador, disapproved of the annexation of East Jerusalem by Israel, and called for "immediate negotiations" with the Palestine Liberation Organization. When it turned out that virtually only the Catholic Church took an unequivocal stand against *Roe vs. Wade*, Falwell realized that the corruption of the liberal church went deeper than he thought. These churches were "secular in every sense of the word," he says. "Previously I knew the liberal churches were a religious morgue. But I didn't know that while the pews were empty, the liberal ministers were full of trouble, supporting antifamily and antimoral legislation." Falwell impugns the double standards of the WCC and NCC, which are ecumenical about doctrine and permit the worst heresies to preserve "unity," but which at the same time divide the church bitterly over political issues like abortion and socialism. "Doctrine does divide," he admits. "It *should* divide, as the Bible does, to separate truth from error." But he feels that nondoctrinal issues should not hamper to Christians' coming together. He does not see a contradiction here. To some extent, Falwell today divides Christians by the strident political stands he takes on issues only tangentially related to Christian doctrine.

Abortion politicized, even radicalized, Falwell, but as he began to be interested in politics, other issues arose. Eventually he came to see all of them as interconnected. His theological style has been to identify two sides, good and evil, in every dispute. Naturally he has extended this style, to politics. For instance, he sees a connection between people who favored abortion and people who opposed national defense, specifically the war in Vietnam. He saw a connection between people who opposed the war and people who spoke of "social justice." And in fact many of the protesters in different causes are the same people, merely turning one placard of protest in for another. And the record of success of these people convinced Falwell that the United States was in a period of moral and social decline. He now says that the preservation of America and of freedom is "the primary moral issue of our time."

Falwell's entry into politics was unwelcome to those who disagreed with his political views. However, they voiced their concerns mainly in terms of Falwell posing a danger to the principle of separation of church and state. Thus the *Christian Science Monitor* said Falwell's "moral zealotry" was not welcomed by Americans, who "can only be grateful for the Constitution's wisdom of erecting a wall of separation between church and state." An article in the *New York Times*, entitled "Fears on Rise about Growing Role of Religion in Election Campaigns" noted that the trend toward fundamentalists like Falwell practicing politics "has caused considerable consternation among some clergy and laymen alike, who feel it threatens the basic separation of church and state." And not to be outdone by the big papers, the *Democrat-Herald* of Oregon editorialized, "The once common marriage of interests between politics and religion has gone out of style. And Falwell should not try to bring it back." Ira Glasser, president of the American Civil Liberties Union, actually charged that Falwell was trying to destroy the American Constitution and subvert the Bill of Rights. Other critics of Falwell took up this hyperbole, apparently feeling that moral passion entitled them to sling such charges.

Falwell's reaction to charges that he is violating church-state separation is to point out a double standard. "Where were our critics when William Sloane Coffin, the Berrigan brothers, and Eugene Carson Blake, and Martin Luther King used the pulpit to advocate their political views?" He may have a point here. Liberal clergymen have, from the start, engaged vigorously in political action; in fact the very theory of social justice is dependent upon political involvement. In the nineteenth century for example, the crusades against slavery, for temperance and for women's suffrage, were led by preachers. Martin Luther King, head of the Southern Christian Leadership Conference, practised a kind of fundamentalism not too far removed from that of Jerry Falwell. Falwell told the *Los Angeles Times* in 1981, "Obviously I am doing now what Martin Luther King did fifteen years ago." Critics of Falwell concede that their favorite clergymen have never drawn up a "hit lists" or engaged in lobbying.

To this Falwell replies that Moral Majority has never drawn up a "hit list" either—it was Christian Voice that did so in 1980. But, he says in defense of that group, the Catholic social justice lobby "network" has been issuing voting records for nine years. Also it is simply not true that left-leaning religious organizations have not lobbied. He points out that the U.S. Catholic Conference has a full-time lobbying staff and has published several of their legislative positions derived from papal encyclicals and rulings by the Synod of Bishops. "But nobody has yelled about these," Falwell maintains, "Because they happen to agree with the views expressed." The same is true for the United Methodists' Board of Church and Society, which employs a dozen full-time lobbyists, and the Society of Friends Committee, a Quaker lobbying group. In 1976 the Reverend James Wall, managing editor of the *Christian Century*, the liberal evangelical magazine, managed Jimmy Carter's campaign in Illinois. And from the 1970s until now, the Reverend William Sloane Coffin has conducted "disarmament seminars" and symposia at Riverside Church in New York City.

Falwell feels that criticism leveled at him on the church-state score is disingenuous. "If I called for the nationalization of major oil companies, every liberal preacher and reporter in the country would be for me," Falwell says. "But because I stand against abortion, against pornography, for the family, all these people say I am a threat to the Constitution." The church-state business is just a matter of whose political ox is being gored, he feels. He is supported in his contention by the mostly conservative small papers. For example, the *Paducah Sun* in Kentucky observed in Falwell's defense, "All that Moral Majority threatens is the virtual monopoly liberal churchmen have had on the attention of the media."

Falwell's argument in favor of clergymen being involved in politics is a historical one. Basically, he is reasserting the Judeo-Christian tradition. He quotes James· Madison, whose *Memorial and Remonstrance*

Against Religious Assessment is more often quoted by liberals. According to Madison, "the whole future of American civilization" depends "upon the capacity for self government, upon the capacity of each and all of us to govern and control ourselves *according to the Ten Commandments of God.*" Before that, Christopher Columbus attributed his discovery of America to "rays of marvelous illumination from the Holy Scriptures." And the first charter of Virginia, drawn up in 1606, defined the mission of its citizens as "propagation of Christian religion to such people as yet live in darkness and miserable ignorance of the true knowledge and worship of God." Falwell also likes to cite Lincoln's "day of prayer" and George Washington's requirement that his troops attend chapel if they were not in combat.

The argument Falwell makes for moral laws such as those regulating abortion or permitting prayer in schools rests on the assumption that while there may be ethnic and lingual diversity in America, there should not be ethical diversity. This is Falwell's solution to what may be called *E Pluribus Unum* paradox. Should unity or university be stressed? Falwell is for theological diversity but moral unity. He believes, with Bruno Bettelheim, that a moral consensus is vital to a society's holding together. When consensus breaks down, coercion takes its place. That is what he claims has happened.

Falwell is content to point out to his liberal critics that in criticizing him for breaking the barriers between church and state they are invoking a dual standard. But to fundamentalists concerned that he is also breaking their tradition of political celibacy, he must be more persuasive. To them he argues, "It is not the religious conservatives in this country who have politicized the gospel. It is the liberal in the church and in the government who has turned the basic moral values that were the foundation of this country into political issues." It is the Left, in particular the leftist establishment, which has invaded the domain of the Church That the state has climbed over the wall of separation. For example, until 1973 abortion was not a political issue. But the Supreme Court made it one. So also the family has been politicized. Falwell justifies his role in politics as essentially defensive; he is securing the ramparts of the church against invasion from an irredentist state. As Joe Sobran said on the CBS program "Spectrum," "The separation of religion and politics ended when the state started trying to redefine right and wrong—in pornography, abortion, race, economics, and the relations between the sexes."

Another point Falwell makes is that the morals of a nation are a reflection of the condition of its churches. This is based on the assumption that Christians and churchmen in general involved in the policy discussions which shape the nation. In America in the last several decades, Falwell maintains, only liberal clergy have engaged in politics, and they have always favored policies that promote secular objectives over religious ones. America has gone bad, he believes, because Christians have been apathetic. As a result the rogues—feminists, pornographers, secular humanists—have triumphed in legislating their agenda.

Falwell feels that "nations, just like men, do not live by bread alone." They need religion. He denies that preachers are unqualified to speak politically because of a supposed lack of knowledge. He says, "There are many things they are discussing in Washington that I believe are out of my area. But when they are dealing with freedom, morality, the family or the home, I believe a preacher has not just a right, but an obligation, to fight." Moral disputes are precisely the domain of the preacher. "When it comes down to the destruction of human life, when it comes down to pornography on the newsstands, or obscenity on the television, set, that's where the preacher's role is."

Falwell's entry into politics did not begin pragmatically. he denounced liberal critics with a roar. In a 1976 sermon he said, "The idea that religion and politics don't mix was invented by the Devil to keep Christians from running their own country." His attacks against immorality took on such ominous tones that it sometimes seemed he was against America. But around 1980, this gave way to his "hopeful vision," when he announced, "I'm optimistic about America. I am convinced that we can turn this nation back to God."

Falwell and some of his students at Liberty Baptist College saw decay of morality clearly illustrated one winter night in 1975. Falwell and his chorale preached and sang to a group of 250 fundamentalists in a Seattle gymnasium. Falwell was successful in drawing people up after the service to receive Christ. But his sermon that evening had been disrupted by loud music coming from a hall nearby. After the service Falwell received people, clasping hands and reciting the usual advice to twice-born converts; "Purchase a Bible, read it every day, ask Christ to forgive your sins, find a born-again believing church in your area." Toward the end of the hand-shaking, a mournful cacophony once again filled the gymnasium. Falwell asked five of his students to come with him to see what the noise was all about.

It was a Led Zepplin concert. "When we arrived it was ninety percent over, but in its seats it was just beginning," Falwell recalls. "The place was filled with the smoke of drugs; the police and paramedics were carrying people out; there was psychedelic lighting." The band was playing a languorous tune, and the audience—"no more than a bunch of children, really"—was tripping and swaying and chanting. On the floor couples were fondling and having sex. There is a mixture of shock and titillation in such scenes, even for a moralist, but Falwell only remembers feeling grief. "It was quite an experience for our kids who were used to the preaching of the gospel, the joyfulness and radiance of Christian life, for them to walk from that into what was really a coliseum of death."

The Led Zepplin concert experience was profoundly upsetting to Falwell. Standing there in the Seattle coliseum, a stranger in every way, he saw the people he witnessed as zombies. But these were no ordinary savages; made rude by their primitive environment. These were barbarians nurtured in the heart of the most civilized nation known to history. Even now Falwell cannot bring himself to acknowledge any good in the decades of the 1960s and 1970s. Weren't those decades worth it, I asked him, since they taught us what we know now about morality. "I think we could have learned without them," he told me. "Twenty million cases of herpes and forty percent divorce rates are a high price to pay. But it may have been the only way, as you say, to learn what we know now."

By 1972 Falwell's TV program was already airing on two hundred stations per week, giving him a large forum for his political preaching. In 1974 a new program called Student Missionary Intern Training for Evangelism (SMITE) was launched. Thomas Road Church would, in the future, send missionaries to foreign countries to provide social service and bring people to Christ. Liberty Baptist College, Falwell's now renamed school, enrolled 1,244 in 1975 and over 1,500 in 1976.

As early as 1973 Falwell began to teach students at Liberty Baptist College patriotic songs. By 1975 even his sermons at Thomas Road began to take on a new intensity. He had realized that living a christian life required taking a position on political issues involving questions of morality. His religious message remained powerful with the famous "five essentials" of fundamentalism stressed as much as ever. He didn't give talks on national defense or the Panama Canal treaty—not yet. For the time being he concentrated on moral issues that had become political issues, but which were largely indistinguishable from religious issues—abortion; the divorce rate, "which is making the institution of marriage extinct"; and "the homosexual epidemic—celebrated by our government and the media." Falwell did not blame the obvious culprits. "We could easily blame the Democrats and the Republicans, the national media, or the entertainment industry," he said. But the real criminals, he insisted, were "the silent pulpits" of America. This has now become a well-known Falwell theme. "The silent pulpits of America are more responsible for the moral decadence and breakdown of the republic than any other contributing force." Sometimes he gets carried away: "Silent pulpits bear in part the responsibility for such atrocities as the Civil War and the holocaust of Jews in Germany." This is hyperbole, but with a subtle point. The Church is often criticized for failing to speak out against Hitler by the same people who demand that Jerry Falwell stay out of anything political.

Falwell begins by asking the "silent pulpits" to do what they have already been doing: preaching the gospel. "Many pastors preach only about loving everybody and everything," he says "Many pastors have been quiet on the issue of abortion and the other burning moral issues of our time." This call to political action is mixed with a call to aggressive proselytization, a cry that always works wonders with fundamentalist crowds. "Many pulpits today are silent on doctrine."

In late 1975, Falwell began to indicate another group for the moral slide of America. He perceived a monopoly of what he was later to term "secular humanists" in Washington; these people were directly responsible for legislating immoral policies.

Falwell has always held that all rulers, good and bad, are ordained by God. He cites Romans 13 in evidence. "Not. . .all persons in places of authority are godly people. . . . However, whether they are aware of it or not, they are in their positions by divine ordination." But Falwell also argues that God, even though he appoints all leaders, sometimes appoints others to scourge them or drive them from office. If leaders do not live up to God's plan for them, or if they are finished with God's task, he may replace them.

A poll taken by the connecticut Mutual Life Insurance Company validates Falwell's claim that there is a gap between the beliefs of the American people and their leaders. The survey, both of random people and of prominent Americans in fields like science, politics, and the media, asked for respondents' views of social issues. Sixty-five percent of the public felt abortion was morally wrong, compared with 36 percent of leaders. Seventy-one percent of the public disapproved of homosexuality, compared to 42 percent of leaders. Fully 85 percent of the public objected to adultery, but only 71 percent of the leaders did. Sixty-eight percent of the public, compared to 56 percent of its leaders, felt pornographic movies should not be aired. Eighty-four percent of the public, but only 73 percent of the leaders, articulated opposition to permitting the legal sale of hard drugs. Falwell cites this poll to illustrate what he calls a "crisis of leadership" in America, which in his view parallels the "crisis of pastoral responsibility" in the churches.

In 1976 Falwell planned a major celebration in Virginia for the nation's bicentennial, and rallies across the country after that. His theme was patriotism. He reasoned that most of the ills facing America were related to a loss of national will and a spiritual aboulia. The purpose of the bicentennial celebration was to reassert America's pride and spirit, to revive the old patriotic feelings, that he had last seen manifest just after the Second World War. He was not sure how to go about achieving the political agenda he sought, if indeed he had an agenda thought through at that time. So patriotism blind, pure, and simple was his solution for the present. Later specific goals would be defined. But for now it was unabashed jingoism for a nation which had forgotten how to salute its flag, at least in the old hand snapping way.

On July 4, 1976, more than 25,000 people rallied on Liberty Mountain, the campus of Liberty Baptist College. They sang hymns and patriotic songs. The fiery old fundamentalist B.R. Lakin, one of Falwell's mentors, preached about the Great Awakening that was to come in American politics. Showing political savvy, the Democratic senator from Virginia, Harry Byrd, appeared at the rally and joined in the prayers and the music. It was a rousing occasion. Not often in the late 1970s did one see a college campus fifteen hundred young men and women in clean matching suits and dresses marching briskly up and down with heads raised, singing about the land and God they loved.

Then Falwell and seventy students from LBC took off for 112 "I Love America" rallies across the country. Careful planning went into these; press coverage was arranged, escorts were planned, meals were selected off restaurant menus in twenty states. Local traditions were researched so that Falwell could appeal to local sentiments in his sermons and call to action. Speakers at the rallies included Senator Paul Laxalt of Nevada, Governor John Dalton of Virginia, Governor James Rhodes of Ohio, and Senator Jesse Helms of North Carolina. The biblical theme for the rallies was II Chronicles 7:14—"If my people, which are called by my name, shall humble themselves, and pray, and seek my face, and turn from their wicked ways: then will I hear from heaven, and will forgive their sin, and will heal the land." The passage summarized what Falwell was after: genuine national religious repentance, followed by assertive steps toward national revival.

Each rally began with a heartfelt rendering of "Faith of Our Fathers" and "America the Beautiful." Then Falwell spoke rousingly of the need for spiritual and political renewal. They finished with more songs and prayers and vows to change the character of Washington. With Falwell was Robbie Hiner, a cherubic youth raised in Hernando, Mississippi, with a Donnie Osmond voice and several records to his name. "I'm just a flag-waving American," Hiner sang as the audience applauded. McCauley Rivera, a strapping young black man, thrilled each audience with a speech in support of the armed forces and the men who had died for America. "I believe that this is the greatest nation on earth," Rivera said. "I am proud to serve this nation, to follow her flag, to honor her, and if necessary to die for her, for I love America."

In 1681 William Penn said, "If you are not governed by God, you will be ruled by tyrants." This was Falwell's message to the hundreds of thousands of people he spoke to in his rallies. And they listened, quietly at first, then more intently. By the time the rally was over, they found themselves cheering for America. Patriotic and religious emotions mixed easily. Many came forward and received Christ, and many who had soured on the United States resolved that she mattered, after all. It was time to take up arms for her, not as guerillas in uncivilized countries do, but with marches and lobbying and votes on election day.

8

Establishing
Moral Majority

With the success of the "I Love America" rallies, Falwell decided to plant some new churches in Washington, D.C. He hoped to bring some of the citizens of the capital to Jesus. McCauley Rivera would pastor the first church in Washington. On February 26, 1976, Falwell flew up to Washington with Rivera to examine the proposed site. It was an impressive structure in a strategic location. That day Rivera preached in a small church, and six people came up the aisles to receive Christ. But it was to be the last effort by the vibrant young black pastor. Two days later he and his fiancé, Sharon, were cut into pieces by a train.

Falwell was stunned. However, he interpreted Rivera's death not as a sign to turn back and leave Washington to others, but as positive proof that he should mount another offensive in the capital. At his urging, several people signed up to replace Rivera.

Falwell believes that God has a script drawn up for every Christian, and "it behooves you to know the differences between God's plan and your own plan." Falwell does not claim personal revelations or to be able to hear God's voice audibly. He takes the practical view that God speaks to His people through His word, the Bible. That is why the Bible must be without error. Would the Almighty talk to His people in a text riddled with mistakes and anachronisms?

Falwell preaches about three kinds of decisions: (1) scriptural decisions, which are spiritual choices with only two alternatives—right or wrong; (2) service decisions, which are guided by prayer but also by intelligence (he warns against the Hamlet-like indecision that often marks fundamentalists); and (3) spontaneous decisions, which require little spiritual preparation. Because some fundamentalists get terribly confused about when to seek divine guidance and when to act on their own, Falwell advocates decisiveness in small matters and spiritual introspection in large ones.

In political matters, Falwell counsels a sober aggressiveness. "I'm not talking about being foolhardy, I'm talking about decisive action," he says. "The Christian life is full of choices for which there is not a verse of Scripture." Even though issues like the revolution in El Salvador touch only generally upon Christian teaching, Falwell asks Christians to get involved, because the issues touch upon the larger moral-political battle, a battle he perceives as nothing less than a war between the forces of good and evil.

On January 21, 1977, 2500 students and faculty from Liberty Baptist College gathered on Candlers Mountain. It was freezing outside, but Falwell had brought this group out into the cold for a purpose. LBC was five years old at a turning point. "Only the blessing of God can keep us going," he said. "You have seen God perform miracles in our midst." These were mundane miracles, mostly: the miracle of a continuing flow of support locally and nationally via his television ministry.

Falwell invoked a sense of mission for his students and faculty. They were doing nothing less than executing a divinely ordained plan for the Christian ministry. "Liberty Mountain is our Promised Land," he told them bluntly. He read Phillipians 4:19 "God shall supply all your need according to his riches in glory by Christ Jesus." The crowd prayed for more money to begin construction of LBC and pay off all indebtedness on the school property.

Either by divine miracle or earthly accident, money began to pour in. New construction on LBC began the next month. Enrollment was by then 1880 students from forty-nine states and ten foreign countries. The Liberty Home Bible Institute, formed the previous year, now enrolled 1400.

Falwell introduced two fund-raising programs: one for the college, the other a "Clean Up America" campaign. The former was educational, the other political—he was not talking about environmental-ism when he introduced "Clean Up America." He had already raised $5 million, which he promised would come in by "Miracle Day," set at September 24, 1978. Falwell broadcast his appeal on television. The call for money was backed by a bleak message: America was morally decrepit. He was not very specific and did not list his usual targets. He simply appealed for Christians to unite. "We think pro-moral Americans who pay taxes, send their sons to fight in our nation's wars, and who are honest, decent citizens, working to build America instead of trying to tear her down, deserve to be heard."

His appeals touched a chord. By "Miracle Day" Falwell had raised more than $7 million, and money was sill pouring in. The donors were mostly viewers of "The Old Time Gospel Hour," by now on 325 stations across America. They gave small amounts, only $25 to $30 on average, but many contributed. The students now refer to the episode as the "Miracle of Liberty Mountain," because they think is was all set in motion by prayers uttered on that freezing day in January 1977.

In 1978 Falwell claimed credit for defeating both a homosexual rights ordinance and an endorsement for the Equal Rights Amendment in the state of Florida. He'd gone to Florida several times the previous year to lend support to Anita Bryant's "Save the Children" campaigns against homosexuality. Why Falwell chose to focus on homosexuality instead of the issue that politicized him, abortion, is not clear. It may be he figured it to be a better issue to raise money on. Indeed Falwell's fund raisers in 1977 and 1978 frequently focused on homosexuality and included questions like "Do you approve of acknowledged homosexuals teaching in our public schools?" Such questions were disingenuous. Falwell's own position is that it's okay for homosexuals to teach in public schools "so long as they don't present their lifestyle as accepted." But there was little nuance in the fund raisers, which is partly due to the character of fund raisers. They invite not polemical hair-splitting but the writing of checks.

In 1978 Russian dissident Alexander Solzhenitsyn sent a message to a meeting of the National Religious Broadcasters that Falwell attended. "There is in our days a prevailing and entirely wrong belief that the contemporary world disasters are the result of this or that political system's imperfections. It is not so, however. The truth is that they all stem from the relentless persecution of the religious spirit in the East, and the fading of that spirit in the systems of the West and the Third world." Hearing that, Falwell decided to start up his "I Love America" rallies again. To this day he regards Solzhenitsyn's observation as one of the most profound moral analyses ever. Since then he has always treated the moral regeneration of America and resistance to the Soviet Union and its "relentless persecution of the religious spirit," as his predominant theme. He introduced his "America, You're Too Young to Die" program on television. Already the tone was changing from that of his "I Love America' ralliers. It was going from a rosy, undiscriminating patriotism to a less certain vision of America *unless* certain reforms were made.

By March 1979 six more buildings, including two dormitories, had been completed at LBC. A gymnasium was dedicated on March 3, and that day Falwell anounced that he was going with his "I Love America" team to all fifty states and assemble locally committed groups of people to fight for moral values. In April, 1979, the first rally was held at the U.S. Capitol Building, with several Congressmen, including Virginia Democrat Harry Byrd, present. The program, which included the usual melange of preaching, patriotic songs, hymns and handing out leaflets, was filmed as the first prime-time special aired by The Old Time Gospel Hour. An I Love America Club was formed, and television viewers were urged to send money to finance the tour of all fifty states by Falwell's singing and preaching crew. Meanwhile Falwell's church had grown to 16,000 members in December 1978, making it the second largest Baptist church in the country.

The United Nations designated 1979 as the "Year of the Child." In typical UN fashion, the legitimate rights of children were not mentioned—particularly the fetus's right to be born, children's right to protection against pornography, and children's right to home care versus feminists' rights to ignore their offspring. Instead the United Nations attempted to strengthen the child's position vis a vis the American family. Falwell, who has never seen the American family as detrimental in any way to the rights of any family members, lashed out in anger. "This International Year of the Child would make it possible for children to get minimum wage for performing household chores. How stupid! It would take a bunch of Liberals to give birth to something like that. Then you go past that. The children's rights to choose their own parents if they don't like the parents they are living with. They can apply to a federal agency and be taken out of that home and select another set of parents. And if parents paddle their children they can be told on and put in jail. You go beyond that. This will give supervised family planning and Planned Parenthood clinics the authority to license parents virtually to be parents. It will take the ownership of the child away from the parents and take it into the hands of the government. It will legalize homosexual marriages and homosexual adoptions. It will produce an Equal Rights Amendment ultimately only for children."

This was typical of Falwell's early style of argument, many aspects of which persist today. He assumes that taking the first step in a certain direction automatically implies that one intends to go all the way. Falwell doesn't like to see this kind of argument used against him particularly in connection with his views on censorship—as in: if you want to censor *Screw* magazine tomorrow you'll soon want to censor Shakespeare—but he uses it himself when it is to his advantage. He is also adept at negative linkage. Notice his tie in of the UN resolution with the Equal Rights Amendment, which was under simultaneous but separate consideration.

In May 1979 Falwell was contacted by Robert Billings, a former director of the National Christian Action Coalition, whom Falwell knew but not intimately. Billings arranged a meeting between Falwell, himself, and "a few politico friends of mine." What was it all about? Billings said simply, "It's to draw up a game plan to save America."

The group met in Falwell's office in Lynchburg a few days later. There was Howard Phllips, the executive director of the Conservative Caucus and a former aide to President Nixon. There was Ed McAteer, founder of the Religious Roundtable, a member of Bellevue Baptist Church in Tennessee, and also associated with Phillip's Conservative caucus. There was Richard Viguerie, the stumpy populist who discovered direct mail for political purposes.

Falwell remembers feeling a little strange that day. He felt a kinship with Billings and, to a lesser extent, McAteer, but the other two guys were professional operators, not ostensibly interested in Christianity. Phillips was actually Jewish.

The men discussed their common goals. They wanted to legislate against abortion. They wanted prayer back in the schools. They wanted to get rid of pornography. They wanted something done about the drug epidemic. They wanted conservative alternatives to the liberal media to reach the American people directly. They wanted to see America stress its Judeo-Christian tradition.

Falwell noticed that these men had crafted their goals to serve as mutual objectives. He could approach them from a religious perspective, the others from a political perspective. He had not given serious thought previously to building a coalition that would aim at political goals. He suggested that a broad educational effort to redirect America would be sufficient. These men disagreed.

Howard Phillips spoke savagely against the sin of indecision, wishy-washiness. "When we can do something about this perversion," he pointedly queried, "why just talk about it?"

To this McAteer added, "And why should any listen to us talk—and do—when we are not ourselves doing?"

Falwell remembers feeling at first that setting up a political organization, which is what these men were proposing, was too much of a hassle. "I worried it would take away from my ministry, which was growing and needed me" Falwell says. He had been approached by conservative strategists as early as 1977 inviting him into the political arena, but he had demurred.

Falwell feared politics for other, very natural reasons. He was not familiar with how one went about influencing the political process. He was not that familiar with the issues. He had never been in a political debate, "I was hoping that someone else would do it. I saw it had to be done. I just didn't want to be the one with the load."

Richard Viguerie addressed Falwell's first concern; arguing that a political role for Falwell would actually benefit his ministry. It would give it a tangible sense of purpose, arousing people all over the country to issues that affected their lives. This might induce them to think about their preparedness for the next world.

Phillips told Falwell how much he admired the activists of the 1960s because morally repulsive through they were, they at least put their sweat behind their ideals. Conservatives ought to be revolutionaries, Phillips felt, not philosophically but temperamentally. He was sick of the business as-usual politics of the Republican Party.

"It's all we've got," Falwell said pragmatically.

Phillips agree. "That's my point. I think our coalition could affect the Republican Party platform in 1980. But we have to act immediately." He wryly paraphrased the radical slogan of the 1960s. "If not now, when? If not Jerry Falwell, who?"

Along with Paul Weyrich, another conservative activist, Phillips and Viguerie had the strategy all figured out. Once they saw Falwell's interest they laid it on the table. The strategy pivoted on one of Weyrich's insights into the issue of abortion. But Weyrich did not feel that Republicans who hated the Communism; high taxes, and liberalism in general would in fact vote Democratic simply because their party opposed abortion. On the other hand, if the Republican Party came out strongly anti-abortion, that would split the powerful Catholic vote within the Democratic Party.

Weyrich proposed that Falwell's group, and the New Right in general, focus attention on the abortion issue, because it would split the

Democratic party, while hardly affecting the Republican vote. This suggestion was attractive to Falwell, because abortion was the main reason he was getting into politics. Now these men were telling him it would also help achieve his other objectives.

At first Falwell did not understand that the suggestion before him was to start a political, not a religious group. Then he realized that the distinction was jesuitical. It would simply be a matter of approaching politics from a Christian perspective. Certainly he would need to distinguish his pastoral duties from his political participation, to head off criticism that he was mingling church and state. Besides, by setting up a separate political group, he would be able to appease those fundamentalists who still disapproved of politics. Also important, the difference between a political and religious group affected tax status. Churches were tax-exempt and could not engage in lobbying; political groups were taxable but could. "The gentlemen of the New Right showed me how I could get up an activist group legally," Falwell says. "they had it all figured out."

Numerous suggestions for a name for the group were tossed around: "People for a Stable America," "Citizens for a Free America," "Moral America," and so on. "What we really need," Weyrich said, shaking his head when McAteer ran down the list of proposed names, "is a moral majority of Americans with a name like—"

McAteer interrupted him. "What did you say? Moral what?" "A moral majority of Americans" Weyrich repeated.

"That's what we'll call it," McAteer said resolutely. "Moral Majority. It has a nice sound to it."

Weyrich wasn't so sure. He liked its inclusiveness—who would not want be part of a moral majority?—but disliked its arrogance, which he feared might alienate.

Falwell and Phillips liked the name. "Look, we've even got a name, Jerry," Phillips said. "With strategy, with common goals, with everthing legal, and now with a name, man, you can't back out of this now."

Falwell said he had no intention of backing out. The activists smiled. They had their man.

On June 6, 1979, "Moral Majority Inc." was formally registered. The board of directors included Jerry Falwell, Charles Stanley of First Baptist Church of Atlanta, Greg Dixon of Indianapolis Baptist Temple, the evangelist Tim LaHaye, and James Kennedy of Coral Ridge Presbyterian Church in Florida. These were Falwell contacts with some political savvy. Ronald Godwin, a bespectacled former Christian school administrator, was hired to be vice-president of the new organization, and Robert Billings was executive director. Godwin, though stodgy and sometimes flat-footed, was an extremely competent manager with a realistic sense of the political limitations of fundamentalists. Moral majority was set up as three organizations: Moral Majority Inc., the political lobby; Moral Majority Foundation, an educational group with tax-exempt status; and the Moral Majority political action committee. Falwell was head of all three.

Falwell and his directors defined four concrete objectives of the newly chartered group. Moral Majority would be pro-life, of course, because, in Falwell's word, "The national crime of America is abortion. We are destroying one and a half million precious lives annually. I feel this is biological holocaust. If God was angry at Hitler for the destruction of the Jews, he is likewise angry with the United States, and particularly with the churches of America, for our silence."

Moral Majority would be pro-family, affirming, the sole legitimacy of the monogamous family. Falwell is scornful of feminists who point to the diversity in American families. "They talk about bread-winning father, homemaking mother, and two-point-four children," he says. "Of course there are small and big families, city and rural families, and so forth. What we are talking about here is one man for one woman for one lifetime. That's all." Falwell opposes the Equal Rights Amendment "a piece of anti-family legislation." The pro-family stand of Moral Majority also explains its hostility to so called homosexual rights. Falwell feels that "homosexuality is moral perversion" that, whether or not it stems from genes or environment, it can be cured by being born again. Homosexuality subverts the institution of the family. When cross-examined he says that he is not opposed to civil rights for homosexuals, only to special privileges, as might be extended under affirmative action programs. Curiously, he accepts the principle of affirmative action for redressing racial inequality.

But unlike blacks, he feels homosexuals are not persecuted because of what they instrinsically are, but because of how they choose to live. "Choices carry with them consequences," Falwell says.

Moral Majority should also be pro-moral. For Falwell "pro-moral" means opposition to pornography and the illegal drug traffic; which he says are eroding the minds and senses of America's children. "All that filth they sell in the stores and put on film—it is degrading to our society." He has little sympathy for the view that if one wants to engage in perversion one should be able to. But he is primarily concerned with children. This emphasis wins Moral Majority considerable support.

Falwell's graduation picture.

Jerry's father Carey Falwell was an aggressive Lynchburg entrepreneur and agnostic. Falwell inherits his business acumen, and uses it to further goals of evangelization.

Jerry (left), at age 2, is seen with his grandfather Carey Falwell; Dave Brown, an employee of the Falwell family; and twin brother Gene.

Jerry (left) and brother Gene (right) flank friends on the Falwell property.

ene (left) and Jerry Falwell went for long bike rides on Candler's Mountain in Lynchburg. As early as age 10, however, both kids were driving automobiles.

Jerry (front row, sixth from left) was 13 and a freshman at Brookville High School.
He topped his class, but was nearly expelled for practical jokes.

The basketball team of Bible Baptist College in Springfield, Missouri, where Falwell ended up after his conversion. He was preparing for the ministry, but played basketball and baseball in college and even contemplated a professional career in the two sports.

Jerry and Macel were married in the newly formed Thomas Road Baptist Church, which Falwell now pastors.

At the fledgling Thomas Road Church, Macel Falwell played piano. Jerry was past fund-raiser, and janitor at $65 a week.

Jerry Jr. was born in 1962.

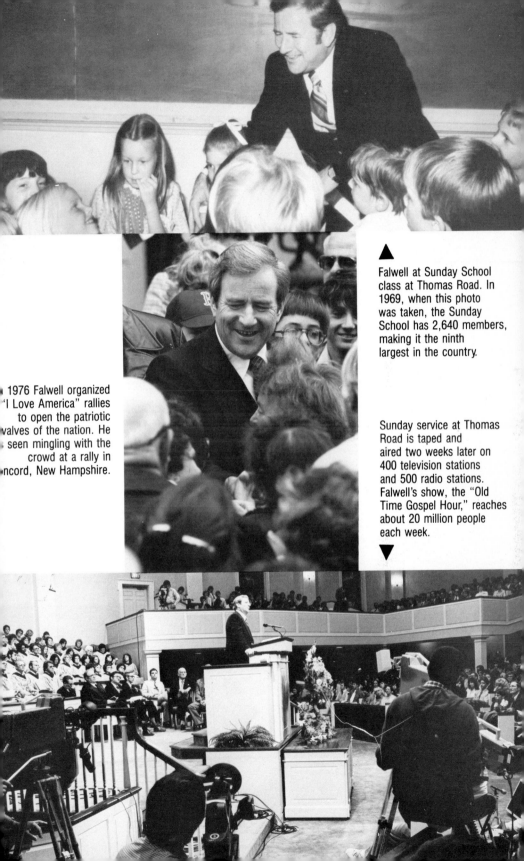

Falwell at Sunday School class at Thomas Road. In 1969, when this photo was taken, the Sunday School has 2,640 members, making it the ninth largest in the country.

1976 Falwell organized "I Love America" rallies to open the patriotic valves of the nation. He seen mingling with the crowd at a rally in ncord, New Hampshire.

Sunday service at Thomas Road is taped and aired two weeks later on 400 television stations and 500 radio stations. Falwell's show, the "Old Time Gospel Hour," reaches about 20 million people each week.

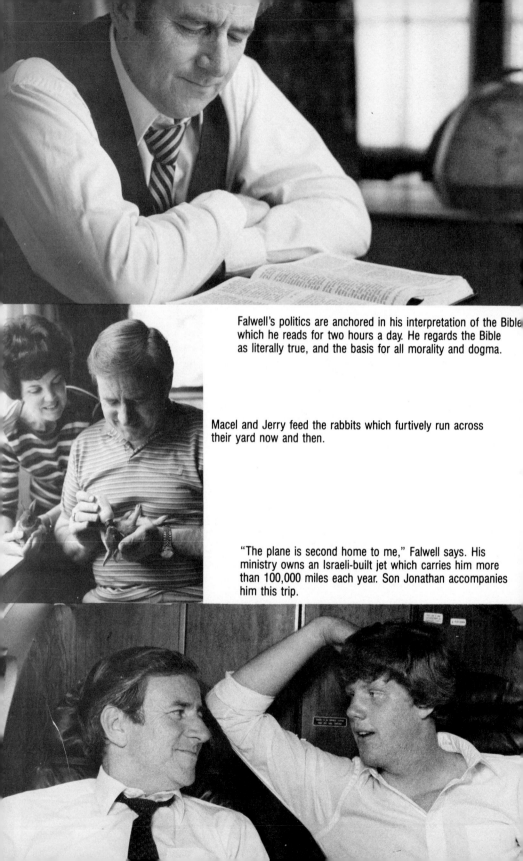

Falwell's politics are anchored in his interpretation of the Bible which he reads for two hours a day. He regards the Bible as literally true, and the basis for all morality and dogma.

Macel and Jerry feed the rabbits which furtively run across their yard now and then.

"The plane is second home to me," Falwell says. His ministry owns an Israeli-built jet which carries him more than 100,000 miles each year. Son Jonathan accompanies him this trip.

Tom Landry, coach of the Dallas Cowboys, is only one in a long list of celebrities who have visited and spoken at Thomas Road Church.

Falwell broke his rule of permitting only fundamentalists to speak at Thomas Road Church when Mrs. Phyllis Schlafly, a Catholic, spoke about the Equal Rights Amendment.

TV host Phil Donahue finds Falwell to be one of his most provocative guests. He has had him on the show no less than 11 times—a record for Donahue.

On one annual vacation Jerry and Jerry Jr. enjoy a successful fishing expedition in Alaska.

The nation would be better off if Watergate was never exposed, Falwell believes, but says "Nixon has only himself to blame" for the outcome.

Candidate Reagan came to the campus of Liberty Baptist College in October 1980 to court Falwell's support. Pollster Lou Harris believes that without Moral Majority, Reagan would have lost by one percentage point to Jimmy Carter in the November '80 election.

David Frost interviews Falwell about the role of religion in American politics. Falwell believes that separation of church and state does not prohibit preachers from speaking out on moral-political issues.

Liberty Baptist College, founded by Falwell in 1971, now has approximately 4000 students on a 150 acre campus, but Falwell hopes that within 15 years it will train 40,000 undergraduates and graduate students, annually.

A sports aficionado, Falwell makes time to attend all LBC games and is frenetic if his team wins.

Falwell's jet is fully equipped. He frequently phones from 50,000 feet u

Menachem Begin, former prime minister of Israel, is a close friend and in 1980 awarded Jerry the Jabotinsky award for distinguished service to Israel.

The Thomas Road Church seats nearly 4,000. Falwell draws nearly 15,000 people to Thomas Road each Sunday, nearly a quarter of the population of Lynchburg.

Reagan and Falwell share strengths of charisma and oratory.

Henry Kissinger and David Hartman chat with Jerry and Macel Falwell during *Newsweek's* 50
anniversary party. All celebrities featured on *Newsweek's* cover were invited.

Vice President George Bush, speaking at LBC, praised Falwell for stressing the Judeo-Christian tradition. Jerry presents Bush with an LBC tie, while Senator John Warner of Virginia applauds.

Falwell visited El Salvador in September 1983 and returned even more resolutely opposed to guerilla attacks.

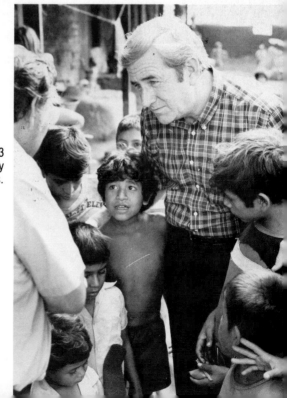

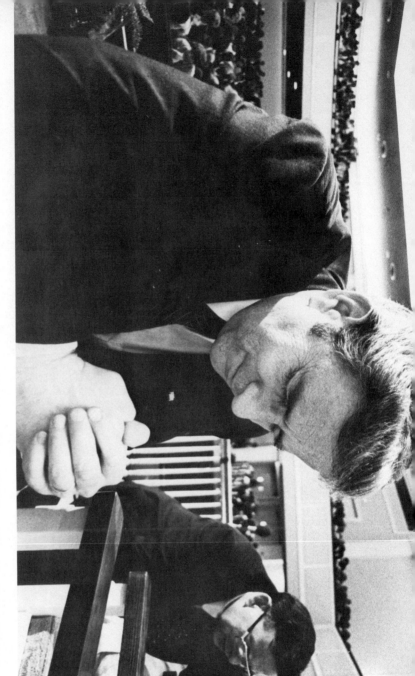

For all his activism, Falwell remains, at heart, a small-town pastor.

People who are not otherwise sympathetic to Falwell's agenda are receptive to his cries to protect children, who are the most vulnerable members of our society. As Daniel Yankelovich observed in his *Psychology Today* article of November 1981, even radicals who call for free love, 1960s style, become nervous when those values are applied to their children. Possibly a return to school prayer also falls under the rubric of "pro-moral." Falwell does not mention it when he catalogs his agenda, but it remains a concern close to his heart, and the issue has been introduced at fund raisers, also because of its overwhelming appeal to conservatives throughout the country.

Finally, Moral Majority would be pro-American. It would stand for a strong defense and, curiously, for support of the state of Israel and Jewish people everywhere."

Falwell's position on defense is a carry-over from the patriotism of the "I Love America" rallies. It may also have been reinforced by Phillips, Weyrich, and the other conservative strategists who, while concerned about morality, are more intent on secular conservative issues such as opposing the Russians and protecting the free market economy.

"Freedom is the basic moral issue of all issues" Falwell says. If we lose our freedom, it would be irrelevant to talk about getting prayers back into public schools—we would not be praying anywhere. There would be no fighting against abortion. Our very lives would be completely dictated and our personal freedom would be gone." Falwell believes that Christianity is all about freedom, spiritual freedom. The Bible says, "You shall know the truth, and the truth shall set you free." And Christ said, "I am the way, the truth, and the life." Ergo, Christ is the liberating force in Christianity. He frees the soul from the bondage of sin.

It is useless to talk to Falwell in the current vocabulary of freedom. He does not regard the right to be homosexual as an exercise in freedom. On the contrary, he regards those things as limiting. They are sins, according to the Bible, and Falwell views all sins as restricting man's freedom. True freedom, he feels with Aquinas, "is the opportunity to do the will of God."

Falwell does make some connections between spiritual and earthly freedoms that are not entirely clear. For example, he thinks there is a connection between spiritual liberty and economic liberty. He goes further—the Book of Proverbs in the Bible positively sanctions free enterprise. I asked him whether he thought the rich or poor were more likely to be saved, according to the Bible, and if the poor, why would he support capitalism, a system designed to make us all rich? Falwell responded that capitalism does not make us rich, only comfortable—we are rewarded according to our talents, and only a few have the talents to be rich. Moreover, his experience is that the rich are as open to the gospel as the poor, but he admits that "wealthy persons often find it difficult to humble themselves before God." However, this is true in both capitalist and socialist countries. So spiritual freedom is connected to economic freedom, which is connected to political freedom. Political freedom means, naturally, keeping the Soviet Union at bay. He feels that an "adequate deterrent" is needed to "guarantee that our children grow up in the same free society that we did," but his goal is not to extinguish communism. That, he feels, is "unrealistic," and he calls for nuclear parity, not superiority.

His position on Israel is one of unabashed support and admiration. Basically nothing Israel does can be wrong. Here Falwell's view derives from theology, not politics. His pro-Israel and pro-Jewish stance is linked to his belief in the Abrahamic Covenant, a religious root of fundamentalism. Fundamentalists believe that the Bible points to historical developments as dependent on divine dispensation, and that prophecies in the Bible show us the unfolding of God's will throughout the course of history. We are in the last historical era, moments away from the second coming of Christ. However, he does not believe that further prophetic developments in Israel are necessary before Christ can come. Others say, the Jews are no longer the "chosen people," having reneged on their covenant with God. Now Christians are God's chosen ones. While Falwell's position has strong biblical roots, his interpretation is controversial even among fundamentalists. However, Falwell has also come to admire the closeness of Jewish families, their culture, their entrepreneurial skills, and Israel's military prowess. That has reinforced his unqualified support for Israel which in 1980 earned him the prestigious Jabotinsky Award for distinguished service to the state of Israel.

The four main thrusts of Moral Majority—pro-life, pro-family, pro-moral, and pro-American—are not primarily religious objectives, although it is possible to arrive at them as Falwell did via adherence to religious principles. But he argues that this does not make Moral Majority religious in character. "Republicans and Democrats may come to their party because, for religious reasons, they agree with its policies," He maintains. "That does not make either party a religious party per se." Although he was initially skeptical, Falwell now sees the enormous advantage of setting up a political group that does not re-

quire acceptance of a particular theological orthodoxy for membership, just agreement on a set of principles. This way his influence can
spread beyond the fundamentalist community to a much larger segment of the American population, a process Weyrich calls "reverse ecumenism." Falwell has targeted five groups: evangelical Christians,
fundamentalists, conservative Jews, Mormons, and Catholics. Naturally many evangelicals and fundamentlist are drawn to Falwell's political program out of religious sympathy. Jews like his position on Israel.
Mormons find his conservative social agenda appealing and his calls to
moralism reassuring. And Catholics are drawn to his pro-life stance.

Presently Moral Majority is 30 percent Roman Catholic. Most people don't realize this; it affirms the truth of Weyrich's strategy.
Falwell's forthright condemnations of abortion have literally flushed
Catholics out of the Democratic Party. While they are not likely to
embrace Falwell's theological fundamentalism, they are susceptible to
his political orthodoxy. The press tends to characterize Moral majority
as a religious group, but even atheists subscribe to its political agendas.
The early Moral Majority fund appeals contained several Bible passages, but pretty soon Falwell realized an inconsistency in that. Now
the organization sends out appeals couched in secular moral terms. It is
Falwell's view now that the only hope for moral reform by judicial and
legislative means is to be realized by coalescing millions of moralist
Americans who may or may not agree theologically.

Moral Majority has not been the only group of its kind in operation.
In 1978 the Reverend Robert Grant started Christian Voice, a group
which became controversial in 1980 for issuing "voting records" of
Congressmen. Unlike Moral Majority, Christian Voice did not have
chapters in the fifty states, but it had a much more active political
action committee, headed by Gary Jarmin, formerly from the American Conservative Union. Besides Christian Voice, there were the constituencies of the other three "angry young men" of TV evangelism:
Pat Robertson, James Robison, and Jim Bakker. Robison agreed to
form the Religious Roundtable, with Ed McAteer as director. The
group, whose name was later changed to simply the Roundtable to
broaden its appeal, was devoted to forming a "Christian coalition"
(later "moral coalition") around the same issues Moral Majority addressed. Besides these Christian Right groups, there were other New
Right groups already in operation, the largest of which was the national conservative Politcal Action Committee headed by Terry Dolan. NCPAC worked in alliance with Howard Phillips' Conservative
Caucus, Paul Weyrich's Committee for the Survival of a Free Con-

gress, and Richard Viguerie's fundraising operation, the Viguerie Company.

While Moral Majority was obviously an attempt by Falwell to expand beyond his fundamentalist constituency, in its initial stages most of his support came from the fundamentalists who already knew and supported him. Given the long-standing political apathy of fundamentalists; many analysts have wondered about the ease with which he recruited their support. Many of them, some 15 million by Falwell's estimate, were not even registered to vote.

Falwell found raising their consciousness about the political process a surprisingly easy task. Of course there were diehards who, on discovering that Falwell advocating political activism, immediately pronounced him the Anti-Christ. But most fundamentalists warmed to Falwell's political message and did not see it as compromising his theological one. They may have accepted Falwell's argument that politics is an earthly extension of theology. But most likely they came to him for psychological reasons. "Fundamentalists have felt left out of everyone else's liberation," Martin Marty wrote in Context. "Women's, black, chicano, gay, and other liberation movements leave them behind. The textbooks have been changed to accommodate the sensibilities of Jews, homosexuals, women, and the like. The only ethnic stereotypes one can still use and misuse are WASP, redneck, or backwoods, and to a lesser degree Catholic ethnic."

Fundamentalists also perceived that the campaign for "rights" was a two-sided operation: as the rights of the minority goups were advanced, the rights of the majority were diminished. "Whenever someone claims he has a right to something," Falwell says, "I wonder what right of mine is being compromised." Fundamentalists perceived the advancement of minority values, for example homosexuality, as directly infringing on the advancement of their values, the monogamous family and traditional morality.

Sociologist Jeffery Hadden feels that fundamentalists became political because of a need to be treated with dignity. "Perhaps what has angered them most of all is the fact that they don't believe the rest of society, and the government in particular, has taken them seriously. They are tired of being treated as a lunatic fringe or just another interest group that isn't strong enough to be factored into political decisions," he wrote. "Alienated, fearful, angry, outraged, frustrated, anxious—they find hope, community, and reason for being in groups like Christian Voice, Moral Majority, and the 700 Club." Another point is that fundamentalists are used to being ridiculed for their religion, and that makes them all the more eager to be taken seriously for their social and political views. They saw that politicians even in their own districts refused to take them seriously. When Falwell and Bakker and Robison told them that they could do something about this, namely, kick the politician out, they rolled up their sleeves in anticipation.

Falwell is a politically savvy man. He started his organization quickly, setting up fifty state chapters of Moral Majority in a few months, outpacing the eighteen-month schedule Weyrich and Phillips had drawn up for him. In doing so, he captured the position of leader of the Christian right and became the most visible figure of the new Right, which was really the oldest Right in America.

In January 1980 he began to publish *Moral Majority Report*. The first edition had a circulation of 77,000. In October 1980 482,000 copies were being printed. But Falwell was also sucked into the political vortex quicker than he'd expected. He was still not knowledgeable enough on the issues, and that sometimes showed at press conferences and on talk shows. He also discovered that using quotations from the Bible and pulpit-style parables was not effective on national television. He came to understand the style of political discourse in this country, but he did not appreciate the parameters of acceptable debate, the code that governs national political discussions, until much later.

Falwell did realize right away that there are two types of argument: rational and theological. the former relies solely on shared principles, empirical evidence, and deductions from those; the latter depends on the theological propositions accepted as an article of faith that often have no persuasive power whatever. While it might be acceptable to tell fundamentalists that adultery is unacceptable because of such-and-such verse in Leviticus, when speaking to the larger American audience he had to frame his argument in different terms: the preservation of the family, the effect on the partners and the children if divorce ensued, etc. Falwell told me, "When I am talking to the press on El Salvador or the nuclear freeze, I don't quote verses [of Scripture] to them. The Bible says don't cast pearls before swine. Scripture is wasted on gainsayers. So I argue issues in secular terms entirely. But I use my scriptural understanding to form my opinions on issues."

He had to learn these things, but Jerry Falwell already enjoyed a terrific control over words. He was not, as his enemies expected, a Southern bumpkin. They may have expected him to rant and rave, but he mustered impressive arguments and analogies that complacent liberals could not answer. For example, when Falwell appeared on the Phil

Donahue show he spoke against homosexuality and invited homosexuals to accept Christ. One hostile questioner said, "You made a comment earlier that you try to reform homosexuals." Falwell: "No, we try to win them to Christ, and that transforms them." Questioner: "Okay, you try to win them to Christ. Okay. You also said you love them but you don't like what they do. I have always been brought up with my Christian education telling me that love is unconditional." Falwell: "Let me ask you this. Do you love thieves? Yes or no?" Questioner: "Sure, Christ did." Falwell: "Do you like what they do?" Questioner: "No, I don't like what they do." Falwell: "That is conditional."

Armed with rhetoric and a small budget, the newly incorporated Moral Majority launched itself into political orbit. Falwell's men arranged press conferences in which he articulated his organization's goals. He was hyperbolic and used unwise phrases like "set up a Christian America." He made analogies between abortion and Hitler's genocide that set the press squirming. He accused the media of being deaf to the cries of God-fearing America.

Meanwhile Moral Majority's state chapters were humming with activity—holding rallies and demonstrations, registering voters. Pretty soon it became obvious that something major was going on here. The grassroots activism of Moral Majority was combined with action from the top—Falwell delivering his message on The Old Time Gospel Hour, proselytizing his religiously committed audience on political themes. These were the people he knew would deliver a surprise in the upcoming election.

9

A Nation
Under God—Again

In his entire lifetime Christ preached to probably no more than 30,000 people. Yet every week millions tune in to the gospel according to Jerry Falwell. This was as true in 1980 as it is now, and it was true of the other TV evangelists—Robison, Bakker, Robertson—as well. The decision by these men to militate for the Republican Party during the 1980 campaign translated into a considerable political wallop that liberals were unaware of until it was too late.

There has been a lot of squabbling about the real power and constituency of these TV preachers. There are those who have wildly exaggerated the influence of Falwell and his cohorts. Ben Armstrong, president of the National Religious Broadcasters, claims that Falwell and the other right-wing preachers "launched a revolution as dramatic as the revolution that began when Martin Luther nailed his 95 theses to the cathedral at Wittenberg." Armstrong estimates that these broadcast preachers reach more than 100 million Americans each week, or 40 percent of the population. Falwell himself once claimed that "The Old Time Gospel Hour" was more widely distributed than "The Johnny Carson Show"—and indeed it is.

On the other extreme there have been regional sociological studies and media reports stating the influence of these evangelicals to be greatly exaggerated. Arbitron studies put the combined viewership of Falwell, Oral Roberts, Rex Humbard, Robert Schuller, Jimmy Swaggart, and Jim Bakker at about 12 million, which is extremely low, even considering that Arbitron does not measure cable television stations, where the evangelical preachers have a large viewing.

The facts lie somewhere in between. On February 25, 1980, the *Los Angeles Times*, one of the papers to catch on to evangelical clout early on, compiled a chart comparing the number of stations and budgets of the television evangelists. According to the *Times*, Oral Roberts was largest, with an annual $60 million budget. Next were Jerry Falwell, Pat Robertson, and Jim Bakker, all with budgets over $50 million, all with over 200 television stations. Falwell was listed with 324, making his the most widely syndicated program in America. *The Times* called Falwell "the first clergyman to become a major right-wing political power." Preachers in the $16–$30 million bracket with over 100 television stations were Billy Graham, Rex Humbard, Jimmy Swaggart, and Robert Schuller. In 1980 there were 30 religious television stations, more than 100 religious radio stations, and four religious networks. Annual expenditure on television ministries grew from $50 million in 1970 to $600 million in 1980, and viewership grew proportionately. Shortly before the election some authorities estimated that his "Old Time Gospel Hour" was reaching 25 million viewers each week.

Before 1980 the secular media were largely oblivious to the evangelical movement, that "other world out there." While people like Jerry Falwell had amassed huge audiences by the mid-1970s, they remained only a vague irritating presence to the reporters in New York and Washington. When more than 500,000 evangelicals marched in a "Washington for Jesus" rally a few months before the election, the demonstration got only brief notice in the major newspapers. At the same time, 100 blacks with banners protesting Reagan's position on civil rights drew front page treatment and raised "serious questions" about black power. Until very recently the media have been closely attuned to the whimpers of the activist left while being blind to the roars of the evangelical right.

Falwell did not show up at the April 29 "Washington for Jesus" rally at the Capitol Mall because he felt it was poorly organized and would not draw its expected 1 million people. It didn't but it was still an impressive show of political muscle. James Robison was there, with his sneering put-downs. "I'm sick and tired of hearing about all the radicals and perverts and the liberals and the leftists and the Communists coming out of closets," Robison said. "It's time for God's people to come out of the closets, out of the churches, and change America." The people applauded, but the media scoffed, and not entirely without reason: Christians had previously demonstrated little ability to organize on political issues.

Meanwhile Falwell and others, were busy planning a rally to be held in Dallas on August 21, 1980. All three political candidates—Ronald Reagan, Jimmy Carter, and John Anderson—were invited. Only Reagan showed. There were 18,000 delegates registered for the assembly, along with thousands of visitors and observers. Some 250 reporters were present. Conservative activists present included Paul Weyrich, Ed McAteer, Phyllis Schlafly, Howard Phillips, Senator Bill Armstrong, Connie Marshner, Congressman Phil Crane, Jerry Falwell, Pat Robertson, and James Robison. Conspicuously absent were Billy Graham, Oral Roberts and Robert Schuller.

Candidate Reagan made a rousing speech to the evangelicals. He promised to "keep government out of the school and the neighborhood, and above all the home." But this did not mean, he stressed, that abortion would go unregulated. He concluded by saying, "Now I know this a nonpartisan gathering and so I know that you can't endorse me, but I only brought that up because I want you to know that I endorse you and what you are doing." Huge cheers and amens. There was a new sense of confidence among evangelicals.

After the Dallas rally there was not much doubt about the power of the evangelical preachers. Figures about their budgets and viewers became much more widely disseminated. These men took in more money than the Republican and Democratic parties combined. And they showed remarkable solidarity, not only among themselves, the Christian Right, but also with the secular conservative activists of the New Right. Harry Cook of the *Detroit Free Press* predicted that Falwell in 1980 "will have a larger impact on the races than any religious leader has ever had in this country's 200-year history." The *New York Times* said of Falwell, shortly after the Dallas rally, "In organizing to arouse a particular electorate, to shape the way it votes, to give it a common language and means of communication, to use it to influence law and policy at state and national levels, to raise funds to support certain candidates for public office, Falwell has created something very similar to a political party." Columnist Carl Rowan put on a brave face and asked everybody to calm down. "It may be that this country needs a right-wing scare badly," he said. "How else to wake up the clergymen, the deacons, the decent church-goers who were such a force for racial and social justice in the early 1960s?"

But the religious Left was not pacified. There was panic in liberal quarters. Episcopal Bishop Paul Moore, in an op-ed piece in the *New York Times*, lamented that Falwell and other preachers "call themselves Christian conservatives, when it is the traditional churches who truly merit the description of conservative." He termed Moral Majority members "a strange breed of Christians." Just how strange Bishop Moore's own Christianity is can be illustrated by comments he made in January 1980 on "The Dick Cavett Show." Of a lesbian aspiring preacher, Moore said, "The lady in question had all the qualities you'd want in a priest except this one thing of being honest about her lesbianism. Can honesty be a bar to ordaining someone to the priesthood?"

Other preachers and theologians spoke out against Falwell and Moral Majority. The Reverend Theodore Edquist of the First Congregational Church of Boise, Idaho, said Falwell "strikes at the very heart of the notion of religious pluralism and religious and political freedom." The Reverend William Howard, president of the National Council of Churches, was quoted in *TV Guide* as saying, "There is an unnerving similarity between Jerry Falwell and the Ayatollah Khomeini." James Dunn, executive director of the Southern Baptists Christian Life Commission in Texas, proclaimed that Moral Majority members "don't want a democracy, a free people, a pluralistic society. They want a theocracy." Daniel Maguire, a theologian at Marquette University, insisted that Jerry Falwell was practicing "religious fascism."

The liberal church organizations could not hope to shake Falwell's people, who have only scorn for them. But they did hope the publicity they generated would boost their membership. The National Council of Churches produced a study of Moral Majority that concluded in an orgy of self-congratulation. "Finding arrogance in others, the National Council of Churches becomes sensitive to its own spiritual arrogance. While noting the provincialism of the religious right, the Council rejoices in the scope of its own internationalism, but recognizes omissions in its domestic concerns."

On October 3, 1980, Ronald Reagan stopped in Lynchburg to address a convention of television preachers. Falwell, host at the gathering, praised Reagan's positions on social issues and expressed the hope that they would bring him victory a month later. Reagan, in turn, told the people in Lynchburg that he believed as they did in separation of church and state. He also said, "I don't think we should have ever expelled God from the classroom," to cheers from the audience. This was Reagan's most concrete statement on school prayer. Earlier, he had expressed personal doubts about the theory of evolution. And at the Dallas rally he'd also claimed that the Bible contained the solution to all the world's problems. All this was surprising and uplifting to most evangelicals, who felt that these perspectives had too long been absent from the national political scene.

When Reagan first got off the plane at Lynchburg airport, he was asked whether he felt that God heard the prayers of the Jews. He replied he was quite sure God did. Reporters who posed the question were trying to involve Reagan in a controversy that Falwell had unintentionally been dragged into. At Dallas the Reverend Bailey Smith, president of the Southern Baptist Conference, said, "With all due respect, God does not hear the prayers of Jews." This statement was attributed to Falwell in the *New York Times*. Even when Falwell said point blank, "I believe God hears the prayers of Jews," columnists blasted him, in effect saying, Falwell may believe God hears Jewish prayers, but he does not think God answers them. Rabbi Alexander Schindler of the United Hebrew Congregation accused Moral Majority of responsibility for "the most serious outbreak of anti-Semitism since the era of World War II."

A few days after Reagan's visit to Lynchburg, Falwell got together with Rabbi Marc Tananbaum of the American Jewish Committee. Falwell convinced Tananbaum he was not anti-Semitic. "Our Lord was a Jew," Falwell said. "God heard his prayers." Falwell and Tananbaum put out a joint testament. "God is a respecter of persons. He loves everyone alike. He hears the heart cry of any sincere person who calls on him." Falwell got along well with Tananbaum. The two even included a little joke in their statement. They stated their joint anticipation of the coming of the messiah. Tanabaum meant, of course, for the first time; Falwell for the second.

Falwell's favor for Israel and Jews embarrassed and angered some conservatives who felt he was selling out to the Jewish lobby. Even some fundamentalists were furious. Pastor Dan Gayman of Schell City, Missouri, published "An open letter to Jerry Falwell" accusing him either of deceiving millions of honest Christian people or being "blinded in ignorance" for his support for Israel. In support of Israel Falwell cites three arguments: (1) UN acknowledgment in 1948 of Israel's legitimate claim to statehood; (2) the historical fact of Jewish occupation of Palestine until they were driven from it; and (3) the "Scripture's word that the land belongs to the Jews." Continuing the argument in scriptural terms, Falwell says that "God deals with nations in accordance with how those nations deal with Israel." He implies portentous consequences for countries opposed to Israel. Following up with secular logic, Falwell argues, "Beyond the scriptural justification, America ought to support Israel because Israel is our only true friend in that part of the world and the only democracy."

Ignoring Falwells' comments supporting Israel and jumping at the chance to embarass Falwell and candidate Reagan, Jimmy Carter's campaign issued a commercial shortly before the election. "Dr. Jerry Falwell has said that God doesn't hear the prayers of Jews," it began. "If Reagan goes on to the White House, Falwell will come with him, and they'll purify the land as someone else did some years ago." This thirty-second spot was run repeatedly on 252 radio stations in areas with heavy Jewish populations. Moral Majority immediately filed an $11 million lawsuit against the Carter-Mondale campaign and its coordinator, Gerald Rafshoon. At first the Carter people pooh-poohed the suit, but when their research could not confirm that Falwell had said what they maintained he had said, they withdrew the commercial, and Falwell withdrew the lawsuit.

The Left also tried to fault Falwell for his views on women, and flip-flopping on segregation. The usual charges of racism and sexism began to surface. Falwell had to spend much time and money combating them. "Racism and sexism are the real bad words of our time," Falwell told me. "It's much worse today to favor segregation than to favor homosexuality." He refused to let his opposition to the Equal Rights Amendment be equated with sexism. "I think there is a certain amount of discrimination that is necessary in favor of women," he said. "That is why I oppose the ERA; it would restrict women's rights."

Falwell blasted the feminist movement as anti-moral and anti-woman. He quoted Gloria Steinem, "By the year 2000 we will, I hope, raise our children to believe in human potential, not God." He drew ferocious support from traditional women who were sickened at being identified with radical feminists but had no voice except for the irrepressible Phyllis Schlafly. With Schlafly, Falwell mobilized the anti-feminists around a moral banner, and their lobbying effect was so intense that sociologist Nathan Glazer referred to them as a "second women's movement." And Betty Friedan, whose *Feminine Mystique* had launched the feminist rebellion two decades earlier, published a hasty disclaimer in the *New York Times Magazine* deploring "sexual politics" that "cast man as enemy and seemed to repudiate the traditional values of family."

Falwell was also vocal about abortion and school prayer. He was on safe political ground on the latter issue, which had wide popular appeal. Falwell's goal was to make people feel intensely about the issue and to steer it to the forefront of public discussion. School prayer supporters were not then likely to make their preference a pivotal issue in their voting.

On abortion Falwell was on more controversial ground. Even Republicans split on abortion. He was often accused of sowing division and jeopardizing votes that would ordinarily fall automatically to the Republicans. But pressure from Falwell and the New Right forced the Republican Party to oppose abortion unequivocally in its platform. Robert Maddox, President Carter's religious liaison, tried to make political hay of Falwell's abortion position. He said the Human Life Amendment then being proposed "would impose a kind of morality on our society that society is not ready to accept." Maddox also maintained that school prayer would "impose morality on people."

The Christian Right used issues like abortion and school prayer to batter its opponents. Various of its groups sent out panicky fund appeals that proved enormously successful but left something to be desired as far as moderation was concerned. Christian Voice asked, "Do you believe America was designed for the avalanche of pornography, abortion, homosexuality, rape and child abuse that has befallen us?" If not, you were to send $25 to Christian Voice. Said a National Conservative Political Action Committee letter, "Your tax dollars are being used to pay for grade school courses that teach your children that cannibalism, wife swapping, and the murder of infants and the elderly are acceptable behavior."

Falwell himself devised various appeals to raise money through direct mail. One of his fund appeals arrived in the form of a telegram. "Fate of the Old Time Gospel Hour hangs in the balance. Stop. Must discover God's will. Stop. Dead serious about closing down unless God sends sign. Stop. Waiting to hear from you." The "sign" Falwell was waiting for was, of course, the clink of the cash register. Another Moral Majority fund appeal quoted Falwell saying, "I have become the victim of a vicious, orchestrated attack by liberal politicians, bureaucrats and amoralists." And you could help poor Jerry meet this attack by sending a small contribution.

Since 1980 Falwell has used the firm of Jerry Huntsinger in Richmond, Virginia, to advise on fundraising. Huntsinger developed many of Falwell's money-raising tactics. They are in the typical screaming style of direct mail fundraising. For example, you can send in $100 and get detailed information on "Armageddon and the Coming War with Russia," as well as a Bible prophecy book, a personalized certificate, and eight cassettes of sermons by Falwell. Or you can send $12 each month for a monthly newsletter from Falwell, a Hotline report on political developments, a special news periodical, and a Bicentennial Bible. If you want to go all the way, you can add $50 and receive your "Parchment Christian Bill of Rights" and the "Beautiful, Easy to Assemble, Flag Kit." That would still leave you without "Jesus First" pins, and you wouldn't be a member of the "15,000 Club," but it would be a good way to start; you could always give more later. Falwell used a large portion of receipts brought in this way in 1980 to buy more television time, thus expanding his influence and increasing the pool for future fundraisers. Falwell is determined to preach the gospel to "every creature."

State chapters of Moral Majority and Christian Voice publicized voting records of liberal Congressmen, many of which were embarassing to the incumbents. Falwell was subsequently denounced for preparing "hit lists" of people he wanted to unseat. His response was, "We don't tell people how to vote. But we tell them how their representatives are voting. The politicians are furious about this, because previously they enjoyed the best of both worlds: liberal in Washington and conservative back home." Certainly Falwell was being partisan. But it was also true that senators like George McGovern were hypocritical in that they voted liberal to radical in Congress while espousing patriotic and conservative themes to their constituencies. McGovern and other liberals who favored abortion were particularly stung by the charges of "baby killing" that fierce NCPAC and Moral Majority supporters levelled at them before the election.

Falwell experienced a setback when Reagan selected George Bush to be his running mate. Reagan had met with Falwell, Weyrich, Schlafly, and Howard Phillips in the Renaissance Plaza Hotel in Washington, D.C., and they had urged him to select Jesse Helms, Jack Kemp, or Phil Crane for vice-presidential candidate. "I told Governor Reagan that conservatives just could not warm to Bush, and with the age factor and all that, this choice may endanger their vote," Falwell says. But Reagan was noncommittal. All he would say was that his vice-presidential choice, whoever it was, would reflect his views and not buck him if he was elected.

The day of the Bush nomination Falwell was in Reagan's hotel suite in Detroit, again warning him against selecting Bush. Reagan, who had already made his choice, said he was sure Bush would defend the values and principles he had campaigned on, and Falwell should trust him on that. "I will," Falwell said, "but you understand that if Bush acts differently, I will have no choice but to attack him." On that note the two parted. Bush was the candidate, and Falwell held his tongue, despite pressure from conservatives to criticize the choice. The day after Bush's nomination, Falwell got a phone call from Billy Graham, which he thinks was at either Reagan or George Bush's urging. Graham basically repeated what Reagan had earlier told Falwell. "Well," Falwell said grumpily, "I hope Reagan is correct; that's all I can say."

A few weeks before the election the Carter campaign released transcripts of a meeting between Falwell and Carter which suggested that Falwell had lied about a conversation with the president. Several months earlier Falwell had told a Moral Majority rally in Alaska a story about meeting with President Carter. Falwell now claims he was speaking in jest, and the context of his speech makes that clear. He had also hypothesized about the Ayatollah Khomeini being in the White House. Nevertheless, Falwell was quoted in the papers as having actually asked Carter why he had avowed homosexuals on his staff, and giving Carter's reply as, he had to, because he was president of all the people. Carter's released transcripts showed that no such conversation had taken place. Falwell apologized to Carter on a network news show but still maintains that he had no intention to deceive. "I knew my speech was being reported on, and I'm not stupid enough to make up a story which the president could easily prove false," he says. But he admits his was a "reckless statement."

When November 4, 1980, produced a Reagan landslide, New Right groups immediately claimed credit for his victory. Falwell himself was reserved, but to listen to Paul Weyrich and Richard Viguerie it was they, not Reagan, who had been elected to the White House. Terry Dolan of NCPAC proclaimed that he could put Mickey Mouse in the presidential seat. For all the hyperbole, there is merit to the claim that the alliance of the New Right and the evangelical Right exerted a powerful influence in the election. Pollster Lou Harris, who should know, said that but for Moral Majority, Reagan would have lost the election by one percentage point.

While evangelicals and fundamentalists had been largely apathetic in elections since the 1920s, they did exert some influence. Those who voted supported Roosevelt heavily in all four elections. In 1964 they backed Johnson over Goldwater. They did not prefer Kennedy in 1960 largely because of his Catholicism. In 1976 Jimmy Carter got a whopping 56 percent of the evangelical-fundamentalist vote. As early as

Carter the Sunday school teacher from Plains, Georgia, was the man to restore sanity to a moral Washington.

That, of course, is exactly what Carter did not do. And the evangelicals and fundamentalists who voted for him were soon alienated when they saw him stumping for the Equal Rights Amendment, for federally funded abortions, for homosexual rights. Shortly before his election Carter noticed the powerful chord he touched when he mentioned the American family. So he promised to form a "Council on the American Family" when he was president to study the problems of the family. The council eventually came to be torn by fractious debate and ended up defining a family as any group of people living together who wanted the name. This angered fundamentalists, who came to regard Carter's Bible-toting as a sham. Falwell had been a little wary of him from the start. He blasted Carter for an interview in *Playboy* magazine, in which the president used words like *screw* to identify with the happy-go-lucky *Playboy* audience.

Falwell's efforts in 1980 were directed less to converting the Carter constituency then to politicizing the huge number of evangelicals who hadn't voted before. But Falwell's call to action also drew response from those conservative Christians who had voted for Carter in 1976. Just how many votes Falwell's people mobilized is hard to say. According to Paul Weyrich, Moral Majority registered some 5 million voters in 1980. Geography was also very significant. Roger Stone, a Reagan aide, told *Newsweek* in September 1980 that the election would depend on the heartland states—Ohio, Illinois, Michigan—all of which had growing evangelical communities. The power of the Christian Right had been manifest as early as 1976, when its first casualties were incumbent senators Tom McIntire of New Hampshire and Dick Clark of Iowa. (McIntire subsequently wrote a book called *The Fear Brokers: Peddling the Hate Politics of the New Right* in which he blamed a religious conspiracy for the repudiation he received at the hands of his constituents.) By 1980 the evangelicals' clout was evident—in the rallies their leaders organized, in statistics revealing their television audience and budgets, in their influence on local government in key states.

So politicians began to bend to the newly discovered constituency. Some of them became quite subservient, realizing that this interest group might well deliver the entire election, other things being constant. All three presidential candidates in 1980 appealed to the 50-million-strong evangelical community. Carter stressed once again that he was a Sunday school teacher from Plains. John Anderson from Illinois pointed to an independent voting record based on his Christian conscience and his participation in prayer breakfasts on Capitol Hill. Reagan's old-time conservatism routinely expressed itself in the rhetoric of God, country, and family. Because Carter seemed to have turned apostate, and as Anderson was small and vague about his independent conscience, Reagan reaped the great harvest of evangelical votes in 1980—but only at the last minute. A Roper poll published only two months before the election suggested that 52 percent of evangelicals were going to vote for Carter, 38 percent for Reagan. It turned out that Reagan got 56 percent of the evangelical vote, to Carter's meager 34 percent. Richard Viguerie estimates that between 5 and 8 million evangelicals switched their vote in 1980. This conservative estimate does not take into account evangelicals who didn't vote in 1976 but were politicized in 1980.

There is evidence that the evangelical preachers also caused a shift in the voting pattern of Catholics and Jews. Reagan got 48 percent of the Catholic vote to Carter's 43 percent, the biggest margin for a Republican among Catholics in more than fifty years. This was probably due to Reagan's opposition to abortion, which was widely stressed and amplified by the Christian Right. Among Jews, only 47 percent backed Carter in 1980, while 37 percent went for Reagan and 17 percent for Anderson. It was the first time since 1928 that a majority of Jews didn't vote for the Democratic nominee. The Orthodox Jewish community of New York voted an astounding 76 percent for Reagan.

Reagan ended up winning 51 percent of the popular vote and just under 91 percent of the electoral college. President Carter won pluralities in only five states and in District of Columbia. The Republican Party gained a 53–47 Senate majority, its first in twenty-six years. The House gained 32 Republican seats. A *New York Times*/CBS poll showed that Reagan won 61 percent of the votes of born-again white Protestants. Carter won 35 percent and Anderson 3 percent. Among Baptists, according to an ABC News/Lou Harris survey on election day, Reagan won over Carter by 55 to 34 percent. Harris claimed that two-thirds of Reagan's popular vote margin came from followers of television preachers.

The political battlefield after 1980 was strewn with defeated liberals. Gone were senators Culver of Iowa, Church of Idaho, McGovern of South Dakota, Bayh of Indiana, and Stewart of Alabama. Gone were representatives Brademas of Indiana, Buchanan of Alabama, Fisher and Harris of Virginia (Falwell's home state), Eckhardt of Texas, and Corman of California. Winning candidates supported by Moral Majority included John East in North Carolina, Frank Murkowski of Alaska,

Jeremiah Denton of Alabama, Paula Hawkins of Florida, Charles Grassley of Iowa, Don Nichols of Oklahoma, Dan Quayle of Indiana, James Abdnor of South Dakota, Steve Symms of Idaho, Paul Laxalt of Nevada, Albert Smith of Alabama, Jack Fields of Texas, and Frank Wolf of Virginia.

Moral Majority suffered a few defeats. Candidates in California, Colorado, Georgia, and Maryland they opposed won reelection. But, as *U.S. News and World Report* observed, Moral Majority's achievement was unprecedented. Twenty-three out of thirty-eight candidates with low scores on Christian Voice "report cards" and Moral Majority evaluations were defeated. "These results were particularly amazing when we consider the overwhelming success which incumbents usually enjoy: in House races 90 percent of those incumbents who seek reelection are successful, while among Senators the record is almost two-thirds." Several successful candidates attributed their success directly to Moral Majority. Jeremiah Denton of Alabama and Don Nickels of Oklahoma publicly admitted that without Moral Majority they would not have been elected. Folsom, the defeated candidate in Alabama, said Moral Majority "had a tremendous effect on my defeat." And John Buchanan, also of Alabama, said, "They beat my brains out with Christian love."

Falwell felt a great elation and enormous relief at the election results. He could sit back now, and let Reagan steer the nation back on a right course. He did not know then that the struggle was just beginning.

Reagan's inaugural address was almost theological in motif. In fact he was sued later for allegedly violating church-state separation. But for Falwell the speech was an emotional lift. At a press conference January 25, 1981, Falwell said, "How it thrilled my heart to hear our president say in his inaugural address that this is a nation under God."

10

After the Election

The media reacted to the 1980 election with panic. They weren't upset over Reagan's election so much as the fact that they had failed to exert much influence on the outcome. Their attacks on evangelicals seemed to have had negligible effect.

News reports after November 1980 continued to express paranoia that Moral Majority was out to "impose its views" on other Americans. Often these reports were quite disingenuous. The Associated Press did a story titled, "Moral Majority Won't Criticize Private Lives." The first sentence: "Moral Majority, conceding that a good public servant doesn't have to be a church-going teetotaler, says it will ignore the personal lives of Reagan administration officials as long as they are true believers in political issues the fundamentalist group considers important." Here again Moral Majority is wrongly characterized as fundamentalist. And the effect of the headline and story was actually to reinforce, not refute, the media-propagated suspicion that Moral Majority pries into personal lives. In fact it does not, and there is no evidence that it wants to. The AP story implies that Moral Majority (a) does poke into the private lives of Reagan administration officials (and others—you could be next!), but (b) won't admit it. The *Washington Post* published a story entitled "Falwell Denies Moral Majority Seeks to Dictate Nation's Philosophy." The lead sentence of that story: "The Rev. Jerry Falwell, television evangelist and head of Moral Majority, yesterday denied that his group is trying to dictate national morality."

Immediately after the election Falwell declared that his group did not expect any appointments from the new Reagan administration. In a January 1981 interview with the *Jewish Veteran*, he said, "I haven't asked for any of my friends to be put in the administration. We simply want to be friendly supporters from the outside." He told the interviewer that Moral Majority had not applied "religious tests" for candidates to support in 1980. The national organization did not officially endorse any candidates, but state chapters did. Of forty-three races in which state Moral Majority chapters were involved, Falwell reported "We won forty and lost three." But not a single victorious candidate supported by Moral Majority was a fundamentalist. "I would feel comfortable voting for a Jew or a Catholic or an atheist," Falwell says, "as long as he or she agrees with me on the issues."

Falwell was very unassuming about his role in the recent election. "It is not fair that any group can take singular credit for anybody's victory or defeat. I know we registered between five and ten million voters, but that's all. The American people elected Reagan, not Moral Majority." He did feel that Christian influence was decisive in the election. "I think that Christian people came out of the pews into the polls and caused this avalanche."

Despite Falwell's modesty, the contention by liberal Congressmen that they had been unseated by Moral Majority and Christian Voice caused many in the Reagan camp to warm to Falwell's people. There were efforts to bridge the cultural distance between traditional Republicans and the new Christian conservatives. Even George Bush defended Moral Majority to a hostile band of reporters. At a news conference on November 10, 1980, Bush said, "A lot of the views of the so-called Moral Majority are not extreme views. Strength of family, belief that this is one nation under God—there's a lot of views that are not extreme."

On inauguration day Ronald Reagan paid a compliment to Falwell and the Christian Right. He held open the Bible to 2 Chronicles when he took his oath of office; 2 Chronicles 7:14 is the verse that Falwell used as the theme for his political preaching in 1980. It reads, "If my people who are called by my name humble themselves, and pray and seek my face, and turn from their wicked ways, then I will hear from heaven, and will forgive their sin and heal the land."

Reagan had quoted that same verse twice in his campaign.

The fiery exchanges of the 1980 election honed Falwell's debating skills. He became more attuned to the modes of political debate in this country. He began to tailor his rhetoric to the particular show or program he appeared on. Not that he stated different views each time, although some of his critics suspect him of this. Falwell knows that virtually everything he says in public now is taped and reported. He cannot afford to be inconsistent. As it is, there is enough of a contradiction in his efforts to separate preaching from politics while at the same time bringing moral issues to bear on political discussion.

In early 1981 President Reagan decided to nominate Sandra Day O'Connor, an Arizona justice and protege of Senator Barry Goldwater, to the Supreme Court. Mrs. O'Connor's nomination was a surprise to legal scholars and people outside the administration. Falwell himself says, "I never knew her. I had never heard of her. She was a judge in Arizona." But when a cursory check revealed that she had voted ambiguously on several court decisions pertaining to abortion and federal funding for abortion, pro-life groups began to criticize her nomination. They blasted the Reagan administration for going back on its promise to appoint a pro-life Supreme Court justice.

Perhaps the pro-life groups had reason to be worried. Their various legislative efforts to regulate abortion had proven ineffective. The most hopeful way to control what they regarded as mass killing was the court. Reagan maintained that Mrs. O'Connor was indeed opposed to abortion but insisted there was no "ideological test" for the court. Another factor that rated in O'Connor's appointment was her gender. Reagan was anxious to clear perceptions that he was hostile to women.

In order to dissipate mounting conservative criticisms of O'Connor that could cost her the appointment, President Reagan phoned Falwell. He assured Falwell that he was perfectly satisfied with O'Connor's views on abortion and the role of the judiciary. "You've got to trust me, Jerry," Reagan said. Falwell told the president the same thing he said when George Bush was nominated: I'll support you as long as Sandra O'Connor's votes reflect your feeling about her. If she votes for abortion even once, then I will have to go on record against her. Reagan said fine, he couldn't ask for more.

But New Right obstructions to Sandra O'Connor drew the ire of Senator Goldwater, her virtual sponsor for the court post and a dear friend. On September 15, 1981, Goldwater launched a tirade accusing Falwell and others like senator Jeremiah Denton and Jesse Helms of using "the muscle of religion toward political ends." This Goldwater regarded as violating the separation of church and state. "The uncompromising position of these groups is a divisive element that could tear apart the very spirit of our representative system if they gain sufficient strength," Goldwater said of Christian right organizations. He said, "I happen to share many of the values emphasized by these organizations," but he feared they were "imposing their views" on him. "The abortion issue has nothing to do with being conservative or liberal," Goldwater said. He opposed abortion, but his wife favored it. But that didn't bother him. "Lord knows, if I expected her to agree with me on every issue, we'd be in a lot of trouble." As for O'Connor's view of abortion, "No single issue should ever decide the fitness of a Supreme Court justice." Later, at a press conference, Goldwater irritably remarked, "Every good American ought to kick Jerry Falwell in the ass."

Falwell was deeply hurt by Goldwater's attack. He felt is was especially unfair, because he had decided to go along with Reagan and back Sandra O'Connor. He was quoted in the *New York Times* as saying, "It appears that time has passed by Senator Goldwater." Later, still offended, "Senator Goldwater should be writing his memoirs instead of kicking his friends in the posterior." Ironically, Goldwater became a darling of the liberal media and anti-Falwell groups as a result of his outburst. Quotations from him were paraded in magazines, and excerpts from his speech were listed in pamphlets put out by People for the American Way, Committee for American Principle, and such groups.

O'Connor won the nomination, of course. Now Falwell is very pleased with her; all her votes on abortion or euthanasia reflect prolife convictions. "We were not wrong to suspect Mrs. O'Connor," Falwell told me. "But we were wrong about her. Sandra Day has voted on the right side of every important issue. That should answer a lot of questions of a lot of people who wondered where she stood. She and Justice Rehnquist are the finest justices sitting on that bench." Of Goldwater's criticism of him, which he does not regard as insubstantial, although he replied to it flippantly at the time, he says, "There is a danger of disunity whenever people are bitterly opposed on issues, but on the issue of abortion we have no choice. I regard abortion as the murder of unborn infants. Should I stop speaking out on it because Senator Goldwater is afraid that I am causing disunity? Why don't people unify behind a banner which supports life, human life, in all forms, and regardless of whether it is white or black, Northern or Southern, in the womb or in the cradle or in the wheelchair."

Falwell does not usually pay a great deal of attention to his critics.

During the 1980 campaign he was downright contemptuous. "I could care less what Walter Cronkite thinks of me, or Jimmy Carter, or people like that. I didn't care before, I don't care now, I won't care tomorrow. I'm not running for anything, so they can't affect my support. My grass roots people are with me. Most important, I think God is with me. So I don't get up in the morning and think about my critics. The amazing thing is that they've done two years of a number on me, and we have more people, more crowds, more support, than we've ever had, so I'm hoping they don't change their script."

That Falwell was stung by Goldwater's criticism shows he had by then begun to identify himself with conservatism. Goldwater's attack was almost like criticism from another fundamentalist, almost. Not so with liberal clergy and the media. Falwell says, "Any work of God has satanic opposition. If you're not being opposed you're probably doing something wrong." And everybody from Walter Cronkite to the president of the National Council of Churches to pornographers fall into the category of satanic opposition. Falwell talks about "that great coalition of secularists who did not build this country, and so have no right to destroy it," He told me, "It's amazing how groups that don't agree with each other on anything join together to fight the gospel. Right here in Lynchburg we have atheists, homosexuals, and local preachers—yes, preachers—getting together to oppose us."

Falwell regards his work as the work of God, so sees obstructions to him as almost equivalent to attacks on God. He has an explanation for the intensity of his critics: "There's a mob out there very angry that this nation is beginning to turn back toward God." As for the press, Falwell noted at service on January 11, 1981, "When you preach the cross you cross people. And this old world is no friend of grace. Whenever you find a reporter, a writer, objective and fair with a minister of the gospel, the chances are you have found a Christian who wrote the article. It's a very, very rare thing that anyone is objective about the gospel. You're either all the way for it, or you are all the way against it."

While Falwell has gotten used to some of the media attacks now, he still cringes when a particularly ferocious denunciation appears in *Newsweek* or on a television show, because they have such an influence. "What I worry about is not that the press is drawing conclusions about me, but they they are creating in people's minds assumptions," Falwell told me. "The people are not even aware of the basis for these. But they may affect the way they behave toward me, or toward God-fearing Christians, many years down the road." Falwell believes that these assumptions are what motivate psychotics and killers to act against him. The people who send him two-hundred death threats a month aren't weighing the evidence against him; they aren't genuinely concerned about separation of church and state. They have been convinced that Falwell is evil and must be eradicated. So the campaign of hate launched against Falwell has been successful to some degree. Falwell is accused of his own hate campaign in the 1980 election, but that of his enemies has surpassed his. No one calls up George McGovern today and threatens to shoot all the members of his family.

Falwell says it annoyed but did not overly upset him when he was criticized in the 1980 election debate. Macel, his wife, told me. "I didn't know how people could write such things."

The adverse effects of media attacks were balanced by some prestigious awards that Falwell received in 1981. First he received the Golden Angel award from Religion in Media, for using television to spread the gospel in a way perhaps unmatched in the history of the medium. He received the Christian Humanitarian of the Year award from Food for the Hungry International, joining previous winners Norman Vincent Peale, Billy Graham, and Francis Cardinal Spellman. In 1980 *People* magazine named him one of the twenty-five "Most Intriguing People of 1980," and he was also listed in several magazines as one of the most influential Americans. But the humanitarian award was particularly welcome to Falwell, who says he was feeling drained at the time, wondering whether his political incursions were worth it after all, what with all the hassle to his family, with his church being deprived of his full-time services, and so on.

However, even during the height of the 1980 campaign, Falwell tried hard not to give so much time to politics that it would force him to neglect church duties. "I would preach at Sunday School, then rush to Washington to speak at a rally, then back to Lynchburg to do critical visitation for sick church members, and off to New York the next day for more press conferences and news shows." He tried to keep up as best he could with his pastoral duties, trying at the same time not to neglect his family. "A lot of times ministers lose their children because they have time for everyone except their own sons and daughters," Falwell says. He has a rule at the office: Calls from his wife and children always go through, no matter how busy he is, no matter who is in his office.

Controversy erupted in the aftermath of the 1980 campaign when *Penthouse* magazine published an exclusive interview with Jerry Falwell that Falwell claims was illicitly obtained. Falwell maintains he granted the interview to freelance reporters on the condition that it not appear in a pornographic magazine like *Playboy* or *Penthouse*. The reporters said they agreed to no such condition. Falwell filed for an injunction to stop the presses, but that failed. His complaint against *Penthouse* seems to have some validity. In the *Penthouse* interview, he blasts Jimmy Carter for granting an interview to *Playboy* before his election in 1976. It is reasonable to assume that Falwell would not have said that if he knew he was being interviewed for *Penthouse*.

Penthouse publisher Bob Guccione turned the issue into one of censorship. The First Amendment attack surprised Falwell. Ordinarily he would have been able to defend himself. But given the book-burner image the media had created for him, nothing he could say could cancel the "censor's" label. But he gave good account of himself on the "Tom Snyder Show," on which he appeared with Guccione. When Snyder asked him about the First Amendment issue and why he objected to a forum where he could obviously preach the gospel to the sinful subscribers of *Penthouse*, Falwell replied, "I like to select my own forum to preach. I think that's a First Amendment right, too. I don't think I have to go into a brothel to win prostitutes to Christ. I don't think I have to become an alcoholic to reach alcoholics."

The hulaballoo Falwell created around the *Penthouse* incident contributed to the image of him as intolerant. At the same time it was probably necessary. While Falwell lost his case, he probably preserved credibility with supporters fearful that fame and success would lead to moral compromise with a corrupt establishment. "If I have left the *Penthouse* situation unchallenged," he says, "that would have damaged me irreparably with my own constituency." And he raised lots of money on the issue, with loudly indignant fundraisers alleging subterfuge.

What about the charge that Falwell wants to burn books? On October 4, 1981, a group of religious extremists in Baltimore, Maryland burned piles of books on a church altar while onlookers applauded. However, the book burners were not "moral majoritarians" who could not tolerate *Ulysses* and *Lady Chatterly's Lover*. They were religious liberals, incensed by "sexism" and "patriarchal emphasis" in the Bible. Books burned included writings by St. Thomas Aquinas, St. Ambrose, St. Augustine, and Old Testament prophets. This book burning ceremony got the implicit sanction of the National Council of Churches when it issued its revised Bible expurgating Scripture of all sexist references and changing facts to suit the sensitivities of feminist Christians.

I asked Falwell what his position on book banning was and to please list specifically the books he wanted censored. Falwell in essence feels that he who destroys a good book destroys reason itself, the image of God. This does not mean that copies of *Hustler* magazine should be placed in the arms of eight-year-olds, that failure to allow this repudiates the First Amendment. It does means an implicit responsibility to keep books of all perspectives on the shelves; this is in the Christian tradition of tolerance. "I would oppose the removal of any book, I repeat, any book, from a public library." Falwell told me, "Not only do I protest the removal of books from the shelves, but our people are busy trying to *return* books to the shelves—conservative and Christian books that are systematically excluded." He feels that the law's forbidding the use of religious books in the classroom amounts to discrimination as well as censorship. Cal Thomas, vice-president of Moral Majority, has written a book protesting media's bestseller lists, which deliberately exclude religious books even if they sell *more* than secular books.

Falwell told me an incident which revealed to him the double standards of liberals crying censorship. "There was a big fight—in Texas, I believe—about school parents who wanted to remove Eldridge Cleaver's *Soul on Ice* from the classroom library. Now that book is filled with obscenities and blasphemies. The librarians won, and the book remained on the shelf. But Cal Thomas called and asked that librarian if she kept a copy of *Soul on Fire*, which Cleaver wrote after he became a Christian. The librarian told Thomas she had never heard of the book."

Now, Falwell *does* support the right of school boards and parents to influence the kinds of books that children read. He does not think that should be purely up to teachers and librarians, and he does think standards of decency should prevail. He jokes about educators who, in protesting efforts by parents to protect children from sedition and blasphemy, give the impression that obscenity, sedition, and blasphemy are the very core of the educational process, without which children would grow up severely stunted.

In order to make light of charges of insidious book burning, Moral Majority has issued thousands of "Moral Majority Book Burning Matches." These are circulated at liberal gatherings and on college campuses at which Falwell speaks. "See official book list inside," the note on the matchbook cover reads. When you flip open the matchbook you see a blank list with the further note: "That's right—there aren't any!"

Falwell was drawn into another censorship controversy when the

Reverend Donald Wildmon formed the Coalition of Decency to monitor sex and violence on television. Wildmon discovered that in the fall of 1977, 1978, and 1979, almost 90 percent of all sex on television was outside of marriage. During an average year of prime-time viewing the television audience was exposed to 11,500 sexually suggestive comments or scenes of explicit or implied sexual intercourse. During 1979 the amount of profanity on television increased 45 percent over a comparable 1978 period, he reported. Falwell and Wildmon announced a planned boycott.

Falwell explained on a radio show how the boycott would work. "If we set date X for the boycott, we would write to five million families instantly, saying: Here are the facts, here are the people, here are the products, here are the things we don't want you to buy anymore, here's why. And so would three-hundred other organizations loosely affiliated with Moral Majority. And then we would buy full-page ads across the nation listing the public enemy number one and his products and urging the boycott. And we would get on the radio and TV and hold press conferences everywhere and eighty-thousand pastors would preach on it next Sunday and would put it in their church bulletins. And within thirty days the dust would by flying."

This drew howls of dismay from media representatives, even though these same people had hailed labor activist Cesar Chavez for boycotting nonunion lettuce in California. Economic pressure was all right so long as it was being applied to the big corporations, not to the media. Gene Mater, CBS vice-president, called Falwell's threat to boycott advertisers of programs that promote sex and violence "censorship." He was quoted in the *New York Times* as saying, "No matter how you couch it, and no matter how well intentioned it is, that's censorship."

Falwell said he found it puzzling that people who didn't watch television programs because they didn't like the values they promoted could be accused of being censors. "The word censorship has lost its meaning if this is the case," he told me. Falwell and Wildmon never did implement their boycott, but they didn't really need to. Procter and Gamble, television's largest advertiser, fearing the possibility of a boycott, decided to withdraw its advertising from programs that Wildmon's surveys listed as promoting sex and violence. This came as a blow to the TV producers, who feared that other companies would join Procter and Gamble. A year later Falwell jubilantly announced that the Wildmon charts showed a marked improvement in the content of television, so he didn't anticipate any boycotts in the near future.

I asked Falwell what his view of decency in TV programming is. Spe-cifically, what programs did he want sanitized? Falwell said, "Moral Majority has never asked that the national airwaves become propaga-tors of any philosophy. We have not asked for a back to "Ozzie and Harriet" calendar or a pervasive religious motif. We have simply said that in the name of reason and common sense, let's get the four-letter words off the air, let's stop at the bedroom door—we don't have to go between the sheets—let's remove gratuitous sex and violence that is offensive to the average American, as far as his children are con-cerned." He said he found "Saturday Night Live" offensive, much of Norman Lear's stuff and "Dallas" sometimes, although "it could be very acceptable. Greed and avarice are real-life themes. Most people who see J.R. on TV don't want to go out and be like him; they know that's entertainment. But when they see J.R. in bed with a woman— not his wife—wrapped up together under the covers, most reasonable people say, that's going too far. A good artist should be able to suggest what is going on without being graphic and offensive about it."

Falwell rejects the argument that watching licentious programs on television is strictly optional, since one can always reach out and turn off the set. "The people own the airwaves," Falwell told me. "Don't ever let anybody tell you that there's a knob on there you can turn on and turn off. You should not have to turn it off. You own the airwaves. If the water coming out of your faucet was filled with poison, the gov-ernment couldn't say, Hey, you have the freedom to turn it on or turn it off. You have a right to clean water. You also have a right to decent programming in your house." However, Falwell seems less concerned with violence on television than Wildmon. "I don't think the re-sponse from violence is commensurate with the response from gratui-tous sex," he told Hodding Carter on a TV show. "I don't think it's been proved that violence on the screen translates into violence in real life."

In order to counter Falwell and Wildmon's influence on television, ABC television ran two programs, "Pray TV" and "I Love Liberty" in 1981. "Pray TV" portrayed an Elmer Gantry-type evangelist who profiteered on the hopes and religious impulses of the people. The show backfired on ABC, though. When the phone preacher came on the screen and said, "If you have a problem of any kind—financial, medical, or spiritual—call the number you see now on the bottom of your screen and let us help you be born again by the spirit of God," more than fifteen-thousand people dialed the number, despite ABC's warnings that this was fiction. The program only confirmed

Falwell's claims of television's influence over the public.

ABC commissioned Norman Lear, Falwell's nemesis, to run the "I Love Liberty" extravaganza, which was made by Lear along with People for the American Way. Lear said ABC paid PAW a $1 million license fee for the show, but he insisted it was "not in the least" intended to counter the religious right. ABC likewise said the show was nonpolitical. The show featured skits of people eating boiled eggs and people eating poached eggs; the narrator said that people who like their eggs different ways should be able to get along. The message was diversity, and the hidden villains were those who were said to oppose this.

Falwell asked ABC for time to reply, but that was denied. Then he asked PAW if the Liberty Baptist choir could sing on the show; Lear said no. Falwell complained, "To me it's amazing that Jane Fonda could be part of an 'I Love Liberty' program. She is the Hanoi Rose." Falwell is adept at names and also has one for Lear: the "Hugh Hefner of television."

In late 1981, Falwell became embroiled in another controversy. On December 7, a group of creationists had their day in court defending an Arkansas law stipulating that if evolution was taught in a classroom, then creation should be given balanced treatment alongside it. The American Civil Liberties Union had challenged the law on the grounds that it violated separation of church and state. Judge William Overton ruled in favor of the ACLU. The Arkansas law, he said, violated all three tests laid down by the Supreme Court for deciding whether a law violates the First Amendment: it had a basically religious purpose, it had no secular educational purpose, and it would involve the state in religious judgments.

Falwell did not participate in the court case, but he did endorse the position of the creationists. In fact he sponsored a "Creation versus Evolution" debate at Liberty Baptist College between creation scientist Duane Gish and a California professor. Gish won rhetorically, according to the next day's *Washington Post*, but the arguments were not adequately presented in the brief debate format. Falwell did print several attacks on the court decision in his *Fundamentalist Journal.* He took the position that because he supported academic freedom—a modern shibboleth—he was for schools teaching both creation and evolution. "Let the students make up their own minds," Falwell announced in a speech at Princeton University. Falwell's *Fundamentalist Journal* research staff had come up with a curious point of detail. In the Scopes trial, John Scopes had argued not for his right to teach evolu-

tion to the exclusion of creation, but for the teaching of both competing theories. "Education means broadening, advancing, and if you
limit a teacher to only one side of anything, the whole country will
eventually have only one thought, one individual. I believe in teaching every aspect of every problem or theory," Scopes said. The irony
was that the Arkansas fundamentalists were asking for precisely what
Scopes wanted.

Falwell's position on evolution is simple. "The Bible says otherwise," he told me. "How can I believe in anything except creation?"
He is unable to see any metaphors and ambiguities in the biblical account that might render the positions of evolution and divine creation
compatible. Falwell's suspicion of evolution is rooted in his acceptance of what Martin Lings wrote in 1970—that "more cases of loss of
religious faith are to be traced to the theory of evolution than to anything else."

Falwell spent most of 1982 expanding his ministry. Moral Majority
was virtually inactive during that time; it served mainly an educational function. Falwell visited South Korea and Australia in May
1982. In Korea he spoke at a prayer breakfast and received the nation's
highest medal from the country's president. He also received an hon-
orary doctorate from Central University, one of Korea's largest. In
Sydney, Falwell filmed a special broadcast of "The Old Time Gospel
Hour" and preached for the Baptist Bible Fellowship there. In Australia only 2 percent of the population attends church, but he was received warmly. He addressed more than 300 church workers at a
growth convention. He spoke to 250 delegates of the Word of Life fellowship.

The 1982 congressional elections came along, but Falwell and Moral
Majority stayed away. Instead of campaigning during the weekend before the election, top state and national Moral Majority leaders held a
convention in the Bahamas. This was a period of political apathy for
Falwell, reflecting his enormous confidence in President Reagan—and
his naivete. Soon after Republican reversals in 1982, Falwell realized
that people in a democracy are often impatient. They do not place
long-term trust in politicians. Activists exercise great influence only so
long as they remain active. If Moral Majority stayed out of the fray, its
constituency would suffer measurably.

11

An Avalanche of Invective

Falwell may have helped Ronald Reagan win the 1980 election, but he did so at the cost of making many enemies. After November 4, 1980, several groups were formed specifically to counter the alleged threat of the religious Right. The American Civil Liberties Union and other organizations joined the Moral Majority hate club, convinced that Falwell was out to subvert precious American values. The following are just some of the volleys aimed at Jerry Falwell.

John Bennett, former president of Union Theological Seminary, averred that the Christian Right has "an authoritarian tendency in religion which meshes well with authoritarian secular structures."

Rabbi Alexander Schindler, president of United Hebrew Congregation, claimed that Falwell's people "ignore and even oppose such religious principles as stewardship of our resources, care for the poor, justice and peace."

Ira Glasser, president of the American Civil Liberties Union, insisted, "There's a strong anti-Bill of Rights movement building in America that is represented by a great deal of what the new evangelical groups represent."

George McGovern, unseated as senator, warned of the "emergence of irrational forces in American politics." Of Falwell McGovern said,

"I personally regard him as a menace to the American political process."

Katherine Helmond, a soap opera actress, said she was so frightened by the Moral Majority that she was moving back to Britain.

Patricia Harris, former secretary of Health and Human Services, citing Falwell's "moral absolutism," said, "I am beginning to fear that we could have an Ayatollah in this country, but he will not have a beard, but a television program."

Black activist Julian Bond wrote in a letter on behalf of Klanwatch, a watchdog organization, "A dangerous new coalition of neo-Nazi and Ku Klux Klan groups is threatening the worst rise in racism and anti-Semitic activity since the 1920s." Naming Falwell as part of this coalition, Bond said, "Television preachers like Jerry Falwell of the Moral Majority feel free to drop racist comments about Jews."

Author Leon Uris sent out a letter sharing his great concern over the recent upsurge of activity by the Ku Klux Klan . . . and the American neo-Nazis." He referred to "public racist comments by the likes of Jerry Falwell and his repressive Moral Majority."

Television producer Norman Lear, accused "single issue zealots" such as Falwell of "fascism masquerading as Christianity." What these people want, Lear suggested, "is the ultimate obscenity, the spiritual pornography of debased religiosity."

Oregon Senator Mark Hatfield, himself an evangelical, accused the Christian Right of spreading "this horrible, cancerous disease of anti-Semitism."

The list could go on. Of the several groups formed to counter Falwell's influence, the most famous is People for the American Way, which Norman Lear assembled to counter the spiritual arrogance he perceived in Moral Majority. PAW's first fund raising letter said, "It is not enough to simply shake our heads in disbelief when we hear Jerry Falwell, head of the Moral Majority, proclaim that if you are not a Christian you are inherently a failure." Citing "hate-mongering" on Falwell's part, PAW urged, "You and I must do something concrete to protect the diversity of opinion, the religious tolerance, and the tradition of personal freedoms that long have been the American way." Concrete actions recommended included "your generous tax-deductible contribution" which, it was noted, "will help us counter the ominous threat to our tradition of freedom, diversity of opinion, and religious tolerance posed by moral majoritarians."

For his newly formed PAW, Lear recruited several big names among the liberal clergy: William Howard, president of the National Council of Churches; Theodore Hesburgh, president of Notre Dame University; Harold Hughes, an evangelical preacher and former Democratic senator from Iowa. The group began a direct-mail campaign to gain more money and adherents. It purchased full-page ads in major newspapers accusing "moral majoritarians" of everything from book-burning to wanting homosexuals executed. "Some groups believe Webster's Dictionary and Robin Hood are dangerous to read," began a full page PAW ad in the *New York Times*. The ad noted that "There are hundreds of books on the moral majoritarians' hit list. Works by Steinbeck and Hemingway and even *Treasure Island* are under attack from groups led by Jerry Falwell, Phyllis Schlafly, and textbook censors Mel and Norma Gabler. But the moral majoritarians' crusade to impose their views on everyone doesn't stop with books. If you're a woman they want to deny you equal rights. They racially segregate private schools, and want to use your tax money to do it. They want to weaken child-abuse protections, as they have already done in Indiana. They want to involve the government in your decision to have children. Or not to. Some want all homosexuals executed. They want to deny your Social Security benefits, calling them inconsistent with the Bible. They want to keep you from going to court to protect your civil rights and religious liberties. In all, they want to force you to practice their particular religious beliefs. By law."

PAW was joined by the Committee for American Principles, another group disgruntled by Moral Majority's presumptuousness. "Can we afford to turn our heads away from the threat of the right wing?" a brochure queried. Birch Bayh, Edward Asner, Frank Church, Dick Clark, Robert Drinan, Charles Mathias, Thomas McIntire, and Gaylord Nelson—several of them toppled Congressmen—endorsed the organization's charges that "the repressive right and its army of political action committees" were "waging guerilla warfare against an open and viable political process."

Clergy and Laity Concerned, another New York-based group, trumpeted that "The religious Right is not what it pretends to be." While Moral Majority and other groups were said to hold "an ideology based on fear, selfishness, greed, and exploitation" that was "financed extensively by giant corporations and millionaire businessmen," CALC claimed to be working for "an immediate freeze" on nuclear weapons, "global and domestic food issues," and "a new multiracial movement in our society."

The American Civil Liberties Union, accused Moral Majority of trying to impose "a nightmare of political and religious orthodoxy." The

New York chapter of the ACLU bought full-page ads in the *New York Times*, the *New York Post*, and the *New York Daily News* which outdid PAW in stridency.

The Moral Majority—and other groups like them—think that children should pray in school. Not just their children. Your children.

They want their religious doctrines enacted into law and imposed on everyone.

If they believe birth control is a sin, then you should not be allowed to use contraceptives.

If they believe that abortion is wrong, then you should not be allowed to have one.

If they believe that the Bible condemns homosexuality, then the law should punish homosexuals.

If they believe that a man should be the breadwinner and head of the family, then the law should keep women in their place.

If they are offended by the ideas in certain books, then the law should ban those books from your libraries and schools.

This incredible barrage invites comment. It is inaccurate. Falwell strongly supports contraception; he does not share the Catholic Church's views that it is morally forbidden. He does not want doctrine enshrined into law. Nothing he has said even remotely suggests that, and the purpose of setting up a political group like Moral Majority was in fact to distinguish it from Thomas Road Baptist Church. Falwell doesn't just believe abortion is wrong, he believes it is murder, so it is not surprising that he wants it prohibited. He does not think that the laws should either punish homosexuals or discriminate against women in the workplace and has never said anything to that effect. And Falwell is not in favor of forced prayer, as the ACLU implies. It is disingenuous for the ACLU to argue that if voluntary prayer is permitted in schools, there may be pressure on children who don't want to pray, so that meant Moral Majority members want "not just their children, but your children" to pray.

The ACLU also invoked the spectre of McCarthyism and charged that Falwell's group stood "against the First Amendment guarantees of freedom of expression and separation of church and state." Falwell's people sought "not to conserve American values, but to overthrow them." This was nothing short of "a major struggle over the Bill of Rights." The ACLU prayer ads raised $100,000 in their first month, one of the most successful funds solicitations in the ACLU's history.

Prominent intellectuals like Timothy Healy, president of Georgetown University, and Bartlett Giamatti, president of Yale, also attacked Falwell. Healy linked Falwell's activities to anti-Semitism and violence. I got a chance to ask Healy about this in an interview with him I did for the *National Catholic Register*. Here is an excert from that interview:

Register: What is your objection to the Christian Right?

Healy: Its element of profound intolerance. In the one campaign I saw it hardest at work, I saw a great deal of anti-Semitism.

Register: From what I've read about the Moral Majority, Jerry Falwell is close pals with Menachem Begin.

Healy: I understand this. I was deliberately not singling out anybody.

Register: Which case did you refer to?

Healy: The individual case that horrified me was what I regarded as the bluntly anti-Semitic campaign against Senator Stone in Florida.

Register: Do you see that particular case as being representative of all New Right groups?

Healy: That is the only one I had direct experience with.

Register: But isn't it unfair to extrapolate from that to—

Healy: One case for me is enough.

Register: In a speech to the University of the District of Columbia, you associated the New Right with the Ku Klux Klan and McCarthyism. What's the parallel?

Healy: Hatred and racism.

Register: Hatred and racism, based solely on the one experience you give me?

Healy: If I see one case, I will yell.

Giamatti welcomed entering freshmen to Yale on August 31, 1981, with, of all things, an attack on Falwell. "A self-proclaimed Moral Majority," Giamatti warned, "and its satellite or client groups, cunning in the use of a native blend of old intimidation and new technology, threaten the values I have named. Angry at change, rigid in the application of chauvinistic slogans, absolutistic in morality, they threaten through political pressure or public denunciation whoever dares to disagree with their authoritarian positions. Using television, direct mail, and economic boycott, they would sweep before them anyone who holds a different opinion." Giamatti went on to call Moral Majority a set of "voices of coercion" which "speak not for liberty but for license, the license to divide in the name of patriotism, the license to deny in the name of Christianity." Falwell's people, he asserted "have licensed a new meanness of spirit in the land, a resurgent bigotry that manifests itself in racist and discriminatory postures, in threats of political retaliation, in injunctions to censorship, in acts of violence." Giamatti's speech made the front page of the *New York Times* and was excerpted in *Time* and *Newsweek*.

Giamatti's unexpected philippic drew several conservatives to Falwell's defense. Columnist William F. Buckley noted that at Yale students may join the Citizen's Party, the Campaign Against the Draft, the Yalesbians, but certainly not the Moral Majority. Buckley wondered why Giamatti had launched his sudden tirade, observing, "To be lectured against the perils of the Moral Majority on entering Yale is on the order of being lectured on the danger of bedbugs on entering a brothel."

About this time a spate of books appeared blasting Falwell and the Christian Right. Some of these were more amusing than injurious, such as Gary Clabaugh's *Thunder on the Right*. Clabaugh admits his book is in retaliation for being attacked as a seventh-grade teacher by fundamentalists who objected to his teaching evolution. He compares fundamentalists to Hitler and McCarthy and provides "a neo-Freudian theory of the etiology of the authoritarian type," which is just the kind of stuff you would expect from a seventh grade teacher.

Perhaps the most widely circulated of the books attacking Falwell was *Holy Terror* by Flo Conway and Jim Siegelman, published by Doubleday. Terming Falwell "the supreme religious huckster of the era," Conway and Siegelman maintained, "The air in Falwell country is heavy with fear" and accused Falwell of having a security force "larger than the Lynchburg Police Department." Error and speculations gave way to sheer absurdity. The two authors concluded that Falwell and others like him were part of an international conspiracy to subjugate, oppress, and in some cases destroy, other nations. Named participants in this conspiracy included Falwell, the Amway Corporation, Baptist Bible College, Jim Bakker, Accelerated Christian Education, Coalition for Decency, Billy Graham, Jesse Helms, Bunker Hunt, Terry Bradshaw, Moody Bible Institute, National Religious Broadcasters, Howard Phillips, Ronald Reagan, Roy Rogers, Francis Schaeffer, and the Wycliffe Bible Translators.

Replying to *Holy Terror* in his *Fundamentalist Journal*, Falwell observed, "The authors are guilty of the very thing they accuse fundamentalists of: 'name calling, glittering generalities, and card stacking.' " Falwell also arranged with Morton Shulman, a Canadian talk show host, to have Conway and Siegelman debate two of Falwell's pastors,

Ed Dobson and Ed Hindson. The show was taped and aired on CITY-TV in Toronto. After a brief and admittedly tough grilling by host Schulman in the first session, Conway and Siegelman got up and walked out during a commercial break. David Sobelman, associate producer of the show, said he thought Conway and Siegelman's experience on talk shows would have prepared them to handle an investigative review of their work. The show went on with Dobson, Hindson, and a representative of People for the American Way. Dobson and Hindson challenged the credibility of Conway and Siegelman's research, accused them of "cultic paranoia," and challenged them to a future debate.

Falwell's numerous critics had their views freely aired by the media, which hoped that the combined religious and secular attacks would whittle away the power of the Christian Right. There was even an obscene record made about Falwell and Moral Majority by a San Francisco group. When it became apparent that the critics were having little effect and Falwell's constituency and influence continued to grow, the press itself entered the fray.

A March 4, 1981, *Washington Post* article entitled "McGovern Back on Campus Runs into Moral Majority" began

She was just a tiny thing, all peaches and cream and honey-blond hair, her pink down vest shiny behind her "Jesus comes first, I'm with Moral Majority" button. But Salley McKenna, a freshman at George Mason University, was mad yesterday, fist-shaking mad, and she rose up to her full 5 feet, 2 inches, and hissed at George McGovern.

"He's nothing but a liberal-commie-atheistic-pinko-faggot. He's got nerve to come here and say the things he did. The Lord Jesus will make him pay for this . . . I hope his dentures fall out."

So went the voice of dissent in George Mason's gleaming new Studio Theatre yesterday, when that famed liberal and dethroned Senator George McGovern, a former student minister and son of an evangelical preacher, came to address the students on the "Effects of the New Right on the Politics of the '80s."

The Post, by its headline indicated that it considered this student representative of Moral Majority. She was a somewhat foolish and unsophisticated girl, depicted as a kind of religious fanatic. Meanwhile McGovern was sympathetically portrayed as a "student minister and son of an evangelical preacher." This kind of partisan characterization, identifying Moral Majority with the rashly expressed views of one angry young student, is typical of the media's efforts at discrediting everyone associated with Falwell and the New Right.

Reporter Christopher Bonner of the *Wichita Eagle-Beacon* in Kansas identified Moral Majority in a lead story as a "right-wing fundamentalist religious group that opposes birth control, abortion, and gay rights, and favors a traditional role for women." This is a fairly common characterization of Moral Majority. There are several things wrong with it. First, Moral Majority is not religious. Second, it is not fundamentalist—Roman Catholics comprise 30 percent of the membership. Third, it does not oppose birth control. Indeed Falwell favors it. He says it prevents unwanted pregnancy and possibly abortion. Fourth, Moral Majority *favors* legislation which would permit abortion for women who are victims of rape and incest or where the life of the mother is at stake. Falwell does not support an all-inclusive Human Life Amendment because it would exclude abortion for these women. Fifth, Moral Majority is not against gay rights, only against special treatment for homosexuals. Falwell believes that homosexuality is morally wrong, but he does not think homosexuals should be denied civil protection. He opposes affirmative action for homosexuals. Finally, Moral Majority supports women's rights but does not believe that the Equal Rights Amendment is a conduit to those rights.

The media barrage against Falwell is expressed in six ways: (1) Falwell is an absolutist, (2) Falwell wants to impose his views on everyone else, (3) Falwell is like the Ayatollah Khomeini, Adolf Hitler, and Jim Jones rolled into one, (4) Falwell is racist, sexist, and anti-Semitic, (5) Falwell is rolling in money, (6) Falwell and his supporters are stupid, weird, and "ultraconservative."

PBS commentator Bill Moyers asserts, "It is not that the evangelicals are taking politics seriously that bothers me. It's the lie they're being told by the demagogues who flatter them into believing that they can achieve politically the certitude they have embraced theologically. The world doesn't work that way." In a symposium on the Christian Right, the *Christian Century* accused Falwell of "self-righteousness that leads to absolutism." *The Christian Science Monitor* lamented in an October 1980 editorial, "All too often religious activism is narrowly and simplistically bound up with one issue."

Falwell's reply to all this is that Moral Majority is absolute about some things and not absolute about others. It does not believe that there is a single Christian position on environmental legislation or SALT II. You can be for the Panama Canal giveaway and still be a Christian. Does this mean that Moral Majority ought not to speak on issues on which there is room for disagreement? Is Moral Majority not

entitled to its view of what is moral and right? May it not seek to convert others to that point of view? When the National Council of
Churches endorses disarmament, is it guilty of moral absolutism, because Christians can favor a strong defense and still be Christians?
When William Sloane Coffin asks people to vote for unilateral arma-
ment reduction, why is it that he is not viewed as "narrowly and simplistically bound up with one issue"?

The other inconsistency about the argument against Falwell's alleged absolutism is that it is made in absolute terms: No one may challenge relativism. Falwell knows that this is an untenable position for
Christians. It is something of an absolute for the media, for whom the
First Amendment is certainly an absolute. "There is no higher good
than the First Amendment," said Judith Krug of the American Library
Association in a moment of pseudo religious afflatus.

David Broder of the *Washington Post* said Falwell wants "to impose
an older-generation view of morality on the younger generation of
Americans." *Inquiry* accused the "Moral imperialists" at Moral Majority of being "intent on enforcing a set of rigid, doctrinaire political
and religious beliefs on an entire nation." *The New York Times* charged
"ignorant fundamentalists" with trying to "ram God down the throats
of America's school-children." Columnist, Burt Wilson has said
Moral Majority's success depends "upon its ability to capture people's
hearts and minds before they have a chance to think." And Mike
Royko, writing in the *Chicago Sun-Times* says he follows Falwell "and
other right-wing fanatics" in order "to see how many constitutional
rights they want to obliterate."

Falwell indicates simply that he is trying to build political coalitions,
not impose religious anything. He asks, "Is it not true that liberals
have been imposing morality on us for the last fifty years? Forced
busing—that's imposed morality. High taxes to fund welfare
programs—that's imposed morality." Even laws against murder and
theft are imposed morality. The notion that morality is entirely personal and must be kept to oneself, or that all public standards of morality are illegitimate, would mean that murder is just a matter of
personal ethics.

"Fascism lives" was the title of an article by news editor Bill
Sullivan's in the *Western Courier* in Illinois. Wrote Sullivan, "Hitler-
ism, unfortunately, is alive and well and flourishing in America,"
in the form, of course, of the "so-called Moral Majority." Citing
"Falwell's fascists" Sullivan went on to say, "These witch-hunting
censors burn books, magazines, rock albums, and anything else."

His conclusion: "The swastika has been replaced by the cross."

The Washington Post paraded this opinion as well when it quoted Representative Parren Mitchell (D-MD) naming the Ku Klux Klan and American Nazis as enemies of blacks. According to Mitchell, the "climate of the Moral Majority feeds into these hate activists." Meanwhile, Haynes Johnson, a *Washington Post* columnist, compared the actions of "Christian zealots" with "the fanatical Mohammedan, the fanatical nationalist, the fanatical Communist, and the fanatical Nazi."

Flora Lewis of the *New York Times* most intensively developed a supposed Falwell-Khomeini parallel. She saw similarities in China's Red Guard rampage, Khomeini's Islamic disciplines, and America's Moral Majority. "They all feel they know better than others what is good and bad for society on the basis of revealed or nostalgic values. They are all moved to attempt what they consider purification of what they see as moral decay. They all proclaim simple rules defining good and evil to save their worlds from devilish confusion." This, from a columnist and newspaper who actively abetted the Shah's downfall and published several columns and articles declaring his successor a moderate leading a truly progressive revolution.

The *St. Louis Globe-Democrat* quoted a local resident as saying, "You know when that Jonestown thing happened, that Jim Jones thing, I heard a lot of people here saying that if Jerry Falwell told his people to drink Grape Kool-Aid, they'd drink Grape Kool-Aid." Columnist Ann Rinaldi wrote that Falwell "reminds me of Guyana" in the *Trentonian* of New Jersey.

What is curious about the Jim Jones analogy is that Jones was an atheist, a this-worldly socialist whose idol was Josef Stalin. He hated the Bible; frequently spat on the Bible in his temple. He was also an antinuclear activist. Jim Jones was the very antithesis of Jerry Falwell. Ironically, on August 18, 1973, the *Washington Post* had praised Jones and his group, referring to "the 660 wonderful members of the People's Temple" and "this spirited group of travelers." In 1976 the *Los Angeles Herald-Examiner* had named Jones "Humanitarian of the Year." Jane Fonda once said of Jonestown, "Much of what America needs to resolve its overwhelming social problems has become embodied in the life of Jonestown and the works of the People's Temple."

Falwell's racism was "exposed" by Channel 2 in Baltimore, Maryland, which covered a protest march against Jerry Falwell, who was at a fundraiser. Ron Olson, the reporter, quoted as his first source not Falwell but one Anne Thompson, an anti-Falwell demonstrator who said, "We're going to have civil liberties wiped away; we're going to have all kinds of progressive legislation, progressive civil rights bills, progressive court decisions—they're going to be wiped out." This did not elicit so much as a single critical question from Olson. In the magazine *Inquiry*, Jere Real misquoted Falwell to the effect that God does not hear the prayers of Jews, and the *Atlanta Constitution* editorialized, without explanation, that "Falwell doesn't much like Jews." All this despite the fact that a significant portion of Moral Majority is Jewish, that Falwell is a close friend of Menachem Begin and Yitzak Shamir, and that Falwell has lost some fundamentalist support because he is willing to form political alliances with Jews. None of this deterred the *New York Times*, whose reporter Adam Clymer assured his readers that "Moral Majority has been widely denounced by Democrats as anti-Semitic and generally narrow-minded." Clymer also repeated the erroneous charge that Falwell had said God does not hear the prayers of Jews.

Falwell is commonly portrayed to be wallowing in money. *Newsweek* inveigled Falwell into letting its photographer take a picture of him reclining on an easy chair before his swimming pool. Then in its September 15, 1980, issue *Newsweek* pasted the picture above a story title, "A $1 Million Habit." The title implied that living luxuriously was Falwell's million-dollar habit, but one discovered umpteen later that the $1 million figure referred to the amount Falwell's television show took in weekly.

Robert Scheer of the *Los Angeles Times* began a front-page feature, "As his private jet begins its descent into Los Angeles, the Rev. Jerry Falwell..." Dudley Clendinen, in an August 20, 1980, series, started off similarly—"When the Rev. Jerry Falwell strode toward his private jet..."

Falwell travels some 250,000 miles per year. "I cannot be expected to travel by commuter airline and make separate reservations all the time," he observes reasonably. "I take my TV people and pastors and assistants with me. Should I buy all of them tickets?" Falwell maintains it's less expensive for his ministry to own a plane, a realization which apparently has come to major newspapers and the networks, which routinely employ their own helicopters and airplanes, even though they find it irregular that Falwell, head of a $100 million organization, does, too. And isn't it hypocritical for people like Dan Rather, who makes twenty times what Falwell does, to impugn him for his salary and lifestyle. Sure, Falwell lives comfortably in a twelve-room house, owned by his church, complete with pool. But drop by the homes of Phil Donahue and Mike Wallace to get a sense of perspective. Look at the homes of liberal clergymen Jesse Jackson and William Sloane Coffin.

It is taken to be a matter of great significance that Falwell has a sensitized fence around his house. But is that surprising for a man who gets two hundred death threats per month, usually from maniacs repeating charges they have read in the newspapers, charges made in hate by people who claim to be trying to combat hate in American politics. Robert Scheer of the *Los Angeles Times* describes Falwell's house as "surrounded by manicured lawns, a large swimming pool, and barking dogs all nestled behind a 10-foot high wall that Falwell feels are necessary for his security but which many local people find offensive." Notice the references to "barking dogs." Falwell owns two dogs, a poodle and a twelve-year-old half-blind Irish setter. These are routinely referred to as "barking dogs" or "attack dogs" by reporters who cannot but know better.

The media also uses the crassest stereotypes to portray Falwell and his followers while themselves denouncing the use of stereotypes among fundamentalists. *The Washington Post* ran a story describing Falwell's viewers as "predominately married or widowed women over 50 who are not well educated and live in the South." The media does not seem to be interested in Falwell's opinions. Is America morally decrepit? Is the family enfeebled? Are the nation's values becoming relativistic? These questions are passed over. Falwell is rejected as ignorant, and his supporters as culturally odd. The intention is to suggest that he and they constitute a group with peculiar propensities whose opinions can be safely dismissed or explained as the outcome of an archaic upbringing. Falwell is identified as an "extremist" and "ultraconservative" in virtually every media report. The implication is that he is outside the mainstream and can only be evaluated in terms of the American tradition as defined by the media.

Given Falwell's coverage in the national media, it is not surprising to hear Cal Thomas say, "Reporting about Falwell and Moral Majority is only slightly better than what we'd expect in *Pravda*." Falwell himself has a more casual explanation, "The whole world loves us or hates us, and the rest are scared of us."

But Thomas and Falwell also know that some Moral Majority members have unwittingly made comments ripe for distortion. The Reverend Dan Fore, former Moral Majority head in New York, was asked how he could justify Christians being political when Christians had persecuted so many during the Inquisition. "Oh, those weren't Christians, those were Roman Catholics," Fore said without batting an eyelid. He soon resigned his position at Moral Majority.

Falwell admits that Moral Majority sometimes gets bad press because "some young leader gets his mouth working before his mind is in gear." Because Moral Majority is a young organization, some of its members are not tutored in the protocol of modern political discourse. Falwell himself has erred on this point. He once said at an "I love America" rally, "I know a few of you here today don't like Jews. And I know why. A Jew can make more money accidentally than you can on purpose." Falwell did not realize then that to refer to Jews making a lot of money is widely regarded as anti-Semitic. He intended the remark as a jocular compliment.

The effect of the media attack on Falwell, however, has been to unify the Christian Right behind him. Richard Zwier correctly notes, "Nothing unites a group so quickly and intensely as the perception of being persecuted by a common enemy—in this case the liberal media." Although Falwell must thank the media for this, he says, he is still hurt and astonished, when rumors and untruths about him are systematically printed, even though proper explanations and evidence have all been provided to the reporters. After all, what can you do if a reporter does not believe you? In an unusual moment of candor, reporter Teresa Carpenter of the *Village Voice* wrote, "You can either give Jerry Falwell the benefit of the doubt, that is, keep an open mind, or you can assume that he is a sophisticated snake-oil salesman. I tend toward the latter, and that, I will be the first to admit, is a purely emotional reaction. Whenever I step within a 10-foot radius of a fundamentalist minister my reason clouds over." Falwell says there is nothing more dangerous in a free society than a mass media whose mind is so made up that not a fact can violate it.

12

The Scene in Lynchburg

Lynchburg, Virginia, lies right in the center of the state. It is surrounded by rolling hills that rub shoulders with the Blue Ridge Mountains. It is a three-hour drive from the nation's capital. It is an industrial town, with a population of about 70,000, growing at the rate of 1 percent per year. There are about 200 small factories in Lynchburg, and they turn out everything from heavy equipment and medical supplies to toys and thread. Its Chamber of Commerce includes mainly small businessmen proud that theirs is one of the oldest industrial towns in the South. Lynchburg is a working city. Plumes of factory smoke attest to that. Homes in the city are characteristically low-slung houses with brick walls and sloping roofs.

The people in and around Lynchburg are laborers, farmers, and small businessmen who mostly live hard lives and go to church on Sunday. They are not much more virtuous than other Americans, but they are able to distinguish virtue from vice. They recognize that it takes standards higher than we often live by to prompt us to live as better men and women.

Not everybody in Lynchburg is fundamentalist, although a plurality of churches in town are Southern Baptist. There are 144 churches listed in the Yellow Pages; 57 of these are Baptist. Some of the Baptist churches are histrionic; others are low-key. All subscribe to the un-adulterated tenets of the Bible, taken literally or at least without much bowdlerization. Thomas Road Baptist Church is the largest church in Lynchburg; it has 21,000 members, about a quarter of the population of greater Lynchburg. The church itself sits squatly in a large parking lot that overwhelms the church, and is filled with cars, mostly American-made and driven by well-dressed people. Other churches—the Presbyterian Church on the upside of town, for instance—are grander, but Thomas Road is the fullest. Each service packs in 4000 people, most of them locals, to listen to Jerry Falwell fulminate on is-sues of morality and salvation.

A Thomas Road traffic controller directs the flow of traffic through the parking lot. Besides cars, school buses pull in too, bringing church members who live on the outskirts of town and have no other trans-portation. There are buses from out of town; I saw a bus from Springfield, Missouri, bring in forty or so young people, all well be-haved and carrying Bibles.

The congregation files into the church through five entrances. They are greeted by ushers and elders handing out bulletins and leading them to their seats.

Inside, the church is shaped as an arc, with a podium at front left. There are no statues or decorations, except for an American flag dan-gling behind the podium. The windows aren't ornate or stained-glass; the door is plain solid oak; the seats aren't plush. "People come here to pray, not to relax," Falwell says, explaining his Spartan decor. There are sections to the right front of the church to accommodate the choir and church deacons. The architecture is Jeffersonian.

Sunday school precedes the regular service. Ten thousand people, young and old, attend. They are all in their Sunday best. On the Sun-day I am in attendance, about 25 percent are over 60; 60 percent are middle-aged adults. Some of the men wear gold watches and rings and carry Bibles under their right arm, like Falwell. The women are metic-ulously made up, with their hair curled and the chains resting on their bosoms. The single young men and women sit next to each other. The young children walk up and about the aisles, uninhibited and secure, even with all the adults around them constrained in prayerful atti-tudes.

The church is predominantly white, with a goodly number of blacks. I also spotted several foreigners. A Japanese man actually took pictures before the service, although there is nothing much distinctive about the church, except perhaps for the television cameras, poised to shoot

Falwell and the musicians from five angles. In fact, that is what the Japanese man took pictures of. Later, during the service, these cameras turned around to get a shot of the crowd of 4000, including the Japanese man and the minority members in church. This, no doubt, stresses the presence of nonwhite fundamentalists, working to erase stereotypes. "The Old Time Gospel Hour" lenses also focus on the two black members of the choir, who sing more vigorously than the others and stand out. For all what may appear tokenism, Falwell's church, with its 400 or so black members, is one of the most racially integrated churches in Lynchburg—or Virginia, for that matter. Ironically, it is the liberal churches in town that tend to be lily white.

Falwell's Sunday services are taped under the supervision of Bruce Braun, a savvy young media-man with curly hair and watery blue eyes. Braun takes care of the show-biz part of the "Old Time Gospel Hour," and is constantly asking Falwell to tone up his performance. After all, Falwell, unlike other TV evangelists, does not have a variety-style show, with news reports, cuts to Israel and the Capitol bulding, and/or various skits pieced carefully together. Falwell's TV show is merely a slightly edited church service broadcast on the air. The only variation Braun is permitted is panning back and forth between Falwell and his people.

Braun tells me that Falwell is resolutely opposed to spiffing up his service. "He wants to keep it dignified, he says," according to Braun. "He doesn't want a circus." But Braun has been counselling Falwell to reduce the amount of time he devotes to fundraising on his show. "It detracts from his overall performance," Braun says. But Falwell has proved reluctant to be subtle about appeals for funds. He does not think that relying on the Lord means being reticent about financial needs. Braun says Falwell feels insecure that one day money may stop coming in, that he will only get it if he stumps for it.

Falwell's television show is edited down to an hour and aired on four hundred television stations across the country two weeks after it is taped. Falwell boasts that he reaches more people than Johnny Carson, that there is no town in the country where you cannot get his show.

The service begins with singing. The music is lively but traditional. Most everyone participates; the elderly sing loudest and least in tune. A woman up front translates the words for the deaf. Some people have their eyes closed, but that is the extent of any overt emotionalism—these people are not charismatics or Pentecostals; they do not raise their arms, pray in tongues, or perform other histrionics. Falwell in fact has criticized "overly emotional types of worship." He feels they may be cathartic, but they are certainly not biblical. He also feels that speaking in tongues stopped with Christ's apostles, that charismatics who fancy they are speaking in Aramaic or Hebrew are in fact speaking gibberish. But, with the moral majority, he openly associates with charismatic preachers, for which he has drawn fire from some traditional fundamentalists.

Ed Dobson, Falwell's associate pastor, usually delivers the sermon at Sunday school. Dobson is a boyish fellow with wavy black hair whose voice emerges from his small frame with surprising volume. He is fancied by Thomas Road members to succeed Falwell, although either Jim Moon or Don Norman seem likely to be placed in charge by Falwell. (Falwell, who fears for his life, has apparently written down plans for his succession, but he refuses to divulge these, for understandable reasons.) Dobson is a lively speaker. He has a sense of humor about himself and sometimes about fundamentalists and that goes over well. His biblical exegeses at times seem a little glib, glossing over questions that can be raised against his position. Every six months or so he holds a question-and-answer session, answering written questions from church members. When doing so often he only repeats the portion of a sermon that prompted the question to begin with. Dobson's question-and-answer session is well liked among church members, however, because it provides a refreshing break from the usual half-hour lecture and signifies an open-mindedness that fundamentalists know is a luxury to them.

Some people file out after Sunday School, but not many. Others now enter, and Pastor Dobson asks people to move close together to make room for the newcomers. Then he leaves. It is while this shuffling is going on that Falwell and the associate pastors make a ceremonious entrance, taking their place on the front chairs and rafters.

Falwell is escorted to his place by Jim Moon and Don Norman. Students from Liberty Baptist college file into the front rows, all well attired. The faculty members are in church, too, because they are born-again Christians, every one. Church attendance is mandatory for all of Falwell's staff—not, as some have speculated, to fill the church for television purposes, but because Falwell believes that the philosophy of his college is determined "not in meetings or in committees, but from the pulpit."

Before Falwell preaches he hands out "prayer packet" to his congregation, which have been put together by Bill Sheehan's prayer team.

These packets contain prayer requests from people across the country. There are at least six thousand of them each week, so everybody in church must take at least one envelope home and pray sometime during the week for the letter-writer(s). Sheehan and his team also conduct a prayer session for all the prayer needs, so, as Falwell explains, "The people who need our prayers are getting a double helping."

Many things come around during the Sunday service: prayer envelopes, cards to sign up for Falwell's "15,000 Club," "Jesus first" pins, a collection for the missionary effort. While he is not threatening or insistent, Falwell is just keen to have his people give more to God than those watching on television. He constantly tells his congregation how they must outdo everyone else in prayer and generosity; they must be an example to the world, especially to those "babes in Christ" who have only recently been born again.

The choir begins the last hymn before the sermon, and I cannot resist opening my prayer envelope. Ignoring a few pairs of eyes on me, I open the envelope and peel out the requests. There are three of them, all hand-written. Two of them are signed. One is from a woman who says her son is living with a woman "in the swamp of sin" and she is helpless to do anything. The other is from a mother whose son shot a man to death. "He is in the hospital, and the doctor's think he will live. But no thanks to my son." The woman writes. "Please pray that he may receive Jesus into his heart. That is the only thing that is wrong with him." I was surprised she had signed her name. The anonymous note was from someone in Omaha who said he had been demoted in his job and wanted "you Jerry" to pray "for my continued success." The choir sits down. Now it is Falwell's turn to speak, and a silence descends upon the church. Falwell begins with a prayer asking for blessing upon his teaching, that it be inspired by God's eternal wisdom that it make its audience and its speaker contrite, aware of their own failings even as they ask virtue of others. The people put their heads down as Falwell prays.

Falwell's theme is "A Mother's Role"; it is one of those nostalgic sermons. He asks, "What kind of mothers do we need in the 1980s? What kind of mothers do we need for all time?" The question is important, he says, since "the basic unit of our society is the family, the home, and no nation can be stronger than the families within her." He quotes Proverbs 31:10–31, in which feminine virtues are outlined. Falwell admits that "It is not easy to be a mother today in this rapidly changing world." He insists that good mothers, today as before, should be submissive to their husbands—not servile, but submissive. He

quotes Ed Dobson, dean at LBC: "Submission in a sense means duck-
ing so God can hit your husband." The point is that only when wives
are acquiescent can husbands realize their responsibility to take charge
of the household. The proper mother, Falwell says, "creatively helps
meet her family's financial needs, as well as caring for the poor and
needy. She is well dressed, so her appearance enhances her husband's
image of her. She is neither extravagant nor haughty, and is feminine,
yet competent. She follows her husband, leads her children, and always speaks with wisdom and kindness." Most important, "she honors
God and her family."

Falwell remembers his own mother. "I thank God my mother loved
to be at home. She didn't feel she was in a prison. Her family was her
delight. She loved to cook three meals a day and keep the house. She
loved to see us off to the school bus in the morning and meet it in the
afternoon. She loved to meet our needs and instruct us in right and
wrong and enforce our behavior habits. I thank God she felt a fulfilled
and happy woman, because she sure made us feel fulfilled and happy."
(Helen Falwell died on April 28, 1977, after a stroke had incapacitated
her some weeks earlier.)

Then it's time for whacks. Falwell observes, "There is a stark contrast between the biblical picture of the ideal mother and that of some
contemporary women with their alcohol, cigarettes, pills, nervous
breakdowns, and generally disgruntled dispositions." He cites statistics: a divorce rate of 40 percent, 1.5 million abortions a year.

Falwell argues that separate duties are the reason for different roles
and capacities in men and women. He is not talking about duties like
hunting and cooking and so is not vulnerable to the counter argument
that separate roles for men and women are anachronistic in this post-
primitive society. Rather, he is speaking of different duties spelled out
in Scripture, which does not accommodate itself to time. This is abstract stuff for most, but Falwell gets down to earth. Men are not
stronger and more aggressive than women because men are trained to
be soldiers, nor do women nurture children because girls play with
dolls. His point is that society merely makes laws in line with biological necessity: it does not write its own history.

Now, Falwell is quick to delineate a Scriptural position for women,
but he realizes that there are exceptions—not just militant feminists,
whom he sometimes refers to as malformed men, but also women like
Phyllis Schlafly who idealize the housewife but perform beyond the
feminist ideal. (When Phyllis Schlafly came to talk at Thomas Road,
Falwell issued the following qualification: "Being a Baptist, I've never

had a women preacher here. We Baptists don't ordain women. But may I say to you that if I ever ordained a woman and if she ever requested it—and I won't, I promise—it would be Mrs. Phyllis Schlafly. You'll be hearing from Phyllis in just a few moments. She is not going to preach, she's going to talk. Don't get nervous, Baptists. She's going to talk.")

Falwell winds up his sermon with a celebration of the demise of the Equal Rights Amendment (ERA), saying "we want equality without the Amendment." And, he bellows, "There is not going to be an Equal Rights Amendment, because Christians believe in superior rights for women; we don't believe in equal rights for women. We help them with their coats, we open the doors for them, we go out to war and fight for them. They ought to be cared for by their husbands, and women don't need to use unisex toilets and go out to the battle fronts to fight and give their lives in doing a job that men ought to do." Then he delivers the coup de grace calling feminists "desperate women who are unfulfilled and who have turned their backs on God."

Now, this reads as hyperbole, but when you hear it in Falwell's church it takes on an arresting power. Falwell's sermons are like that. They are devastatingly candid: Abortion is "baby killing," Senator Chris Dodd is a "socialist," feminists are "to the left of Andropov." Falwell is a down-to-earth preacher with an uncanny ability to evoke deep longings, loves, and fears even in the most sophisticated people. He uses symbols—the flag, the family—very effectively. He organizes his material for easy comprehension—for example, "Five Ways to Pray" or "Three Sins of America" that we must correct. All his sermons are comprehensive on the issues. Every one blasts abortion and pornography and includes jokes about homosexuals and calls for a return to godly living.

At the end of the sermon, which lasts a half hour or so, there is silence in the church. Even for outsiders, the experience is rousing and cathartic. You begin to see how deeply affected people are about things like abortion and homosexual "rights." Interestingly, even in church Falwell's appeal is less theological than moral-political. The loudest "Amens" are evoked by political statements. People seem most disturbed by court decisions and the media and the way leaders behave, rather than because not enough people are reading the Bible, although they generally feel these things are closely related. Falwell's television crew, I am told, edits his sermon carefully, so that it is more neatly packaged, if somewhat less moving when it flashes across the screen. Somehow his unedited sermons kindle emotions most of all because like Ronald Reagan, Falwell is a brilliant ad-libber whose strongest asset is that he shoots from the hip and usually aims well.

Cal Thomas, the burly vice-president of moral Majority calls Falwell "basically a country preacher." He feels that in the past "There were things that could have been said differently" but sees Falwell as more sophisticated now. "There's a tendency among fundamentalist preachers to go after the big Amen," Thomas explains. "Jerry's getting over that temptation." That is not to say that Falwell has become more liberal. Thomas is very quick to observe that Falwell "won't compromise his beliefs."

Falwell is happy to be where he is, with the cameras rolling whenever he turns, but he is also conscious of duties undone at this local church, where the people need him and where the rewards for service are instantaneous. "One thing about politics," Falwell once told me, "is that you're not always sure you're doing the right thing."

Cal Thomas feels that this ambivalence makes Falwell careless about his fame. "He would rather throw it away in a moment than compromise himself. That's because he has an alternative—possibly a better alternative. Tomorrow if Moral Majority dried up, it the TV show went bankrupt, Jerry would be just as content to go back to being full-time pastor of Thomas Road Church."

Indeed, there is something touching about Falwell's performance as pastor at Thomas Road. After the sermon and the closing hymns, he makes the final announcements—there will be a seminary picnic at Treasure Island; tickets to the LCA basketball game will be available at the church office; etc. He reads off the names of church member moving away or getting married, recalling anecdotes about them so people laugh with cognition. He asks his people to pray for pastor B.R. Lakin, a mentor who is now ailing, and for a baby born to two church members. ("The parents are doing fine, expected to recover.") He asks visiting pastors from faraway fundamentalist churches to come up to the podium and say hello and advertises for a church youth who is selling his bicycle, a family who needs a house sitter, and a young man back from military service who needs a job.

At the same time Falwell can be a shameless name dropper. "I talked to Menachem Begin on the phone yesterday," he tells his amazed audience. "We discussed the Lebanese situation. He wanted me to understand that the P.L.O. are terrorists, and he is only doing what he has to. I told him, Mr. Begin, I only pray that you will not leave Lebanon until you have finished the job. Christian people are praying for the success of your efforts."

Falwell's people do not seem to mind his success. They are honored to be in a church where the preacher is being taped all the time. They look for their faces on television. To his people Falwell is the kid next door who made it big. For all his success, he manages to stay humble, so his people identify with him. They are not frequent movie-goers, so he is their star. Yet, Falwell does not consider himself a celebrity, only an instrument in God's hand.

Several local pastors in Lynchburg have recently come out against Falwell. One of these is the Reverend John Killinger of the First Presbyterian church in Lynchburg. Killinger is a tall, distinguished-looing fellow who looks like an Ivy League professor. Last year Mr. Killinger preached a sermon charging Falwell with rapacity and self-aggrandizement. If Christ appeared on "The Old Time Gospel Hour," according to Killinger, He would say to Falwell, "you appear to be very religious before your TV audience. But inside you are rapacious, unconverted wolves, seeking only a greater share of the evangelical TV market, without really caring about the sheep you devour."

Killinger told me that the population of Lynchburg would probably split fifty-fifty for or against Falwell. Killinger believes that one reason Lynchburg residents don't openly speak out against Falwell is economic. The Falwell ministries and Moral Majority bring in millions in revenue to the city. "Many people are afraid of Lynchburg being called Falwell city, and so on," Killinger says. "But they have a financial stake in Falwell; this city does."

Killinger says his attacks on Falwell don't hurt him because his own appeal is to a different kind of person, the man or woman whom he sees as Lynchburg's intelligentsia. While conceding that Falwell's people are "basically good," Killinger feels that, because of their lack of education, they are vulnerable to harangue— "They are more susceptible to doctrinaire statements," he also thinks that the poor, more than the rich, are obsessed with personal morality."For them sex, drugs, and rock-and-roll are the real mortal sins."

Killinger sees his own congregation as above moralism. His people don't share what he calls the "unbudging truths," "intolerance," "dogmatism," and "simplistic statements" of Falwell. They are not sexually repressed, as are Falwell's people. They do not, like Thomas Road members, "love to be victimized by a lawless and godless society." Rather, they understand that they are part of that society. "The church is not the institution that ought to be shoring up public morality. Jesus ate with sinners and was condemned as a glutton and a wine-drinker." Killinger believes that the Church should deal exclusively with "grace," noting that "In the Bible, moralism is always balanced by God's grace." I learned later that many of Killinger's members support Falwell financially, and they feel Killinger's attacks on Falwell stem from sheer jealousy.

I asked Killinger why he accused Falwell of violating the principle of separation of church and state, given that the World Council of Churches, William Sloane Coffin, Martin Luther King, and the Berrigan brothers were actively involved in political activity. Killinger maintained that their participation was justified "They're calling for justice for the poor." He added that "That is why they get easily identified with communism." On the other hand, "Falwell is identified with capitalism." And "it is easy to see which view is religious."

I asked, "If Falwell's view is not religious, then how can he violate edicts against separation of church and state? Secondly, are you saying that communism is more religious than capitalism?"

No, Reverend Killinger said hastily. "Being identified with the poor is." He declined to comment further on my first question. He declared his conviction that Falwell is being "manipulated by the financial wizards of the far Right," which makes his religion suspect, whether or not it is a constitutional violation.

Two other ordained ministers, William Goodman and Jim Price, are also vociferous critics of Falwell. The two, who teach at Lynchburg college, have written a critical biography of Falwell and an article in *Penthouse* alleging an atmosphere of repression in Lynchburg because of Falwell's presence. "Life down home with Jerry Falwell can be less than comfortable, particularly for those of who dare to raise questions about his myopic theology." Goodman and Price don't pretend to be objective critics of Falwell. In their book they admit that most articles and books written about Falwell are viciously negative, but see them as "a healthy antidote" to Falwell's "self-serving doses of public relations material." Price and Goodman keep files on Falwell and his top aides. They tape everything Falwell says, from his Sunday broadcast to statements at rallies. This irritates Falwell, who blasts them from the pulpit, invariably (and probably willfully) getting their names wrong. But Price and Goodman don't mind; they're delighted with the mention.

When I spoke with Goodman, he had brought along a number of press clippings from his archives. Some of these were meant to show *The Daily News and Advance,* the local newspaper, as subservient to Falwell. Several clippings went back as far as the 1950s. Admittedly Falwell had changed some of his positions since the fifties, Goodman said, citing Falwell's turnabout on segregation, "but the past cannot go away." Goodman believes that "Falwell has been very insensitive to the pluralism of American society. Now that he wants to move into the mainstream he's saddled with baggage from the past." Since, Falwell talked about Senator Ted Kennedy's past—notably Chappaquiddick—Falwell's own past could fairly be mined for evidence of extremism, according to Goodman.

Goodman sees Falwell as schizophrenic—on the one hand "an ordinary personable guy" and on the other a "TV personality." Was this a contradiction, I asked, or merely Goodman's own conviction that no personable guy could have the views Falwell did. No it wasn't, Goodman said. He wished Falwell would either show his true fundamentalist stripe or "greater flexibility" in his positions. He feels Falwell is fence-sitting; that Falwell cannot make up his mind whether he wants to be a hard-core separatist or a coalition-builder. Goodman's own view is that "Falwell is definitely moving in the direction of Billy Graham." He expressed resentment that Falwell is taking many fundamentalists with him. This Goodman sees as deceitful, because, after all, it is the separatists who are in the true fundamentalist tradition. Goodman told me he feels that Falwell's reading of the Bible is arbitrary and eclectic. In his *Penthouse* article he went much further, claiming that Falwell's Scriptural interpretations contained "definite overtones of megalomania and a distinct flavor of fascism."

I decided to drop in on Reverend Falwell at his home. Winding his cab up to Falwell's driveway the taxi-driver turned to me and said, "that Reverend lives it up quite, don't he?"

I said the house was very nice; I wouldn't mind living there.

"Nor me, man," the driver said. "How come you get to see Falwell?"

I shrugged. "I'm writing a manuscript. What do you think about him?"

The driver, who was black, said, "Don't really know. There's folks that say he don't like niggers. But I've heard different, too. I guess he's not much different than the other preachers around here, only he's on TV."

I wondered aloud whether people in Lynchburg resent Falwell's house, surrounded as it is by sensitized fence.

"Naw, there's better houses in town. But there's people that worry about him mixin' the gospel with politics, you know."

I said I knew.

"Three dollars," the cab driver said.

I slung my bag across my shoulder and walked to the gate. A security guard opened it. I gave my name and said I had an appointment.

Falwell's home is a two-story structure with sloping roof, an ornate front door with brass knockers, and a patio projecting on the side leading to the pool The house was purchased for the ministry in 1979 by Claude Brown of Brown Transport. Falwell does not own it. He says guard and fence are necessary for protection—not so much of himself as for his wife and children. "I'm gone most of the time."

Falwell has received some chilling threats. Most are crank letters. However, in September 1983 an anonymous caller detailed to the Lynchburg police the precise clothing and movement of Falwell's wife and children; then threatened their lives. The FBI was immediately called in. By and large Falwell is not intimidated by threats. He takes the view that "God's man is indestructible. God will take care of him until He is finished with him."

The Falwell house is nicely decorated. The walls are decked with family portraits; the living room has an enormous picture of Falwell standing, Bible under arm, in front of Thomas Road Church.

Falwell told me that Brown purchased the house for $160,000 and then spent additional money on renovation. We sat in the living room.

I asked Falwell to clarify his position on abortion. For all his talk about the "politics of convenience," did he think it was an easy decision for a woman to have an abortion.

He looked at me, surprised. "It never is, except in rare cases. When you're talking about life a thousand miles away—in Afghanistan, for example—it's one thing, but when you're talking about life within you, life you helped create, it is very rare for a human being not to care. That is why almost always you can sit down with a woman and she understands why you are asking her to have that baby, because she knows it is life within her. Because of this, even if we get objective or neutral counselors out there, we could stop most of the abortions." Then unable to resist a jibe, "Unfortunately Planned Parenthood and the abortion clinics recommend abortion first, even before they get the name of the person they are counseling—in my opinion."

I asked Falwell what he was doing for unwed mothers, or what he proposed. He pointed to his Save-a-Baby ministry, started a year ago when he purchased the Florence Crittenden home in Lynchburg. The organization takes in unwed mothers from across the country. When Falwell announced the program on his televison show hundreds of viewers wrote letters of support, some telling of their abortion experience. The pregnant women who participate in the Save-a-Baby program come voluntarily. They are brought to Lynchburg at Falwell's expense, live free at the home, and deliver the child away from small-town friends and relatives. Falwell concedes that fundamentalists can be "excessively judgmental" and that small towns are "places where those judgments circulate very fast." But he stresses that his Save-a-Baby ministry has been successful, helping 1,400 women so far. Counseling, education, personal assistance, and adoption assistance are provided by the ministry. If an unwed Lynchburg girl gets pregnant—and some do, even at Falwell's school and church—he says he will arrrange, at her request, to have her sent to a sister church in another state where she can get counseling, attend school or work, and deliver the baby in relative quietude.

David Fleming, the director of Falwell's Save-a-Baby ministry, admits that not all pregnant women who dial his hotline choose to deliver. "But of those who contact us, eighty-five percent changed their mind about abortion when they received information about fetal development." The ministry also is a licensed adoption agency.

I asked Falwell about his support for anti-abortion legislation that makes exceptions for women who get pregnant as a result of rape or incest. Falwell announced his backing for such legislation in a controversial article he wrote in the March 1983 issue of *Fundamentalist Journal.* The article, titled "A Pragmatic Proposal," was blasted by some fundamentalists because it implied that Falwell was selling out. If abortion was murder, the critics said, how could Falwell let even raped women slaughter their infants? That would add homicide to the existing catastrophe of rape. Falwell told me that he does not personally favor abortion even in case of rape or incest, but "realistically, we are never going to prohibit abortion in this country unless those exceptions are made. That is why he opposes a Human Life Amendment, which makes no exceptions.

I pointed out to Falwell that his "pragmatic proposal" seemed to epitomize a general political realism that accommodated his principles to real possibilities.

Falwell admitted that today he is more realistic, more pragmatic, and, yes more moderate than he was a few years ago. In fact, he astonished many when he said on "Meet the Press" that he was "more sensitive now to the pluralism of our society." In the April 1983 issue of *Fundamentalist Journal* Falwell wrote an article entitled "Moderation: A Biblical Command," which noted that "Every Christian has an obligation to be moderate."

I asked Falwell whether fundamentalists were not often anti-Catholic and anti-Semitic. He acknowledged that fundamentalists have traditionally been anti-Catholic, "although that is changing." Anti-Semitic? "No more than other groups." Then he pointed to the Catholic Church's opposition to abortion. "It is to the great credit of the Catholic Church that they fought the battle single-handedly on abortion." But now, he says, "reinforcements have arrived." He is a staunch admirer of Pope John Paul II. "I say about John Paul II what I say about Ronald Reagan: They are the greatest in my lifetime. He spoke with delight of the Pope's unflinching courage. "The Pope came to America, and the media tried to put words in his mouth. But he addressed abortion, homosexuality, and the ordination of women here just as he does at home. He didn't cut any corner regardless of whether people agreed with him or not. He told it the way its was; he couldn't care less what Cronkite thought of him."

While loving Catholic people, Falwell has major doctrinal differences. "Papal infallibility would be a problem, because you would be equating the Pope with Christ." I asked Falwell whether he understood infallibility to mean that the Pope does not sin. He said yes. I pointed out that infallibility is a theological concept. He became uneasy but countered, "There are many Catholics who believe what I just said." Then he made amends. "I know many Catholic priests who are born again and who preach the same message I do," he said. "I receive mail from them and they tell me this."

Falwell pointed to his friendship with Begin and his consistent and vigorous support of Israel to show that he was not anti-Semitic. "Israel stands as a shining testimony to the faithfulness of God," he said. He lamented that he had lost some support from evangelicals, Catholics, and others because of his unconditional support for Jews and Israel. As Gabriel Fackre wrote in *The Religious Right and Christian Faith*, "some who strongly agree on many other matters with the Religious Right feel particularly betrayed by the latter's friendly relations with Jews and with the state of Israel." Falwell has visited Israel several times. A study commissioned by the American Jewish Committee in October 1980 concluded that Falwell and the Christian Right were *not* anti-Semitic. "This latter-day populist movement has no discernible anti-Semitic element." Instead, "The religious right potentially is a strong American ally of the Jewish state."

We turned to the issue of homosexuality. Falwell is famous for the quotation, "God created Adam and Eve, not Adam and Steve." He uses passages from Leviticus to justify his position on homosexuality, which he regards as "moral perversion." At a speech in Florida he went further; calling homosexuality "reprobate." He feels homosexuality is learned—and can be unlearned. At the same time, he supports full civil rights for homosexuals, including housing and jobs. He reaffirmed his opposition to affirmative action for homosexuals. He defends the distinction by pointing out that "I have talked to numerous men and women who used to be homosexual. But I have never met a former black."

Falwell is convinced that homosexuality is a choice, not an innate trait. He says being born again is a sure antidote to homosexuality and is willing to produce erstwhile homosexuals in evidence Falwell regrets incidents of violence against homosexuals but refuses to abandon his strident rehetoric. When Virginia Appuzzo, executive director of the Fund for Human Dignity, a homosexual organization, accused Falwell of "declaring war on homosexuals" and called for more understanding, Falwell replied, "The Bible tells me homosexuality is wrong. I cannot help people unless I tell them it is wrong. When I'm dealing with an alcoholic, for example, I cannot say, this is a nice habit you have, but I can teach you to control it."

I told Falwell that while I understood that he had four hundred black members in his church, but there was nevertheless a perception that Thomas Road was racist. Falwell said, "I just don't know what to say. Why don't you talk to Hiram Crawford?"

Crawford is the black pastor who heads Moral Majority in Chicago. He is an ardent Falwell supporter. When I asked him whether he knew that Falwell had been a segregationist, Crawford said, "I'm not so much interested in where a man was twenty-five years ago as where he is today."

Falwell has spoken in the Watts ghetto and on the South Side of Chicago, courtesy of black preachers like Crawford. He has drawn strong support from those areas. Blacks are socially very conservative; Falwell points out. A survey by Shupe and Stacey showed that 73 percent of minorities, as opposed to 52 percent of whites, are against abortion. And 77 percent, as opposed to 67 percent of whites, are opposed to ERA. Futhermore, 74 percent, against 62 percent of whites, do not believe in evolution; 83 percent of minorities favor school prayer; 81 percent oppose sex education in schools. "Minorities are more in agreement with Moral Majority in terms of specific issues than are the white respondents, yet only two percent of our minority sample sup- the liberal establishment, who recruit black support but work against black interest.

In order to help the minority poor in Lynchburg, Falwell started a "Family Center" two years ago. There 1350 poor familes who are not Thomas Road members collect free clothing and groceries. Admittedly, this is a small effort. But Falwell has also announced an "Inner City Ministry" for his and other fundmentalist churches. The plan, developed by E.V. Hill, a black California preacher, calls for suburban churches to "adopt" a minority inner city church and to provide supportive money, personnel, and training. "We work under the direction of inner city ministers," Falwell explains. "The approach will be spiritual, employment-oriented, medical. All the needs of the church will be taken care of." He believes "the climate is right in America for the churches to once again seize the opportunity and responsibility that has always been ours. We *are* our brothers' and sisters' keeper."

But this alternative, or supplement to welfare programs has not been well received by the civil rights establishment. When Falwell announced his urban ministry for the underprivileged, Jack Gravely, president of the Virginia NAACP, blasted the move as a "Madison Avenue Sham."

13

Accusations of Apostasy

Jerry Falwell's involvement in the 1980 election stirred up one group that he may not have expected to provoke—a faction of fundamentalists under the leadership of Bob Jones, whose Bob Jones University was recently involved in a fracas with the Internal Revenue Service over tax exemption. When Bob Jones called Jerry Falwell "the most dangerous man in America," liberals cheered confusedly. That was what they had been saying. But they had no inkling why Jones—who visited Thomas Road Church in 1971; whose university graduated Pierre Guillermin, president of Falwell's Liberty Baptist College, and Ron Godwin, vice-president of Moral Majority—would condemn a fellow fundamentalist like Falwell. Jones did not stop at calling Falwell dangerous. He also accused him of "spiritual betrayal" and asked him to "quit compromising...and get back to God." In his magazine, *Faith for the Family*, Jones insisted that "disobedient preachers (like Falwell) are to a large degree responsible for the moral decay of America" because "they preach morality, but live disobediently." Jones asked fundamentalist to "turn their back on the Moral Majority and seek the soul-satisfying contentment of being a scriptural minority."

In June 1980, primarily through Jones's influence, the Fundamentalist Baptist Fellowship (FBF) passed a resolution condemning the "subtle ecumenicity" of Moral Majority; which includes Jews, Catholics, and Mormons. And the August 1983 World Congress on Fundamentalism, meeting at Bob Jones University in Greenville, South Carolina, passed several resolutions against the Moral Majority. Said Jones cryptically, "Moral Majority, if it achieves its goal in measure, will make this nation harder to evangelize."

There is a major split developing in American fundamentalism, and Bob Jones and Jerry Falwell are likely to be heading rival factions. Jones is on the offensive, probably because Jerry Falwell is stealing his constituency from him. For years fundamentalists quietly followed Jones and his predecessors. From the outset, Falwell himself accepted the tenets of Jones and company regarding the expression of his faith. But now he is separating himself from Jones, mapping out a new road for American fundamentalism, a road that Jones has no intention of taking. Falwell claims his is the only road for fundamentalists. Bob Jones, he says, is on a "suicide course" that can only lead to "total oblivion."

Fundamentalists across the country are only just aware of the impending schism. But pretty soon the various fundamentalist organizations—Baptist Bible Fellowship, World Baptist Fellowship, Grace Bretheren, Southwide Baptist Fellowship, Orthodox Presbyterina Church—will have to take sides and go either Falwell's way or Jones's way. (They are presently resisting making the choice.) The groups represent the 110,000 fundamentalist churches in this country, with perhaps 20 million members. The fundamentalist schools, too— Baptist Bible College, Tennessee Temple University, Cedarville College, Moody Bible Institute—will have to decide whether to take direction from Falwell or Jones.

The issue here concerns the scriptural command to "be in the world but not of it." How is that to be interpreted?

Bob Jones and his followers have taken their interpretation of separation from the world to great lengths. When they see Jerry Falwell having breakfast with a charismatic Christian, Catholic, or Jew, they are appalled. Falwell cannot do that and be one of them—he cannot be a legitimate fundamentalist. Students at Bob Jones University are not even allowed to leave campus for fear of being polluted by worldly influences. "Some fundamentalists are trying to out fundamental other fundamentalists," charges Cal Thomas. But Jones is deadly serious about being separate from the world. He realizes such a position puts him in the minority, but it doesn't bother him. Unlike Falwell, he says, he doesn't want power. Besides, the Bible predicts that only a few will be obedient to God.

The core of Jones's objection is that Falwell's engaging in political action undermines chances for evangelization. Falwell's political work, which in itself Jones has no quarrel with, is akin to "polishing brass on a sinking ship," as Dwight Moody once put it. It is futile. It does not solve many problems yet it creates the *impression* that no further solutions are required. Jones charges not only that good works are irrelevant to gospel preaching, but that they are positively detrimental to evangelism because, alas, they alter the atmosphere of sin that steers people to salvation. According to Jones, "Moral sinners are not the ones who turn to Christ for his saving grace. Lucifer did not show his rebellion to God in heaven by promoting abortion clinics, women's lib, pornography, distilleries, houses of prostitution, gambling casinos, etc. He thought his perfection entitles him to have a throne higher than God's throne. He liked the morality that was there, but he wanted to be the one worshipped. Moral self-righteousness is the devil's thing and leads men to the devil, not to God."

Jones feels that Falwell's concern with moral regeneration is too this-worldly. It addresses the problems of the here and now while ignoring the plight of man's eternal soul. He fears that people who live righteously as Falwell asked them to will not feel that they must be justified by faith, as Protestants should. Rather, they will fall into the "Catholic" error of expecting salvation as payment for good works. The Fundamental Baptist Fellowship, which in June 1980 passed a resolution criticizing Moral Majority and Falwell, explained, "We believe that the saving of America's morals is a mere cosmetic treatment of the deeper problem of sin, that correcting the nation's morals gives the false impression that America's ills would be solved if her morality were reformed, that moral reformation is not the mission of the Church but instead the preaching of the saving grace of Christ." This is what prompted Jones to write in *Faith for the Family*, "[Moral Majority] works against the purpose of God, not for it."

Jerry Falwell laughs when confronted with these criticisms, which are more serious than they appear to the non fundamentalist. But he is aware of the force of Jones's argument, particularly because he is keen to retain his fundamentalist credentials. In the September 1982 issue of *Fundamentalist Journal* he wrote, "I am a fundamentalist by doctrine, by conviction and by practice."

Jones clearly adheres to the tradition of American fundamentalism as expressed since the early part of this century. It is Falwell who is the renegade. In fact, as late as 1965 Falwell, too, believed the same things Jones does about political action. In a sermon entitled "Ministers and

Marches," he counseled preachers to stay out of politics. He was talking to civil rights activists, of course, and some feel that he objected
primarily to the politics of the involved churchmen. But in fact his objection was theological, and there is no evidence that it was insincere.
In "Ministers and Marches" Falwell said many positive things about
the civil rights movement, but nevertheless he counseled restraint, because "nowhere in the Bible are we commissioned to reform the externals. We are not told to wage wars against bootleggers, liquor stores,
gamblers, murderers, prostitutes, racketeers, prejudiced persons or institutions, or any other existing evil as such." This reads just like Jones's injunction. But Falwell has since changed his position and is
applying muscle and persuasion to get other fundamentalists to do the
same.

Falwell says, "Until very recently I believed, like Bob Jones, that
fundamentalists should treat politics like the devil." But the devil,
whom Falwell jokingly calls "the first liberal," has politicized everything. Since politics has invaded even the most private aspects of our
being, it is no longer possible to stay out of politics. Falwell's point is
that the state has invaded the domain of the church, which he thinks
is a violation of the edict of separation of church and state. "Separation of church and state is intended to restrict the power of the state,
not of the church. It is meant to protect the church from the state."
And since the ACLU isn't affirming church sovereignty from state
control, Falwell feels that his people must assert their own rights
through political action.

Until recently, Falwell says, citing author Edward Row's *Saving
America*, "Many of those who profess faith in God were living as if
God were dead." They stayed out of politics, even though their faith
was being politically invaded. Falwell also believes that Christians
should be involved in political reform in order to improve their society. "We have been irresponsible as Christian citizens," he maintains.
"For too many years we sat back, as if waiting for apostasy to take over
at any moment, and nearly let our country destroy itself because of in-
ward decay." He admitted to me that "if politics becomes our priority,
it is a violation. Our number one purpose is a spiritual one. But we also
have a responsibility to society, to render unto Caesar the things that
are his."

I told Falwell I could understand his involvement in issues like abortion and school prayer. If he saw the state invading the domain of the
church, surely he was entitled to make a stand. But what about national defense and the economy? Surely the Panama Canal treaty and

El Salvador weren't moral issues? But they were, said Falwell. "The Bible says that a husband and a father who does not protect his household is worse than an infidel. I'd like to extend that and say that a government which does not protect its citizens is worse than an infidel." The issue, according to him, is "Will we defend ourselves as a free society against evil and totalitarianism?" For him defense is, in a sense, the ultimate moral issue, because failure in this area renders all moral issues moot. "If we lose our freedom tomorrow, we cannot talk about abortion and pornography," Falwell said. "People in the Soviet Union cannot stand in Red Square and protest about anything. Well, they can do it once. . . ."

One argument Falwell has used to lure fundamentalists into politics is that God has blessed America in a special way that confers divine responsibility upon her citizens as they engage in political discussion. "Let God give America the right to bless the world," he says, arguing in favor of aid to indigent countries. (This is one of his several positions outside the Republican party line.) Falwell also praises America's three interlocking freedoms—freedom of the press, economic freedom, and freedom of religion—as divinely sanctioned.

Falwell's view of America has drawn savage criticism from the liberal clergy, especially form those who view the role of religion as breaking down the barriers of nations setting up global egalitarianism. The barrages fired at him by social gospel advocates who charge him with religious jingoism, are rather ironic, because the first exponents of social gospel theology, such as Walter Rauschenbusch, also viewed America as God's chosen nation. In fact, this was at the heart of Rauschenbusch's social gospel: Since America is a select nation, it should strive to help other countries attain similar divine bounty. Modern social gospel advocates, however, see America as working against a divine plan to bring about global harmony, not for it.

Falwell has qualified his view of America as divinely ordained, however, because it causes him theological problems. How can he believe this and also that Israel remains God's country, awaiting final liberation in the Second Advent? If Israel remains a chosen nation, can America be one also? Can there be two chosen nations? Falwell explains himself thus; "I am not proposing that America is the kingdom of God. It is not. We have as wicked a nation, if not more so , than other nations in the world. I am not saying that America has a special corner on God's blessings. That is not true. For God is no respecter of persons. But I am saying that in the past two centuries in human history, God has raised up a nation, an instrument, a tool, blessed that instrument and called it his own."

This does not clarify things very much. Of course Americans sin. But so do Jews. Does that make Israel any less God's chosen nation? What is America's status *vis a vis* Israel in the eyes of God? Falwell does not explain this. He takes a somewhat romantic view of America's emergence as a nation. Prudent as the Founding Fathers proved to be, it seems an exaggeration to attribute their writings to divine writ. Perhaps Falwell's critics have a point about his taking patriotism too far.

Falwell is reluctant to talk about the emerging split in fundamentalism. He appears to be sorry that he called some miltant fundamentalists a "lunatic fringe." "I don't mean these people don't have minds or anything like that," he says. "But there is that segment of fundamentalism headed up by Bob Jones and a few lesser lights that way back chose to become the only bastion of truth in the world. Only those who live by their rules are fundamentalists. They have added to the word of God. So today the liberals take away from the word of God, and the fundamentalists add to the word of God."

Falwell likens Bob Jones to the preacher in *Tom Sawyer* who "dealt in limitless fire and brimstone and thinned the predestined elect down to a company so small as to be hardly worth saving." Falwell believes that "a generation from now, that segment of fundamentalism will either be more moderate or be nonexistent or held in disdain by believers and nonbelievers."

Naturally he is irritated that Bob Jones keeps passing resolutions against him. But he does not want to take on Jones on the issue of religion and politics, because Jones is in the tradition. Falwell could point to the grossness of social evils, which cry for Christian reform, Jones would triumphantly reply that the epidemic of evil only makes things ripe for conversion and is also a sign that Christ's return is imminent. Jones could also accuse Falwell, as he has, of being myopically concerned with the present and not with eternity. To this Falwell could reply in words much like those of Cal Thomas—"You know Christ is coming soon, but you're supposed to work in the meantime." Jones would counter this by arguing that political action reflects lack of faith in the imminent Second Coming and also that the interim work that is required is evangelization, not social action.

The debate could go on and on. Falwell is somewhat on the defensive when it comes to fundamentalist doctrine here, so he prefers to attack Jones on a different level—"legalism." Legalism refers to the myriad rules and regulations that govern the lives of ultrafundamentalists. In the words of the Reverend Truman Dollar, pastor of Kansas City Baptist Temple, "It is unfortunate and painful to admit, but some modern fundamentalists have actually become the successors of the Scribes." Bob Jones may not be concerned about the immorality of others, but he is eagle-eyed when it comes to the behavior of his own people. It is virtually impossible to have even a minor vice—including association with persons Jones dosen't like—and be a member of an ultrafundamentalist church. There is even an implicit dress code. If you wear bell bottoms, sideburns, or a beard, you might find a negative reaction in some of these churches. Falwell protests, "There is no verse in the Bible against wearing a beard. It is a man's relationship with God that is of consequence." He also impugns the unforgiving nature of those fundamentalists who erect legalistic rules and then punish church members who, despite good intentions, slip up. This, he says, ignores the facts of original sin and the saving grace of Christ.

So we have parallel accusations. Jones says Falwell, by engaging in political activism, ignores the transcendant nature of sin and justification by faith alone, not works. Falwell says that it is Jones who, by concentrating on myriad rules of behavior, ignores the transcendant nature of sin and justification by faith alone, not works. Falwell decries the "rigid, separatist view" that holds "we should not live in the world but in a shell." Unlike Jones, Falwell interprets the theological concept of "separation" to mean not total detachment from the secular world but, in his words, "a refusal to be seduced into the sins of the world." He argues, "The Bible teaches that we should be the salt of the earth. Salt is a preservative. It keeps meat from going bad. So Christians must be a force for good, for preservation." The obligation to be political stems not just from citizenship in a democracy, but also, for Christians, from divine mandates. So now we have not a divine right of kings, but the divine obligation of subjects.

Falwell also maintains that the isolationist tendencies of the ultrafundamentalists which cause them to demand "secondary separation" of their people is self-destructive. They withdraw fellowship from persons who associate with persons with whom they have differences. While Liberty Baptist College has very strict rules regarding personal behavior, they do not subject their people to draconian rules and operate on a basis of fear. Falwell says the Liberty rules are designed to teach discipline, not produce a sense of self-righteousness.

Falwell defends his rules: "We have nothing against Disney movies, of course, but we don't like to support Hollywood." It's all a question of proportion, he says. "Of course the Bible asks us to live moral lives, and requires parents and schools to impose rules on students." But human nature is frail, and too many rules and unreasonable rules put the law into disrepute. "Plato said that, too," Falwell tells me. He is keen to cite sources like Plato and Burke even in arcane theological disputes. It is a sign of how far he's come from Jones and others, who would regard these philosophers as nothing but heretics and unbelievers.

According to Falwell, the weakness of extreme legalism is not just that it takes attention away from faith and the recognition of man's sinful nature that It also tends to make fundamentalists judgmental. "I am guilty of this sometimes," he admits. "I do not mean that I should compromise my views. But sometimes I am too tough on people. I condemn them out of proportion to their sin." He quotes Scripture: "The letter killeth, but the spirit giveth life." "Let he who is without sin cast the first stone." What about passages that clearly call for righteous living? Falwell says, "You know the law; you know the truth, But if it isn't mixed with the compassion of God, with the spirit of God, it can be very judgmental and vindictive." Has he himself been judgmental and vindictive? "I hate to admit it, but yes, sometimes." It's a matter of establishing a balance. "If you have a double portion of compassion and don't know the law, you can be very permissive, and both are wrong. Somewhere in between lies the ideal, that mixture of firmness and compassion." He adds, "The fundamentalist church in America today is becoming aware of reality. They are learning to hate sin but love the sinner, to wrap their arms around people in their own groups who have fallen, rather than following the old philosophy of shooting their own wounded."

He concedes the fact of differences between him and Jones. He also admits that there is a serious split, although they have not drawn attention in the national media, which is oblivious to these things. As for the political ramifications, Falwell is not worried. He has been successful so far in drawing fundamentalists out of political apathy and feels he will continue to be successful.

Bob Jones is not as articulate and well known as Falwell. "Jerry is the best-known fundamentalist since William Jennings Bryan," one Fundamentalist told me. "Fundamentalists have been outside the mainline culture, so when they see someone like Falwell recognized by the other Protestants and by the secular media, they are impressed by it. They listen to the man." Falwell's supporters are convinced that it is envy of Falwell's success that has provoked anger from Bob Jones and others. Comments B.R. Lakin, the venerable Florida evangelist, "They can't tree the 'coon, so they shoot the dog who can."

Falwell's organization is much richer than Jones and uses his considerable resources to upstage his theological opponent. He imports influential fundamentalist pastors to his college to speak. He holds large conferences and brings luminaries like George Bush and Ted Kennedy to the LBC campus. He travels across the country to little fundamentalist churches and delivers an unadulterated gospel message that instantly belies Jones's frenzied accusations of heterodoxy. Observers of the developing rift between Falwell and Jones say that it should be a short battle, which Falwell should easily win.

The virulent attacks on Falwell from Bob Jones and others like him bring to mind another figure who started as their idol but ended up receiving their hate mail—Billy Graham. Now Graham is the best-known evangelist in the world, having spoken before an estimated 900 million people. Falwell, a regional preacher only recently gone national, enjoys a smaller constituency, although it is more loyal than Graham's. Even so, in April 1982 Newsweek speculated that Falwell was likely to succeed Graham. Many liberal evangelicals dispute that, and the speculation has made Falwell nervous. "I am not the next Billy Graham," he told me.

Billy Graham started out in the forties as a fiery fundamentalist and then turned into a tame evangelical. In 1949, he said, "Communism is inspired, directed, and motivated by the devil himself." The next year he thundered, "America is at a crossroads. Will we turn to the left-wingers and atheists, or will we turn to the right and embrace the cross?" He was candid about both the evils of communism and his affection for Republican politicians. He also preached that "Salvation comes by Jesus Christ alone, and none can enter the kingdom of heaven except in Christ's name." In other words, he believed that Jews, Hindus, and Moslems who did not call on Christ were damned.

But Graham has moderated since—a great deal, in fact. He made a highly publicized trip to the Soviet Union in early 1983, after which he implied that there was no religious persecution there. And since 1950 Graham has been drifting into ecumenism; he no longer seems to hold that only born-again Christians go to heaven. To the chagrin and horror of fundamentalists, he is frequently seen at prayer meetings with Catholics and Jews, and he has powerful political and religious friends of different beliefs and origins. Recently he told Parade magazine, "I have lost some of the rigidity I once had. I've come to understand that there are no simplistic answers to the exceedingly complex problems we face as a country—and as a planet." Graham is not only dabbling in the anti-nuclear movement, he has also lost some of his old evangelical zeal. Now he spends a good deal of his time condemning "simplistic" solutions and assuring his audience that the world is "complex."

Falwell, unlike Graham, has not moved to the left theologically since the sixties. He has, however, become far more loving and tolerant. It is unclear whether moving out of religious exclusivity and entering politics,' even right-wing politics, constitutes leftist drifting, although Bob Jones and company certainly believe it does. Certainly Falwell has become more moderate politically since he started out. He has become more gracious—he is more accepting of Roman Catholics and orthodox Jews. It appears that his political attachment to these people—because they share a moral program for America—makes them theological allies, too, though Falwell denies that his association with Catholics and Jews is anything more than political. However, Falwell told me that he very much respects the moral stand being taken by John Paul II, and he also reveres (that is not too strong a word) Menachem Begin, who he felt was courageous and correct in his drive against the Palestine Liberation Organization in Lebanon. Fundamentalists who follow Jones wonder whether it is possible for a true fundamentalist to have such strong ties to nonbelievers. They note that Billy Graham, too, began with political and personal associations with unbelievers; theological "compromise" came later.

However it is a mistake to misinterpret Falwell's graciousness as weakness. He appears to be unshakeable on his doctrinal positions. He has a thorough and deep understanding of what he believes and why he believes it. But his friends say that he is much less outspoken in his denunciations of other religious denominations than when he was younger. In this respect, Falwell has softened theologically.

Falwell has also softened politically. His early Moral Majority fundraisers stuck to a conservative hard line—"Liberate the Soviet bloc!" "Stop abortion and homosexuality!" Now Falwell is much more temperate. He concedes that it is impossible to eradicate communism. The best we can do, he told me, is "keep the free world free." He opposes U.S. efforts to achieve nuclear superiority because he regards that concept as meaningless by now. Falwell does not believe that homosexuality should meet with state sanction, but homosexuals should be allowed to teach in schools "as long as they do not promote their lifestyle as normal and healthy." Perhaps because of charges of censorship which have stung, Falwell has also softened his views on censorship. He often condemns books as "immoral" but insists, in the same breath, that they have a constitutional right to be distributed.

I asked Falwell if ten years from now we could expect *him* to take a trip to the Soviet Union and then challenge reports of religious persecution there. He laughed. "Billy Graham is a friend, and I admire his great success. But Billy made some very serious tactical errors. Back in the early days of his ministry, he decided that in order to effectively evangelize the world, he would need to invite to his meetings unbelieving pastors—pastors who did not accept the deity of Christ, the infallibility of Scripture, and so on. The problem is that Graham gave his tacit endorsement to liberal Christianity. So today he finds himself unable to take a position on Marxist-Leninism; he has to be very careful about what he says on Central America. Now, with his Third World people, with his evangelist friends in Amsterdam, the only way he can hold his coalition is to be on both sides of the street. I could never do that." Falwell does feel that God has used Graham and recognizes him as an orthodox believer in Christ, but "I could never go the route of Billy Graham. If I did I would feel I was deserting my calling. Do people really say that I am going the way of Graham? Do they really?"

Graham spoke out obliquely against Falwell in 1982 in a statement amplified by the media. "I think the church has to take stands on moral and social issues, but I do not think we should be involved in partisan politics. It dilutes the gospel." Falwell was certainly injured by the implicit reference to his political involvement. Bob Jones and his people meanwhile blasted Graham for his comment, not only because it was Billy Graham the heretic who said it, but also because it put distance between Falwell and Graham. The ultra fundamentalists had consistently been telling their people that Falwell and Graham were two of a kind.

Graham himself was distressed by the gleeful media accounts quoting him as "blasting" and "excoriating" Falwell, which he never intended to do. He sent a personal note to Falwell being made public here for the first time: "Dear Jerry, I am deeply disturbed that there seems to be an attempt to drive a wedge between us. I am deeply grateful for your faithful proclamation of the Gospel of Jesus Christ, the same Gospel I preach, and feel that all of us who know and love our Lord Jesus Christ stand together." Graham praised Falwell's boldness in speaking out, his efforts on behalf of the hungry and underprivileged. He said, "You know that from time to time I have expressed reservations about evangelical Christians becoming so absorbed in political issues that they lose sight of the priority of the Gospel. I am also concerned that such issues could be used to divide us by those who do not agree with the Gospel."

He added, "In recent months I have discussed both in private conversation and media interviews the fact that the term "Moral Majority" has often been misunderstood and caricatured. Some for example think that it is exclusively a white Protestant organization with racial overtones or one which has no concern for some of the deeper social issues which face our world. Over and over again, especially in other countries, I have explained that this is a faulty picture and that it is composed of people from a cross-section of our pluralistic nation including Protestant, Catholic, Jews and various ethnic groups who are concerned about the moral drift in our country."

Falwell is interested in the endorsement of Billy Graham, not just for personal satisfaction, but also because Graham has great prestige among evangelicals, who are just as numerous as fundamentalists and whom Falwell is trying just as eagerly to politicize. Evangelicals, like fundamentalists, tend to be socially conservative, although there is more diversity among them. They are certainly more serious about their faith than Protestants in general. Eighty nine percent of evangelicals versus 60 percent of all Protestants hope to get to heaven by faith in Christ; 67 percent of evangelicals compared to 40 percent of all Protestants view the Devil as real; 45 percent of evangelicals but only 16 percent of Protestants say they read the Bible daily; 81 percent of evangelicals versus 58 percent of Protestants believe in creationism; 46 percent of evangelicals versus 22 percent of Protestants donate at least one-tenth of their income to the church. Falwell is trying to convert his religious devoutness into political fire power. "We are working on both sides of the road—fundamentalist and evangelical," he told me.

"There is a great deal of debate over the difference between an evangelical and a fundamentalist," Falwell observes. "Doctrinally there is no difference. I define fundamentalist as anyone who believes the fundamentals of the faith and has the guts to call himself that." But in the presence of evangelicals Falwell is more diplomatic. "I have to be more receptive and willing to listen," he says. He concedes that both the evangelical and fundamentalist strategies have merit. "We must reject pride in ourselves and our positions. Evangelicals have a tendency to pride themselves on their intelligent comprehension and defense of the faith. Fundamentalists tend to pride themselves on their strong, uncompromising stand for the faith. We must have both."

The extent to which Falwell is successful in politicizing evangelicals depends on the extent to which he can build on theological commonalities between them. It's not like his relations with Jews and Catholics. Their religious differences are accepted as fact on both sides, and the alliance is political. Theology doesn't enter the picture. But as his appeal to conservative Protestants is both religious *and* political, he is to some extent vulnerable to attack on issues of faith. And the ultra-fundamentalists are now on the offensive over that very issue.

14

A Fundamentalist
Notre Dame

Where will Falwell be ten years from now? Probably just where he is today—or doing better. This is best seen by nosing around the city of Lynchburg, where Falwell has invested in the future.

With the revenue Falwell has generated from television and the various programs of his ministry, he has established a veritable empire in Lynchburg. The city is sprawling with Falwell organization. There is Thomas Road Church, the television studios, the Liberty Bible Institute, the Missions project, Liberty Baptist College, Lynchburg Christian Academy, The Elim Home for Alcoholics, the Counseling Center, Treasure Island (a resort for school children and a summer camp for underprivileged kids), Moral Majority offices, and the Sports Center. These building accommodate literally hundreds of programs, which Falwell calls "ministries." Each fundamentalist participates in a "ministry." There is the Sunday School ministry, the senior Saints ministry, the neighborhood evangelism ministry, the inner city ministry, the ministry to the handicapped, the Sounds of Liberty, the telephone ministry, even the bus ministry.

Of all ministries and supporting structures, Falwell places the most emphasis on Liberty Baptist College which he wants to turn into what he calls a "fundamentalist Notre Dame" in fifteen years. It now enrolls six thousand students.

The LBC catalog cites the original charter of Harvard University, drawn up in 1646; "Everyone shall consider the main end of life and studies to know God and Jesus Christ which is eternal life." That tradition continues strong at LBC, even though Harvard has long since abandoned it. However, while LBC's main aim is spiritual refinement, there are other objectives. In the words of the catalog, "The college aggressively supports the free enterprise system" and "traditional American values." The college "is committed to integrating ageless Judeo-Christian values with a contemporary curriculum of liberal arts and sciences."

I met with LBC President A. Pierre Guillermin in his office. As Falwell is not involved in the day-to-day operation of LBC, Guillermin is sovereign at the college. I asked him whether LBC is a genuine liberal arts school or merely a cover for a missionary school. The former, Guillermin says. "But it is possible to be liberal arts and Christian at the same time." I asked whether LBC's requirement that all faculty members be born-again Christians restricts the college's ability to acquire the best scholars in each field. Guillermin answered, yes, but noted that faculty who are not fundamentalist or even Christian may lecture at LBC. "It is important to have a Christian faculty; because that is the primary value we want to communicate to our students. We provide knowledge—we don't exclude anything—but in a Christian context."

At my request, President Guillermin showed me the regulation book applying to faculty and students. Both are required to attend three church services and three chapel services each week. Both must demonstrate exemplary Christian behavior, loosely defined (but with the Bible as second handbook), with penalties for infraction. The LBC catalog says bluntly, " the student who is interested in doing his own thing will not be happy in the atmosphere of Liberty Baptist College." Rules are defended as necessary to proper conduct, and authority is praised as biblical. Then the codes are set forth: "Men are not to have long hair or beards. This regulation means that sideburns may not be longer than the bottom of the earlobe, and that hair may not come down over the top of the ear or touch the back of the collar." For women, "dresses and skirts with slits shorter than two inches from the middle of the knee are unacceptable. Anything tight, scant, backless, and low in the neckline is unacceptable. Pant suits should follow these guidelines: no skin should show at the waist at any time nor at any position, color and material must be complimentary, pants may not be hip-huggers, women will refrain from wearing men's cords or men's jeans or shorts."

The penalties are classified according to seriousness of the offense. A reprimand can be incurred for breach of the dress code, hair over the ears (for men), or tardiness to church, chapel, or other required meeting. A "weekend violation," equivalent to three reprimands comes for disturbance during church, "horseplay," writing bad checks, or dating without permission." The "ten day violation," equivalent to six reprimands is earned by attending motion pictures, gambling, or possession or use of tobacco. More adventurous types can incur a one-week suspension by dancing or attending a bar, nightclub, or disco; discharging a false alarm; plagiarism; or "obscene or abusive language or behavior." Finally, there is expulsion, equivalent to fifteen reprimands, which comes with forgery of an official document, stealing, participation in an "unauthorized demonstration, petition, or riot," or "spending the night in a single person's apartment of the opposite sex."

President Guillermin points out that most young people who attend LBC have been raised under the same edicts in Christian families. They sign a document beforehand saying they will abide by Christian tenets of behavior. They know the rules before they arrive on campus. He insists the rules are applied kindly and equitably, with counseling and pardon for some first offenses. Guillermin calls LBC one of the most progressive of fundamentalist colleges and it has, in fact, been impugned by some ultrafundamentalists as libertine.

The LBC admissions application asks students, "Have you received Jesus Christ as your personal savior?" and instructs "Explain in detail your salvation experience," but no effort is made to validate answers given. The undergraduate catalog lists these doctrinal tenets, which students must subscribe to before they come: belief in the "verbal inspiration, inerrancy, and authority" of Scripture; in man's fallen condition; in the Trinity; in salvation by faith alone; in the imminent Second Coming; and in "everlasting conscious blessedness of the saved and the everlasting conscious punishment of the lost." The graduate catalog is more advanced, listing no less than twenty doctrinal positions to be affirmed by students. No new tenets are introduced as such. It is a matter of refinement of those listed for undergraduates.

I asked President Guillermin whether all students who sign the doctrinal statements are in fact born-again fundamentalists. No. "Some of them are born again when they attend church here." This means they either lied or misunderstood the college application, I observed. Guillermin agreed. I asked what penalty goes along with this? What happens to a student who signs the doctrinal statement but is discovered upon arrival on campus not to have been born again? Nothing happens, "as long as the student abides by the rules." And a student engaging in premarital sex is expelled from school? Yes, that is a serious infraction. Isn't fornication a lesser crime than unbelief, according to the Bible? For a moment Guillermin's face went blank. "I didn't think of it that way."

Guillermin told me that, in fact, no girls have to his knowledge gotten pregnant at LBC. "If one did we would counsel her but ask her to leave school. Repeated drinking is also a crime that merits expulsion. but smoking earns suspension at most. Movies are a no-no, but "We do bring films to campus sometimes." LBC has screened "Star Wars," "Sound of Music," and surprisingly "Raiders of the Lost Ark." Students are discouraged from listening to rock music, but they are permitted to have radios in their rooms.. Interracial dating is permitted only with permission of both students' parents.

I could see Guillermin was uncomfortable spelling out these edicts. "We're hoping that our preferences will become habits and convictions with students. we don't want to have to police their lives." although he admitted that LBC has some of the same problems other schools have—experimenting with drugs, "horsing around"—he says these are the exception, not the rule. Generally students abide by the regulations quite diligently.

Is the theory of creation or evolution taught in biology classes at LBC? "We teach both theories. We believe in academic freedom." However, the perspective is that evolution has not been proven. "We present evolution as a theory to our students, not a fact. "We present the biblical account of creation as a belief." Guillermin feels that the scientific evidence for special creation is as strong, if not stronger, than that for evolution.

After talking to Guillermin, I visited the library of Liberty Baptist College, which boasts over 200,000 volumes. I found books by Marx, Eliot, Defoe, Nietzsche, Plato, and Aquinas. Conspicuously absent were books of modernist biblical criticism.

LBC also has a smallish bookstore, which displays textbooks, Christian books by LBC faculty members and by evangelists like Tim LaHaye and Billy Graham. Stationery, cassettes of Falwell sermons, and shirts saying "I Love Virginia" were also for sale.

I talked to some LBC students about life at the school. It is rather normal, I was surprised to discover. Students attend four hours or so of

class each day, including an hour of religion—courses in fundamentalism are mandatory. In addition to twenty hours of religion, the students must also participate in a church ministry—the choir, the bus
ministry, missionary work, door-to-door evangelism, the inner-city
ministry, etc. There is a sense of fellowship in these things that makes
them fun. The students enjoy each other's company, and no, they
aren't stuffy, even if they spend a good deal of time talking about
Christ.

I noticed a curious tension at LBC between students from the deep
South and everyone else. I sat in on several classes. Professor Jerry
Combee, who chairs the political science department, invited me to a
guest lecture in his government class by Morton Blackwell, aide to
President Reagan. Blackwell is one in a long list of conservative luminaries who have spoken at LBC. Vice-President Bush, former Interior
Secretary Watt, Education Secretary Bell and author Francis Schaeffer
have lectured. There have been some distinguished liberals too: Senator Ted Kennedy and evolution scientist Dr. Doolittle from California.
The speakers are invited in to provide LBC student a sophisticaton
about the political process.

Ted Kennedy's appearance at LBC on October 3, 1983, was not only
an education for students, it was a major political triumph for Falwell.
Kennedy delivered what he called his most important address since
the Democratic Convention in 1980. He began his talk by joking,
"Most of you probably think that it is easier for a camel to pass
through the eye of a needle than for Ted Kennedy to speak at Liberty
Baptist College." He spoke about pluralism and tolerance, chastising
fundamentalist's for excessive narrow-mindedness. He urged Falwell to
give his students an extra hour out after curfew that night, in return
for which he promised to turn on The Old Time Gospel Hour.
Applause.

Before his talk, Kennedy, his sister Jean Smith, and daughter Kara
dined with the Falwell family at the latter's home. The two men confess to having been charmed by the other. The next day Kennedy
called up Falwell to say how impressed he was at the behavior of LBC
students. Falwell says, "He was a little nervous when he spoke. He
didn't know what to expect of our kids—maybe stone throwing from
backwoods fundamentalists. But he told me he was surprised. And he
apologized for the way some few treated me when I spoke at Harvard.
He said that was not Harvard's finest hour."

Yet to the press Falwell denied that he would curtail his attacks on
the Massachussetts senator in fund-raisers. "Kennedy is head of the

Fund for a Democratic Majority," he said. "I'm the lighting rod for his fundraising, and he is for mine. I don't think that he's going to cut off his main source of income, and neither am I."

At LBC I also attended an English class taught by professor Maud Sly. She began class with a brief discussion of Interior Secretary James Watt's resignation. After this preliminary discussion, she bade the students to bow their heads in prayer. All classes at LBC begin with a prayer, usually a spontaneous prayer uttered by some student. A red-haired youth asked God to heal his calculus teacher, to inspire President Reagan, to help him with studies. Other's raised their voices in prayer. The subject for the day was Shakespeare's *Hamlet,* which Sly called "a truly classic work." She passed around Delacroix's illustrations for *Hamlet.* She asked the students to write a three-page paper analysing a single character in the play.

I found a peculiar system of reasoning at work in LBC classes. It is what I call "theological reasoning" and operates in parallel to normal logic. For example, in the English class, the objectives of reading *Hamlet* seemed to be to draw moral and Christian lessons from the text. This seem to be the strategy at LBC: to discover God's hidden message in all events and texts. Thus we learn from Shakespeare that thou shalt not kill and thou shalt not covet they brother's wife; the sins of Claudius. Of course, attention was paid to the esthetics of the text and to the meaning of the text. *Hamlet* served also as a conduit for teaching, not only as a work worthy in and of itself. When I raised this point with some LBC faculty members, they replied that attention should be paid to both esthetic and moral considerations. "We study both the Christian lessons of the play and appreciate the beautiful poesy."

Except for sports which Falwell strongly encourages, LBC kids do not have much to do for entertainment. Falwell regards winning as part of being a Christian. "We have to show people that Christianity is not some sissy religion," he says. "Jesus was a he-man." He urges LBC students to be "champions for Christ." He wants LBC students to be as competitive as he was in his adolescent days. But underclassmen may not date without approval, and students cannot go out for a beer after an exam or go to the movies. Most fun things done by kids across the country are taboo for them. About as far as they can go with a girl is to kiss her, maybe by the ninth or tenth date.

LBC students enroll with their eyes wide open. They receive a list of rules and regulations long before they arrive on campus. They understand LBC is not for everyone—only those young people who, as

Falwell says it, "not only want to learn how to make a living but to learn how to live."

Falwell has been criticized by educators for the moral restrictiveness of LBC and its faculty. When he criticized the amoral philosophy of public schools in the interview sprung on him for *Penthouse*, the interviewers demanded, "But when you say the state schools don't provide character building, surely that's a bit simplistic, because they do provide what they assume is character building. What you mean is that they don't provide what *you* see as character building." Falwell shot back, "Well, if the total vacuum of discipline, if the drug epidemic, if the amoral position of the National Education Association and the teaching profession of this day are building character, then that's the kind of character we don't want built in our young people."

Falwell has been criticized for placing facts and theories in a strictly moral framework. "Here at LBC we teach every ideology," he says, "but we also teach what's wrong." He does not have much regard for talk of academic freedom. To a question on that issue raised by a reporter, he replied, "We give all kinds of academic freedom as long as it concurs wtih this book [the Bible]." Asked if he ever had trouble with teachers dissenting from fundamentalist teaching, he said glibly, "Anytime they start teaching something we don't like, we cut the money off. It's amazing how that changes philosophy."

I stopped in to see Ed Dobson, dean of LBC and co-author of *The Fundamentalist Phenomenon*. I found him to be a reformist fundamentalist, like his boss Falwell and like others I was to meet. Dobson concedes that "fundamentalism is a movement of the people, not of scholars." He defends this to some extent. "Fundamentalists sometimes give simple answers to complex questions, as we are accused of doing. But then liberals often give complex answers to simple questions." He points to the decline of liberal religion. "The liberal preacher quotes Kafka to an empty pew," he says. For Dobson everything hinges on the inerrancy of Scripture, because "if you preach a Bible full of error, about a Christ who wasn't God, didn't die, and isn't coming back, then you have nothing to convert people to."

In his book Dobson claims that now there is a "greater moderation" in fundamentalism, which he tells me is also evident in Falwell's behavior. "The lunatic fringe has for too long set the agenda," Dobson feels. He acknowledges that Falwell and he were part of that fringe— captive to it, he says—but now he is less constricted. He is convinced that Falwell's brand of fundamentalism is faithful to the Bible without adding gratuitously to it. He feels that fundamentalists should have been involved in the civil rights movement. He claims, the "Bob Jones mentality" prevented this. "The Scripture is full of commands that we be vigilant until the coming of the Lord," Dobson says. "Fundamentalists should have been at the forefront of the fight against segregation, which was a moral issue. "We should have spoken out. We, of all people, should have been willing to recognize the equality of all people under God."

Dobson showed me a copy of a satirical journal that interviewed him about fundamentalism. The purpose of the interview was to expose him as narrow-minded, but he was so humorous and genial that he came off well. Asked about the difference between evangelicals and fundamentalists, he replied, "An evangelical is concerned, whereas a fundamentalist is mad. An evangelical has a great deal of concern for issues but does nothing about them. A fundamentalist, right or wrong, is never satisfied unless he has his way." He criticized the "negativism, pessimism, extreme separatism, and exclusism" of the "hyper-fundamentalists." Asked whether this remark might anger Bob Jones and his people, Dobson said, "I doubt it, since most hypers rarely read books, let alone satirical magazines."

Both Dobson and Ed Hindson, his co-author, reveal a capacity to ponder the weaknesses of fundamentalism in their book *The Fundamentalist Phenomenon*. They catalog "ten characteristic weaknesses of fundamentalism," including "little capacity for self-criticism," "the temptation to add to the gospel" with confining strictures, "the extreme tendency" to excommunicate all critics including other fundamentalists, "a kind of paranoid mentality toward the world," and "the sin of exclusivism" or hyperorthodoxy. That Dobson and Hindson could even list weaknesses suggests that they themselves have, to some extent, transcended them. They echo Falwell's reassurance that the fact that he cannot compromise on the essentials of his faith does not mean that he won't even listen to his critics. Christianity, after all, is a religion of sharing and fellowship with all those who seek to partake of the truth.

I also spoke to Nelson Keener, who is in charge of the administration of church programs and editor of *Fundamentalist Journal*. He is candid about himself. He was a renegade at first, he confessed. "When I came to work for Jerry and I heard him call himself a fundamentalist, I said to myself, 'Give me a break, man.' I wondered why Jerry was associating himself with people, some of whom were thought of as ridiculous in their thought and behavior. But soon I saw what he was up to."

I got the point. What Falwell was up to was nothing less than a healing and correcting of fundamentalism.

Keener calls himself a "fundamentalist," but he can be quite "progressive" on some issues, For example, he is "genuinely concerned" about "sexism."

Keener, Cal Thomas, and Ron Godwin make up Falwell's second rank triumvirate. The three men share an ability of organizing and speaking. Two of them—Thomas and Keener—are outsiders to old-style fundamentalsim. Keener was raised in the fundamentalist camp but came to realize it needed patching up. Thomas explodes all the stereotypes. He majored in English at New York University, after which he worked for more than twenty years in radio and television journalism, reaching his peak as national radio correspondent for NBC News. Thomas is vice-president of Moral Majority in charge of dealing with the media. He has a knack for wit and self disparagement. He once began a speech to the Alabama chapter of Moral Majority with, "Good evening, fellow fanatic. It is good to be with a group ready to take over America." He commented to me, "People ask me, What do you do? I say, 'Oh, I'm in charge of forcing values down people's throats.' " Other of his lines are more pointed. Among those he's written for Falwell to deliver in speeches are "We are becoming a society with a chicken in every pot and a baby in every trash can" and "the ACLU ought to apologize to the American people for having performed a religious lobotomy on this republic."

In contrast with Keener, who is quietly efficient, and Godwin, a born fundamentalist complete with Southern drawl, Thomas is garrulous and speaks in a clipped Midwestern accent. He specializes in pointing out the double standard applied to conservative writers and spokesmen. In *Book Burning,* published in 1983, he points out that religious books are systematically excluded from the *New York Times* bestseller list even though they routinely outsell secular "bestsellers." He draws a parallel between this sort of segregation of religion and segregation of blacks prior to 1954.

Falwell's entire staff is intensely loyal to him. "We're called followers—and we are," says Jeanette Hogan, his secretary. No matter what their personal brand of fundamentalism, or their hopes for the future of the Church or Moral Majority, all seem to think that Falwell is doing the right thing.

Falwell's greatest strength is his tremendous organizational ability, tied to a broad, powerful vision for the future. His greatest weakness is his inability to confront people who cannot be regarded as enemies.

15

The Importance of Jerry Falwell

With the exception of Ireland, America is the most religious country in the world. Yet America's laws, as formulated and interpreted in the last several decades, seem to militate actively against religion. Religion has been denigrated in the name of "rights." This has led to a growing backlash. Americans are a tolerant people, by and large, but their moral parameters are not fully elastic. Jerry Falwell is a voice for the many Americans whose concern about moral issues has led to demands for a reaffirmation of Judeo-Christian values and tradition.

Falwell has altered the terms of political discourse in this country. Today he sets the agenda. Only a decade ago, when the media needed a religious spokesman to consult on issues of morality—drugs, promiscuity, etc.—it approached William Sloane Coffin or Jesse Jackson. Today these people are proponents of secular perspectives. Their words are interpreted almost exclusively in a political context. Today it is Falwell who is put on camera to comment about the moral issues as such—the pornography epidemic, homosexuality, even about the morality of defense policies. Admittedly, Falwell has sought out the public eye, but ten years ago it would have been denied him no matter how much he jumped up and down. He has successfully made himself the spokesman for moral America.

He has also changed the political agenda in this country. As he himself says, "When Nixon ran for President in 1972, or when Ford ran in 1976, abortion and school prayer were not issues. They simply were not a serious part of the national debate. They were taken as resolved. But today things are different. Today the moral issues are once again important. It is hard these days to run for dogcatcher in Bangor, Maine, without announcing your position on abortion, and it had better be the right one."

Moral Majority takes credit, along with NCPAC and Christian Voice, for eliminating the electoral hypocrisy by which politicians mostly Democratic talked conservative at him, invoking the family and traditional morals, and then in Washington voted federal funds for abortion and the feminist agenda. Whether or not one agrees with Falwell, one must recognize that he has provided a service to the process of democracy. Democracy after all, assumes that the people's representatives live up to their stated commitment. When they do not, the people may vote them out of office. Senators Church, Bayh, McIntire, and others interpret their political downfall to, in McIntire's words, "the politics of hate peddled by the New Right." But it was the democratically expressed resentment of their own constituencies that put them out of office.

Falwell's has brought millions of evangelicals and fundamentalists into the political process. He has convinced them they should take part in political discussion. This may be theological heresy, according to certain fundamentalist doctrine, but his promotion of citizen involvement in politics and government is healthy for our democracy.

Falwell told everyday Americans that their country's historically accepted traditions were under attack. These people sat up and took notice. They know it is true. They feel their right to continue following those traditions being trampled on by people claiming to be progressive. Falwell made them realize their power to affect the direction of government, to protect their own way of life. Since 1980 Falwell has registered as many as five million voters; in 1984 he will sign up half that figure again. These numbers do not include the millions of people prodded into political awareness by Falwell who did not sign up with him but took their own political initiative.

Twenty-five million Americans (eight million families) are in Falwell's computers. These are his supporters who write to him, pray for him, and give financially to his ministries. They are Protestants, Catholics, Jews, Mormons and other religious Americans. If these persons are as loyal to Falwell and his positions as some observers believe they are, then these people constitute America's largest and most influential voting bloc.

Fundamentalists, therefore, are not the only religious people in America, and Falwell appeals to many more than just those in the fundamentalist community. Fundamentalists are a formidable political force, but Falwell's appeal is broader. He frames the issues in terms that do not merely state fundamentalist theology, but broaden into a moral-political vision for America. That vision for America dates back to the founding of this republic. It is the American dream. Falwell's critics realize how appealing his vision is to many, so they try to tar it with accusations of religious fanaticism and orthodoxy, to make it sound exclusive rather than inclusive. But Falwell is such an effective spokesman for the American ideal that his critics have not had much success with gnarling his message.

According to Pastor Richard Neuhaus, "The Moral Majority has kicked, or perhaps tumbled over, a cultural trip wire and set off an alarm alerting us to a much more fundamental change in modern society: the collapse of the 200-year hegemony of the secular Enlightenment in Western culture." In this Neuhaus is correct, the decade of the 1970s, widely considered a secular decade, was in fact not so. It was, in James Hitchcock's words, "a kind of religious greenhouse, in which every kind of exotic plant bloomed."

People in the 1970s showed signs of spiritual want, but they were alienated from traditional religion. Instead they pursued secular alternatives such as cultic worship and the nature movement. Religious feelings were channeled into the secular Left because the Left made such startling moral claims for itself. But as illusions failed and disenchantment set in, many bailed out of left wing political activism and joined churches or cults. They recognized their impulse for what it was, a religious not a political impulse, and found a church the logical place to express themselves. These churches gradually moved to the right. By 1980 many erstwhile radicals had grown weary of radicalism. They revolted into orthodoxy, to use Camus's phrase. They were ready to listen to a man they would have despised a few years earlier, Jerry Falwell.

Another large group Falwell has widely affected is that vast body of average citizens previously committed to no political program in particular, anxious to pursue decent policies but equally determined that these should take their interests into account. These people had gone along with liberalism all the way from the New Deal. They found liberal spokesmen apparently intelligent and were willing to entrust nation-running to them.

But in 1980 a great feeling of protest rose in the country. The average American had deferred to the liberals long enough! As a result he was overtaxed, inadequately defended, and morally abused. Poll after poll found people saying they were fed up and were going to do something about it. They were sick of seeing criminals get off with light sentences or none at all. They were concerned that promiscuous attitudes among their children were being encouraged in the public schools and by "mainstream" churches. They saw America spurned time after time by posturing, pompous Third World functionaries whom liberal spokesmen fawned over.

It is impossible to make too much of the abortion and school prayer decisions. *Roe vs. Wade* in 1973 legalized abortion on demand, leading to a 1½ million-a-year abortion rate. *Engels vs. Vitale* purged voluntary prayer from public schools.

The 1973 abortion ruling generated a reaction that at first went unnoticed because it was gradual. But it built to a loud crescendo, playing a deciding role in the defeat of liberal candidates for office, particularly in 1980.

Decisions to prohibit prayer in public schools have always been widely unpopular. They have played no small part in the exodus from our public schools and the concomitant burgeoning of private education in America. Chesterton once called America "the nation with the soul of a church." The school prayer ruling had the effect of plucking out the soul from America's education system. We may have the Supreme Court to thank for the destruction of our public school system. The logic of the Court's prayer decision has never been apparent to many constitutional scholars and the public at large. Does separation of church and state really mean that a child who observes a moment of prayerful silence is in violation of the law of the land? Did the Founding Fathers really favor pornography and promiscuity in our schools over a simple nonsectarian prayer? Even many who were not Christian—Jews and Mormons, for example—and those who were not religious but were moral were disturbed by the prayer rulings. These were symptomatic of something deeply amiss with our government.

The fundamentalists felt the pain of society's worsening ills more acutely than anyone else. They could easily compare the way things were turning out to the way things had been. Still holding to long-established principles of morality and social order, fundamentalists were horrified at the breakdown of society in the 1970s. They could see the difference, and they were onto the sham of progress being promoted by pseudo intellectuals who specialized in replacing self-evident truths with absurd, esoteric jargon. And when fundamentalists took their anger into the political arena, they were able to command the attention not only of their own ample numbers, but also of the majority of well-meaning Americans. And the liberals have only themselves to blame for this. They created the ferment that drove the fundamentalists into effective action. They made it hard for moral Americans to stay in the Democratic camp.

Of course, not all moral Americans agree with every item of the fundamentalist manifesto. Many of them probably feel uncomfortable about Jerry Falwell. Even so, when they see him on television, they know what he is saying. They understand his anger and fear and urgency. It is theirs, too. So they are perplexed at people who dismiss Falwell's concerns as mere demagoguery or activism aimed at fame or fortune. They are perplexed because Falwell's anger, fear, and sense of urgency are also their own. Liberals who scoff at Falwell do not realize how widely held and deeply felt the convictions are that he gives voice to. They do not realize that their scoffing offends and angers millions across America. This lack of awareness will be their undoing. Their attacks on Falwell may be effective with those who know nothing about Falwell; they backfire for those who have seen or heard him speak and recognize the ferocious attacks on him as attacks on the very same things they believe. So they rally around him, pull out their checkbooks and write him checks, thump out angry letters to newspapers and network executives. Even fundamentalists who would ordinarily be ambivalent about Falwell hang tight with him when he is attacked by the secular media, because in the fundamentalist world, being attacked from the outside is a sign of being biblically sound.

Most people see Falwell in his political role as chairman of Moral Majority or on television as host of "The Old Time Gospel Hour." But essential as these commitments are, they are but part of his life. Since 1979, when he founded Moral Majority, Falwell's political involvements have increased greatly, and there are some signs they are taking a toll of his family and religious life. At heart, Falwell remains a country preacher. You have to see him in church to realize that. You have to see him when he is not being taped, when he is preaching on penance on Wednesday, when he is counseling an old lady whose husband is ill or a girl who has gotten herself pregnant. You have to see him at funerals for simple people who loved him, at potluck suppers and at annual Lynchburg festivities. Then you see the real Jerry Falwell, the man at his most comfortable, doing what he most wants to do, pastor a congregation and be part of it. Falwell feels no different from thousands of preachers across the country. He does not claim to be a better man than any of them, nor more religious or pious. Like them he has a family he dearly loves to take care of. Unlike many pastors, Falwell is affluent and famous, but he regards wealth as at best something to be employed to the greater glory of God.

Falwell's people are the everyday, simple people who comprise the great heartland of America. Their problems are the same family and money problems many of us face. Their distinction lies not in what they have done but in what they are and what they stand for—America, a country facing difficulties because of her desire to be moral in an amoral world. Falwell's followers have no pretensions. They make up their own minds and do not worry too much about what the experts say or what is written in the newspapers. They do not have to consult studies to discover that their children are rebelling and being subjected to peer pressure and violence in the schools, they find solace in prayer, and they try to work out their problems in a disciplined context.

Falwell's people feel it is preferable to be moralistic and fall short than either to eschew morals because they are difficult to abide by or to construct a false system of morals simply because it is more easy to abide by. They feel it is more honorable to be a sinner come to repentance before God than a skeptic who pretends that he does not sin or that God caused him to sin. They genuinely believe that America is morally sick and needs to be set on a right course.

Falwell's people are accused of being vicious and intolerant. Meanwhile, the "forces of tolerance" accuse Falwell of being a Hitler and an Ayatollah, of trying to subvert the Bill of Rights, of persecuting Jews and blacks and Catholics, of controlling minds and feeding McCarthyism and hysteria, of appealing to the hateful and divisive impulses in people. The forces of tolerance call for Falwell to be taken off the air, so that only their spokesmen may have a national voice. The forces of tolerance want the government to cut off tax-exemption for Falwell's school and hundreds of Christian schools, while their political organs—Planned Parenthood and the National Organization for Women, for example—continue to be funded. The forces of tolerance boycott Falwell's speeches, throw pies and rocks at him, make obscene phone calls to his wife and children, and send him two hundred death threats per month.

I have often wondered what makes the so-called forces of tolerance so intolerant, indeed brutal. Liberals seem to have a self-righteousness about them. They see themselves as victims. Being victims makes them feel psychologically entitled to hurt others in the name of underdog justice. "The old tyrants invoked the past," Chesterton wrote. "The new tyrants will invoke the future." The liberal vision, which characterizes itself as progressive, feels that sacrifices enroute to the goal of blissful world government or "liberating" socialism are worth the prize ahead. With glazed eyes set on the future, liberals ignore the tyrannies of the present and the liberal failings of the past. They speak of having gotten a raw deal at the hands of society, even though they have been running society for the last fifty years.

The liberal churches are in a crisis of failures. Theologically, they pursue what Harvard Dean William Sperry has called a "Yes, but" religion—Yes, I believe in God, but the language of the Bible cannot be discerned; Yes, I accept the deity of Christ, but the virgin birth is irrelevant, and the important thing is not facts but that God loves us. The liberal church ends up conceding so much to its secular critics that it ends up defending an abstract concept of religion that only finds expression in secular terms, such as helping the poor. So religion for the liberal becomes indistinguishable from secular social work. Its objective is not the sanctification of God or even God's creatures, but the here-and-now goal of feeding this village, building this dam, or fomenting this revolution. It is materialistic, even as liberals decry materialism.

Liberal theology is fraught with contradictions. For example, it is inconsistent about situational ethics. While on doctrinal matters liberals welcome differences of opinion, on social issues they demand conformity. It is permissible to challenge Church teaching on the Resurrection and the Trinity, but it is most unwelcome to criticize the goal of racial integration however achieved. In liberal circles it is considered an understandable show of moral conviction to hate and denounce people who are not in line with the liberal social and political orthodoxy. When confronted with biblical texts that demand traditional morality, liberal Christians snort and say the Bible is not to be taken literally—it is antiquated, it was written for a different century and a different culture. But while liberals cite biblical mandates supporting social justice, they are clearly citing incontrovertible absolutes. They seem to want it both ways. It is almost as if they set the standard by which the Bible is judged, rather than the Bible setting a standard by which they can be judged.

Now, Falwell and his people do have weaknesses. They remain hostile to science and derivative streams of thought. They tend to be sticklers about orthodoxy, not just on essential tenets such as the death and resurrection of Christ, but insisting on a sub-agenda that is merely the result of custom and habit. They are unduly fearful of associating with other traditional Christian denominations that have a great deal in common with them. Often they do not see that a conservative Catholic and a conservative Protestant have more shared beliefs than a conservative Protestant and a liberal Protestant. The great religious struggle of this century is not interdenominational, as it was in previous centuries, but between conservative and liberal Christianity.

Falwell's people, so long apart from the mainstream of American life as far as politics are concerned, also still have much to learn about how to behave in the political process. They easily fall into hyperbole and sometimes appear to endorse extremist solutions to political or social problems. For example, a California Moral Majority spokesman joined a $3 million crusade against San Francisco's gay community and during a press conference called homosexuality a sin akin to murder. Then he called for a return to capital punishment. Falwell immediately distanced himself from any suggestion that Moral Majority endorsed the death penalty for homosexuals. "That to me is ridiculous and unthinkable." Falwell also refused to support Jim Wright, a twenty-three year-old Moral Majority representative in Maryland who launched a crusade against a bakery selling anatomically explicit cookies. Wright was deservedly lampooned in the media, and the cookie store actually doubled its business.

In general, Falwell's candor and down-to-earth tone, especially on subjects like abortion, speak directly to the people. They reflect his populist conservatism.

One of Falwell's supporters advanced this defense of Falwell's use of hyperbole. Obviously Moral Majority is strident, he said, but it has reason to be. Our nation is in dire peril. In times of less threatening uncertainty or challange, Moral Majority would be more temperate. A man is unwise to temporize with vague nonsense while teetering on the edge of an abyss.

My thought is that it is precisely in times of hazard that we must be particularly careful to show calm to discuss the issues precisely and not give way to heat and emotion. In Reinhold Niebuhr's words, "Political controversies are always conflicts between sinners, and not between righteous men and sinners." Falwell is now in the pulpit. The Bible speaks of good and evil, and in the Bible the two do not mix. But in politics distinctions are often less vivid. Falwell's rhetoric, however, frequently does not distinguish between liberals, socialists, and Communists. He sometimes regards his enemies as opposing not just his programs, but God Himself. So he demonizes his critics the way they do him. There is a potential danger in this. Seymour Lipset and Earl Raab write, "If a political opponent is just wrong or stupid or misguided, he can presumably be dealt with in the marketplace of ideas. But when his political opinions arise from a deliberate moral wickedness, a case can be made that he does not deserve to be in the debate at all." Also, Falwell does not seem sufficiently cautious that his political views do not work to estrange people from the Bible.

Falwell feels that ordinarily he would welcome liberals as allies in his fight against atheists, but overt atheism is not a serious opponent presently. Falwell suspects, however, that liberalism is the guise in which atheism prefers to appear in our time and sees atheism dressed as liberalism as much more dangerous than atheism standing nude.

Because of Falwell, religious morality is now part of our political discourse. This fact has been obscured by press treatment of Falwell, but it has not been lost on Pastor Neuhaus, who remarks,

They [Falwell and his followers] are not Yahoos and rednecks and Ku Kluxers and neo-Nazis. We blind ourselves by the caricatures we use in order to dismiss them. The secular media sniff around the Jerry Falwells and Jim Robisons and so forth trying to find out if they can't confirm once again the Elmer Gantry syndrome. It's the only way they can think about these rednecks from the South. And so they have all kinds of investigative reporters out there hoping they're going to find Jerry Falwell sleeping around with little girls, preferably little boys, preferably little black boys. They're hoping to find masses of embezzled funds, and so forth. No, these are people of impressive and sometimes insufferable moral rectitude. They and their followers believe that in the past they have been excluded from and despised by the leadership elites of America. And you know why they feel that way? Because in general they have been excluded and despised.

Rabbi Marc Tanenbaum of the American Jewish Committee comments, "We need to understand that one of the reasons for the success of Jerry Falwell is that he is addressing himself to some of the real issues in America, namely, the moral malaise of the American people."

Falwell has introduced the argument, which as far as I know is original with him, that it is the moral issues that presidents should address if they wish to endure through history. Falwell has told President Reagan that if he wants to be remembered one hundred years from now as a great President, he would do well to focus on abortion, prayer, and the Judeo-Christian ethic. Presidents are not remembered for economic programs or defense buildup, Falwell says. "Which presidents balanced budgets?" Falwell asked me rhetorically. "Who knows! But which President freed the slaves? That is less difficult to answer." Even Franklin Roosevelt, who more than any other president shaped the politics of this century, is remembered not so much for the size of his programs—many were modest—but for the new moral direction he gave government, turning it away from a mere security operation to a "welfare state." Falwell is confident that Ronald Reagan will increasingly address the moral malaise of America, although the president has proferred mostly rhetoric and little action so far.

It is fine to talk unspecifically about moral decline and moral malaise, but Falwell is after something considerably more specific. He never puts it this way, but his criticism is really a criticism of the philosophies of the eighteenth century—the rationalism of the French Revolution *philosophies*, the romantic sentimentalism of Rousseau, the nascent utilitarianism of Bentham—of which modern liberalism is an inconsistent amalgam. Falwell wants to restore to America the concept of an immutable natural law, the natural law that Burke and, to a lesser extent, Locke talked about. In Burke's words, "There is an order which keeps things fast in their place. It is made to us, and we are made to it." Falwell realizes that it is sometimes difficult to discern the absolutely right thing to do in a given circumstance, but he does not use that as an excuse for indifference to whatever good can be achieved.

Falwell is eager to restore harmony between law and religion. He does not want a theocracy. But he does understand, as Montesquien observed, that it is virtue that holds a republic together, just as it is honor that cements aristocracy, and legality that supports monarchy. In a republic as in other forms of government, people are bad enough to need virtuous laws, but good enough to be improved by them. Of course law is, by definition, a lowest common denominator. It tells people what they cannot do, or more precisely what they will be punished for doing. The law does not tell people how to live. That is a religious choice—even if the choice is not to be religious. Falwell understands the different, though interrelated functions of law and religion in a democracy.

A democracy based on virtue will enact good laws. However, it is not a simple matter of identifying the good and enshrining it in laws. As Plato recognized, an unenforceable good law that is widely disobeyed casts all the law into disrepute. Falwell realizes, for example, the error of Prohibition in the 1920s, which his fellow fundamentalists actively lobbied for. But good laws that will be obeyed and can be implemented should be passed. And the good society generated by good citizens freely living in accordance with good laws should put itself in opposition to societies devoted to totalitarianism, such as the Soviet Union.

The most insidious thing about Communism is its deceit of indigent people, who are taught to judge Communism only by what it predicts. As Jean Francois-Revel remarks, "They judge communism by its promise, but fascism by its record." Falwell is determined to fight the false promises of Communism, which preys on the suffering and ignorance of the impoverished. He likens Communist promises to Satan's efforts to deceive Christ into accepting the kingdoms of this world in preference to striving for realization of a higher truth. Falwell believes that the "peace" offered by Communism is but the indifference of the grave. But he also feels that Americans must accomplish something infinitely more difficult than disciplining the Soviet Union—they must discipline themselves.

That is Falwell's moral challenge to America. Americans have been seduced into the politics of pleasure and convenience, which in the long run is the politics of frustration and great inconvenience. They have been taught that it is all right to sin "under certain circumstances," that virtue is boring, that guilt is just a neurosis, that one's own gratification is more important than the well-being of one's spouse or one's children. Simone Weil once wrote, "Nothing is so beautiful, so continually fresh and surprising, so full of sweet and perpetual ecstasy, as the good. No desert is so dreary, monotonous, and boring as evil. But with fantasy it's the other way round. Fictional good is boring and flat, while fictional evil is varied, intriguing, attractive, and full of charm." Falwell sees Americans subjected to a modern deception that substitutes fiction for reality. We are continually told we can create our own reality and substitute that as an improvement upon the existing state of things.

Liberalism represents an acute discontent with reality. One offshoot, feminism, cannot bear the fact that men and women were created different with consequently different roles to play in society. Falwell realizes the difference and cherishes it as part of God's exquisite plan. He has an intuitive understanding of people as people and of the family. His knowledge is based on practical experience—the experience of his own family and of the thousands of parents and children he has counseled over twenty-five years as pastor of Thomas Road Church. His laboratory is the real world. He does not have the liberal tendency to devise abstract ideals that do not jibe with human experience or recognize a need to take human frailties into account.

Listening to Falwell speak, one gets a sense that something is right about America, after all, and that much of what is not can be set right if politics is placed in its right context. Politics is not the supreme art. Living a life in accord with what is good is the supreme art. And because true religion concentrates on the ultimate good, rather than on convenience or the fashion of the day, it justly plays a part in the political process, which properly aims at promoting the good of society in its day-to-day functioning. Politics is not the supreme art.

In Falwell's words, "the time has come for you to line up with the churches, the pastors, and the religious institutions that stand for and teach what you believe in and that are putting all their efforts toward saving this nation. Go to a Bible-believing, soul-winning church. Give your time and talent and treasure there. We only have one life to give, so put yours in the right place doing the right thing. Support those men of God and those churches which stand for what is right. Get involved. Freedom is everybody's business. Become a good citizen. Register to vote, and know what the issues are. Know what's vital, know what's important, and forget the labels: Democratic, Republican, Independent, and so on. Find out who is standing for the issues, who is standing for the principles, who is closest to what's right. Stand by that man or woman. According to George Gallup, there are enough of us to turn this country round. By God's grace we are going to do it. I don't know how much time we have, but I pray we have enough."

And "...If God will give us the time, I believe that—through the 110,000 fundamentalist churches, the 34,000 Christian day schools, and dozens of Christian colleges and universities across this country, and hundreds of TV and radio outlets and preachers and programs, and Christian businessman, we can turn this nation to God." "...We're in a battle, we're in a struggle, we're in a fight. We may go down. God willing, we will go down not looking but swinging. But I really don't believe we are going down at all. I firmly believe that God is going to heal this land."